W9-DBE-687

Landmarks in Modern American Business

Landmarks in Modern American Business

Volume 2

1944–1974

Edited by

The Editors of Salem Press

SALEM PRESS, INC.
Pasadena, California
Hackensack, New Jersey

Essays originally appeared in *Great Events from History II: Business and Commerce*, 1994; new material has been added.

∞ The paper used in these volumes conforms to the American National Standard for Permanence of Paper for Printed Library Materials, Z39.48-1992 (R1997).

Library of Congress Cataloging-in-Publication Data

Landmarks in modern American business / edited by the editors of Salem Press
  p. cm. — (Magill's choice)
Includes bibliographical references and index.
  ISBN 0-89356-135-5 (set : alk. paper). — ISBN 0-89356-139-8 (v. 1 : alk. paper). — ISBN 0-89356-143-6 (v. 2 : alk. paper). — ISBN 0-89356-149-5 (v. 3 : alk. paper)
  1. United States — Commerce — History — 20th century — Chronology. 2. Industries — United States — History — 20th century — Chronology. 3. Corporations — United States — History — 20th century — Chronology. 4. Commercial law — United States — History — 20th century — Chronology. I. Series.

  HF3021 .L36 2000
  338.0973—dc21

                00-032962

First Printing

Contents
Volume 2

Landmarks in Modern American Business

ROOSEVELT SIGNS THE G.I. BILL

CATEGORY OF EVENT: Government and business
TIME: June 22, 1944
LOCALE: Washington, D.C.

The G.I. Bill provided veterans with readjustment benefits such as unemployment compensation; loan guarantees for purchases of homes, farms, and businesses; and tuition and subsistence for education and training

Principal personages:

FREDERIC DELANO (1863-1953), the planning agency head who raised the idea of veterans' benefits in 1942

FRANKLIN D. ROOSEVELT (1882-1945), the president who spoke on radio and before Congress in favor of veterans' benefits in 1943

WARREN ATHERTON (1891-1976), the American Legion leader who appointed the committee that drafted the original version of the G.I. Bill

JOEL BENNETT "CHAMP" CLARK (1890-1954), the Missouri Democrat and veterans' subcommittee chair who shepherded the G.I. Bill through the Senate

JOHN RANKIN (1882-1960), the Mississippi Democrat who dominated House veterans' committee hearings on the G.I. Bill

Summary of Event

The Servicemen's Readjustment Act of 1944 (Public Law 346), commonly known as the G.I. Bill of Rights or G. I. Bill, provided economic and educational benefits for World War II veterans. Individuals who had served ninety or more days in the U.S. armed forces after September 16, 1940, could take advantage of readjustment benefits to ease their transition into

In 1932 World War I veterans converged on Washington, D.C., demanding payment of the bonuses they had been promised. The government drove the "bonus army" away and burned out its encampments in an ugly confrontation that the Roosevelt administration did not wish to see repeated after World War II. (National Archives)

the civilian economy. The federal government sought to provide temporary help in finding postwar employment, assistance in obtaining educational credentials, and loan guarantees for purchases of homes, as well as farms and businesses.

Between July, 1942, and June, 1944, government agencies, the president, veterans' groups, and Congress worked out the provisions of the G.I. Bill in a complicated policy-making process. Discussion of readjustment benefits centered on unemployment, federal loan guarantees, and education. Temporary benefits included counseling for return to prewar jobs, job placement by a new Veterans' Placement Service Board working with the U.S. Employment Service and veterans' centers, and unemployment compensation, for a maximum of fifty-two weeks, of $20 per month. Veterans could apply for loan guarantees up to a maximum of 50 percent of a $4,000 loan, payable in full within twenty years, to purchase a home, farm, or business. Loans would be administered through the Veterans Administration (VA), which would work with private banks, lending agencies, and businesses. Educational opportunities involved tuition payments up to $500 per year and subsistence allowances of $50 per month for single veterans and $75 per month for married veterans or those with dependents, for a maximum of four years. Through the educational program, veterans could earn high school diplomas, attend trade and business schools, or receive college or graduate school educations.

The G.I. Bill enabled veterans of World War II to become one of the best educated, most prosperous, and successful middle-class generations in U.S. history. During previous wars, the government had made few plans for veterans. From the 1780's to the 1930's, land grants for Revolutionary War veterans, pensions for Union troops of the Civil War, and controversial cash bonuses for World War I doughboys had been the extent of federal assistance. Remembering controversial bonus bills in the interwar years, veterans' lobbying power, and high unemployment during the Depression, the administration of Franklin D. Roosevelt haltingly began postwar planning in 1942.

Frederic Delano, head of the National Resources Planning Board (NRPB), made the first overture. In July, 1942, Delano sought the president's support for postwar planning. Roosevelt denied approval for any public effort but reluctantly accepted a small interagency group. Between July, 1942, and April, 1943, the NRPB's Conference on the Post-War Readjustment of Civilian and Military Personnel conducted its work, submitting its final report four days after Congress abolished the NRPB. Recommendations included a postwar full employment policy and specific educational and reemployment benefits for veterans and war workers. Roosevelt created the Armed Forces Committee on Post-War Educational Opportunities for Service Personnel (the Osborn Committee) knowing that benefits for military veterans would receive a friendly hearing in Congress.

Although Roosevelt never endorsed any specific group's proposals, he called publicly for a range of veterans' benefits in national fireside radio chats on July 28 and October 27, 1943. On the latter date, he submitted the NRPB/Osborn Committee recommendations to Congress, following up with a strong message to Congress on November 23, 1943.

Warren Atherton, national commander of the American Legion, a veterans' organization founded in 1919, received instructions at the group's convention in September, 1943, to appoint a committee to draft a comprehensive veterans' benefits bill. That committee's omnibus bill included previous ideas and new provisions for loan guarantees for purchasing homes, farms, and businesses. Promoted as the "G.I. Bill of Rights," the American Legion bill restricted unemployment compensation benefits, especially for striking workers, more than had previous federal proposals. Legion officials released the omnibus bill on January 8, 1944, and introduced it into Congress two days later.

Congressional hearings and negotiation over an amended Legion bill proceeded with dispatch. Conservative Mississippi Democrat John Rankin, a longtime veterans advocate with close links to the Legion, sponsored the

House bill, while maverick Senator Joel Bennett "Champ" Clark (D-Missouri) and nine other senators introduced the Senate version.

Between January 10 and March 10, 1944, Clark's Senate Subcommittee on Veterans' Legislation of the Finance Committee held nine hearings sessions. Key veterans' groups including the Veterans of Foreign Wars, the Military Order of the Purple Heart, the Disabled American Veterans, and the Regular Veterans Association initially opposed passage, arguing that the bill would overlook disabled veterans in favor of able-bodied ones. A compromise bill incorporating educational provisions of a bill sponsored by Senator Elbert Thomas (D-Utah) passed the full Senate on March 24, 1944, by a vote of 50-0.

Between January and May, 1944, Congressman Rankin's Committee on World War Legislation held sixteen public and nineteen executive sessions. Rankin insisted on changes restricting unemployment benefits for striking workers, so the bill was amended. On May 18, 1944, the full House approved the bill by a unanimous vote of 388-0. House support included the votes of 149 representatives who were Legion members.

A grassroots letter campaign mounted by the American Legion broke a temporary deadlock in the conference committee. One week after the Allied invasion of France across the English Channel, both houses of Congress unanimously approved the amended compromise bill. President Roosevelt used ten pens to sign the bill into law on June 22, 1944. The final version of the bill provided for VA hospital construction as well as unemployment compensation, loan guarantees, and educational benefits.

Impact of Event

Between 1944 and 1956, millions of veterans used their readjustment benefits to great advantage. In the short term, veterans received help in obtaining work; loans to buy homes, farms, or businesses; and financing for education. In the long term, G.I. Bill expenditures helped promote growth of the postwar mixed economy, improved the educational level of an entire generation of the work force, and generated advantages that made World War II veterans part of an expanding middle class.

Unemployment compensation in 1946 and 1947 assisted about one million veterans per year. The readjustment allowances of $20 per week for up to fifty-two weeks led to permanent reemployment of veterans moving into a postwar economy that many Americans feared would see the return of high unemployment. In limiting the amount and length of compensation, the act marked a retreat from original recommendations while establishing the principle that veterans joined the "52-20 Club" while looking for permanent employment.

In 1945 and 1946, the United States suffered a severe housing shortage. Between 1945 and 1955, lending agencies approved 4.3 million home loans totaling $33 billion. Twenty percent of those loans were made possible by the Veterans Administration (VA). Some veterans combined New Deal-era federal mortgage insurance with a VA loan to purchase houses worth as much as $10,000. The postwar baby boom generation, including survivors of the Depression and World War II, saw VA-financed housing as a valuable commodity in the postwar United States.

Guarantees for loans to purchase farms and businesses were among the more controversial G.I. Bill programs. During the original debate, some argued that small-scale farm ownership through a VA loan made little sense in urban-industrial America. Others feared that unscrupulous business owners would take advantage of veterans interested in going into business for themselves by overstating the prospects of businesses they wanted to sell. Legally, a veteran could use a loan guarantee only to buy into a partnership or to set up a new business. No VA loan money could be used as working capital to pay operating expenses or inventory costs in any business. Small business leaders viewed the idea as an opportunity to regain ground lost to the large industrial manufacturing firms that had dominated wartime defense contracting.

In 1945, more than twelve million Americans served in the armed forces. By 1946, slightly more than three million people remained in the services. That fall, more than one million veterans enrolled in colleges and universities. Of 15.6 million eligible veterans, 7.8 million obtained education or training under the generous educational provisions of the G.I. Bill. Although only 30 percent of World War II veterans went on to earn college degrees, their numbers included 2,232,000 under the G.I. Bill. Although perhaps 80 percent of those probably would have gone to college even without the G.I. Bill, some estimates showed that 20 percent of those graduates could not have afforded a higher education without the G.I. Bill.

G.I. Bill students were the most talented, highly achieving, and oldest college students in U.S. history. Older and married veterans paved the way for later generations in becoming part of the undergraduate and graduate student populations. According to the Veterans Administration, the G.I. Bill helped to educate 450,000 engineers; 360,000 teachers; 243,000 accountants; 180,000 physicians, dentists, and nurses; 150,000 scientists; 107,000 lawyers; and 36,000 members of the clergy. Vocational training at private business schools proved more problematic, as millions of dollars were lost through waste, fraud, and student withdrawals before completion of programs. Some veterans used their benefits to finish interrupted high school programs or received credit for General Educational Development tests begun during the war.

Over the long term, the G.I. Bill represented the emergence of the postwar mixed economy of increased cooperation between the public and private sectors. By 1956, the federal government had paid out $14.5 billion in G.I. Bill educational benefits, including $5.5 billion in college loans. This investment in the nation's human capital was on the scale and of the same importance as the Marshall Plan, which rebuilt Western European economies, and the 1964 tax cut, which helped to spur economic growth. By 1955, the total cost of G.I. Bill programs was at least $20 billion. By 1968, total expenditures had reached $120 billion. In return, the U.S. economy obtained the best-trained work force in its history.

The Servicemen's Readjustment Act of 1944 proved to be among the most successful pieces of economic and social legislation in U.S. history, rivaling the Social Security Act (1935), the National Labor Relations Act (1935), the Fair Labor Standards Act (1938), the 1964 tax cut, the Civil Rights Act of 1964, the Medicare and Medicaid health care programs (1965), and the Americans with Disabilities Act (1990). The complicated policy process leading to passage and implementation of the G.I. Bill brought together veterans, federal agencies, the president, Congress, veterans' organizations, and private businesspeople to promote the principles of federal assistance for military veterans and sustained economic growth and prosperity. The bill led to a range of precedent-setting programs in postwar America. More limited versions of the original G.I. Bill would assist veterans of later wars. The Employment Act of 1958, and the social welfare programs of the 1960's built on the successful precedent of the G.I. Bill.

Bibliography

Ballard, Jack Stokes. *The Shock of Peace: Military and Economic Demobilization After World War II*. Washington, D.C.: University Press of America, 1983. Superbly researched narration of U.S. demobilization efforts during and after World War II. Places the G.I. Bill in context with other readjustment measures.

Blum, John Morton. *V Was for Victory: Politics and American Culture During World War II*. New York: Harcourt Brace Jovanovich, 1976. The most sophisticated account of mobilization on the home front. Discusses the G.I. Bill in the light of congressional politics, weakening of New Deal reforms, and Roosevelt's 1944 "Economic Bill of Rights." The epilogue gives a moving picture of returning veterans.

Mosch, Theodore R. *The G.I. Bill: A Breakthrough in Educational and Social Policy in the United States*. Hicksville, N.Y.: Exposition Press, 1975. Overview of educational sections of G.I. bills of 1944, 1952, and 1966. Valuable tables. Mosch discusses state as well as national programs and includes comparison of U.S. veterans' benefits with those in other countries.

Olson, Keith W. *The G.I. Bill, the Veterans, and the Colleges*. Lexington: University Press of Kentucky, 1974. The best study of educational aspects of the G.I. Bill, with topical chapters including excellent summaries of the origins of the G.I. Bill, a case study of the University of Wisconsin, and a conclusion comparing the World War II, Korean War, and Vietnam War-era G.I. bills.

Pencak, William. *For God and Country: The American Legion, 1919-1941*. Boston: Northeastern University Press, 1989. The first scholarly history of the American Legion in its formative years of the 1920's and 1930's. Chapter 7, "Veterans Benefits and Adjusted Compensation," gives background on the bonus for World War I veterans and how it affected the provisions of the Legion's omnibus bill, which in amended form became the G.I. Bill.

Perrett, Geoffrey. *Days of Sadness, Years of Triumph: The American People, 1939-1945*. New York: Coward, McCann & Geoghegan, 1973. Reprint. Madison: University of Wisconsin Press, 1986. The most comprehensive history of the American home front. Written in a lively style, packed with information, and persuasive in showing the period as "the last great collective social experience" in American history. One of the few histories to show the significance of the G.I. Bill in both the short and long terms.

Ross, Davis R. B. *Preparing for Ulysses: Politics and Veterans During World War II*. New York: Columbia University Press, 1969. The most comprehensive analysis of veterans' benefits, including mustering out pay, the G.I. Bill, demobilization, reconversion, and housing. Ross's view of the complicated policy-making process makes this work the single best account of the G.I. Bill. The concluding chapter is the best summary of the ways in which World War II veterans were treated better than those of other wars.

Severo, Richard, and Lewis Milford. *The Wages of War: When America's Soldiers Came Home—from Valley Forge to Vietnam*. New York: Simon & Schuster, 1989. Severo, a reporter for *The New York Times* nominated several times for the Pulitzer Prize, and Milford, a onetime lawyer for the National Veterans Law Center in Washington, D.C., provide a comprehensive review of the postwar treatment of military veterans over the sweep of U.S. history, helping to place the exceptional positive case of World War II veterans in proper historical perspective.

Patrick D. Reagan

Cross-References

The Wagner Act Promotes Union Organization (1935); The Social Security Act Provides Benefits for Workers (1935); The Truman Administration Launches the Marshall Plan (1947); Congress Creates the Small Business Administration (1953); The Kennedy-Johnson Tax Cuts Stimulate the U.S. Economy (1964); Johnson Signs the Medicare and Medicaid Amendments (1965); Bush Signs the Americans with Disabilities Act of 1990 (1990).

TRUMAN ORDERS THE SEIZURE OF RAILWAYS

CATEGORIES OF EVENT: Government and business; transportation
TIME: May 17-25, 1946
LOCALE: Washington, D.C.

Amid the crises of postwar reconversion, President Harry S Truman ordered seizure of the railroads, accelerating a reconsideration of relations among government, business, and labor

Principal personages:
HARRY S TRUMAN (1884-1972), the U.S. president who ordered federal seizure of the railroads in the public interest
JOHN ROY STEELMAN (b. 1900), a Truman aide and a negotiator with the railroad unions
ALVANLEY JOHNSTON (1875-1951), the president of the striking Brotherhood of Locomotive Engineers
ALEXANDER FELL WHITNEY (1873-1949), the president of the striking Brotherhood of Railway Trainmen
CLARK CLIFFORD (1906-1998), a White House aide who helped draft Truman's nationwide speech on the rail strike
ROBERT A. TAFT (1889-1953), a Senate Republican leader who opposed Truman's proposal to draft strikers

Summary of Event

The year following the end of World War II was filled with a succession of crises in the United States attending domestic readjustments to peace. Organized labor had fared well between 1939 and 1945, relative to the Depression years of the 1930's, but the swift demobilization of thirteen million service personnel, the lasting effects of many wartime economic restrictions, and the destabilizing results of industrial reconversions, rising

309

prices, and unslaked consumption provoked an unprecedented eruption of labor unrest.

During the spring and summer of 1946, the United States was paralyzed by a record wave of strikes, and still more and worse strikes were feared. Despite full employment during wartime, comparatively high wages, and much overtime work, organized labor felt restrained by the imposition of many wartime regulations and by the results of its wartime cooperation with management. The consolidations and mergers of many industries—that is, what appeared to be a continuing trend toward monopoly—and suspicions that management had used patriotism to garner exorbitant shares of profits while abusing labor's voluntarism as a means of regaining control of the workplace were only a few of the factors that exacerbated labor leaders' growing discontent with the postwar world.

The strikes of 1945 and 1946 affected only about 1 percent of the total labor force. In many respects industrial reconversion was proceeding satisfactorily, if not smoothly. At the peak of these stoppages, nearly 550 strikes were in progress, constituting a loss of more than 3 percent of available workers' time and directly involving about 1.4 million men and women. Statistics obscure the critical economic importance of the industries that were being struck: steel, automobiles, petroleum, meatpacking, and, more important because the nation's power was so dependent upon it, coal mining. Additional threats of a nationwide railroad strike, one capable of paralyzing nearly all economic activity, further aggravated President Harry S Truman.

Until the spring of 1946, Truman had been a model of patience in dealing with the nation's labor problems. From the beginning of his political career in Missouri through his days in the U.S. Senate, Truman had been a trusted friend of organized labor and had enjoyed its staunch support in all of his elections, including his run for the vice presidency during Franklin D. Roosevelt's fourth and last presidential campaign. In addition, during his years in the Senate Truman had earned high repute as an expert in railroad affairs. Consequently, at the first hint of a rail strike in early 1946, Truman invoked the Railway Labor Act (1926), which called for a sixty-day mediation period while the principal issue, a wage hike, was negotiated. To oversee negotiations between railroad management and representatives of twenty rail unions, Truman appointed Secretary of Labor Lewis Schwellenbach. Negotiations languished for months despite the passage of Schwellenbach's responsibilities as mediator to economist and White House staffer John Roy Steelman.

In April, although eighteen of the disaffected unions had agreed to an accommodation, two of them, each essential to railroad operations, notified the Truman Administration of a strike to begin on May 18. Together, the two unions were capable of pulling 280,000 railroad workers from their jobs. This potentially disastrous situation was further complicated by the fact that Alvanley Johnston, president of the Brotherhood of Locomotive Engineers, and Alexander Fell Whitney, president of the Brotherhood of Railroad Trainmen—the heads of the holdout unions—were longtime political allies of Truman. Both were distinguished veteran union men whose quarrels with railroad management were venerable. Both had supported Truman in his 1940 Senate race as well as in his run for the vice presidency.

On May 17, the president summoned Whitney and Johnston to the White House. There the union leaders argued that their men were demanding a work stoppage. Truman responded by signing an executive order authorizing government seizure and operation of the railroads. Under this pressure, Whitney and Johnston agreed to a strike delay of five days. In the interim, troops seized the railroads and Truman called upon other political figures to urge compromise upon the union leaders. He proposed an 18.5-cent-per-hour pay raise for railroad workers, more generous than suggested by a fact-finding commission. Whitney and Johnston remained intractable.

Media attention focused on the White House as the strike deadline approached. An hour before the scheduled strike, on May 23, Truman addressed nearly nine hundred wounded veterans on the South Lawn, conscious of the contrast between their sacrifices and the dangers posed to the country by two union leaders. Behind him, inside the White House, negotiations remained stalemated. At five o'clock, as scheduled, the strike began. Its impact was immediate. Neither the great rail strike of 1877 nor the American Railway Union's strike of 1894 had so completely paralyzed rail traffic. Of the nation's nearly two hundred thousand freight and passenger trains, about four hundred remained operative amid the vast disruption. The White House at once came under fire for its apparent failure to steer negotiations to a successful conclusion.

Truman's reaction—one opposed by many of his cabinet members, friends, and aides—was rage. The following day, he drafted a blistering radio speech. In its original version, the speech bitterly denounced the unions' leaders, sharply and inaccurately contrasting their pay with his own and, with equal inaccuracy, comparing the pay of railroad workers with that of soldiers. It simultaneously vilified other labor leaders, along with Congress, and virtually called for vigilantism against those who jeopardized the nation's welfare. Although it remained tough, the draft speech was materially refined and softened by White House aide Clark Clifford before its 10:00 P.M. delivery. As negotiations resumed on May 25, Truman delivered an extended version to Congress, urging approval to draft strikers. Even as Truman spoke, he was handed a note confirming a strike settlement.

Impact of Event

The deep issues involved in the strike conflict reasserted themselves over the following months and years. One such issue concerned the extent of, or limitations on, presidential powers. The issue had surfaced regularly during each of Franklin D. Roosevelt's administrations. Truman's proposal to use federal authority not only to break a strike but to do so by drafting strikers into the armed forces dramatically revived that issue. Although manage-ment and a majority of the public praised Truman's toughness and his forceful display of public character, many of his associates, aides, and friends believed that his radio and congressional addresses were patently unconstitutional as well as intemperate.

Stronger denunciations came from Truman's former friends, Whitney and Johnston. Their views were echoed loudly by virtually every major U.S. labor leader. These leaders variously depicted the president as a dictator, a fascist, or a communist, vowing a complete withdrawal of their support. This was a predictable reaction considering that labor's battles against hostile uses of federal authority were integral parts of labor history. Unions, at least until the mid-1930's, not only had to contend with masses of antilabor legislation but also had been obliged to fight for their existence against the government's employment or support of strikebreaking court injunctions, judicial repression of organizing and strike tactics through dubious applications of the Sherman Act, federal resort to the Army to quell labor disturbances, and government prosecution and imprisonment of labor leaders. Reforms embodied in the National Labor Relations Act (1935) and other prolabor legislation during the 1930's were of too recent vintage in 1946 to erase such memories.

Broader than the issue of presidential power, therefore, was the issue of what role government should play, if any, in critical disputes between management and labor. This in turn was just one part of a more general and widely discussed question about the role of government in the economy as a whole.

Immediately after settlement of the rail strike, there were two related matters before Congress: Truman's earlier proposal for a mandatory cool-ing off period and specified fact-finding procedures before strikes occurred, and the counterpoint to this in the form of a conservative bill authored in February, 1946, by Representative Clifford Case of South Dakota. The Case bill called for a thirty-day cooling off period before a strike could take effect; the use of injunctions, particularly in regard to boycotts; and provi-sions to make both labor and management liable for breaching labor contracts. Each of these provisos sounded alarms in labor's camp.

The flow of the Case bill through Congress coincided with a series of national emergencies caused by conflicts between workers and management. Nationwide coal strikes and two seizures of that industry by presidential fiat were followed by Truman's seizure of the country's major meatpacking plants, oil producing and refining facilities, and tugboat and towing company equipment. Truman coped simultaneously with major steel, electrical, and auto industry strikes. These crises and responses exhausted patience—and often judgment—in all quarters. Reflecting popular sentiments, the congressional stance toward labor hardened. As might have been expected, the Case bill was sharper by the time it came under Senate consideration. It struck Truman as so antilabor that he vetoed the bill. The veto was sustained, but Truman did not regain the favor that he had lost among labor leaders by his handling of the railroad strike.

The notion persisted inside and outside Congress that the National Labor Relations Act of 1935 (the Wagner Act) had tipped the bargaining scale too far to labor's side. For decades before, lawmakers and the country at large had cried out for curbs on business trusts and would-be monopolies, pleas in time sanctified in legislation and eventually in judicial interpretations. This progress toward restraining management seemed only to have whetted the greed and monopolistic impulses of labor organizations. Justifiably or not, what presidents and Congress sought were viable formulas by which to right this apparent imbalance, which now appeared overly favorable to labor.

The Labor Management Relations Act (the Taft-Hartley Act) of 1947, coming hard on the labor tumult of 1946, appeared to be the most politic solution, although it would soon be contested bitterly as a "slave labor law," and become a burning issue in the 1948 and 1952 presidential elections. The Taft-Hartley Act retained labor's rights under the Wagner Act, but it juxtaposed to the list of prohibited "unfair" practices of management a corresponding list of "unfair" labor practices of unions.

Bibliography

Ayers, Eben A. *Truman in the White House: The Diary of Eben A. Ayers.* Edited by Robert H. Ferrell. Columbia: University of Missouri Press, 1991. Edited by a leading authority on Truman, this is a literate, intelligent, abbreviated account of the flow of events, rail strike included, during the Truman Administration. Needs to be supplemented, but useful. Many photos, useful index.

Donovan, Robert J. *Conflict and Crisis: The Presidency of Harry S. Truman, 1945-1948.* New York: W. W. Norton, 1977. Accurate and detailed. Written by a national columnist. Superior to most academic works. Many photos, chapter notes, splendid index.

Gosnell, Harold F. *Truman's Crises: A Political Biography of Harry S. Truman*. Westport, Conn.: Greenwood Press, 1980. The author is a noted political scientist. The prose is uninspired but well organized. Chapter notes, useful bibliography, good index. Chapter 22 pertains to the railroad strike and its context.

McCullough, David. *Truman*. New York: Simon & Schuster, 1992. Overwritten and duplicative of many other works on Truman and his presidency. The writing falls below the standard of McCullough's usually exciting prose. A weighty synthesis worth reading by those who previously knew little of Truman's presidency. Many photos, source notes, fine bibliography, and index.

Miller, Merle. *Plain Speaking: An Oral Biography of Harry S. Truman*. New York: Berkley, 1974. Miller's observations are acute and affectionate. Much on Truman's special knowledge of railroads. Good index.

Miller, Richard Lawrence. *Truman: The Rise to Power*. New York: McGraw-Hill, 1986. Excellent reading, accurate and informative. Fine background on Truman's experience and character, including his understanding of railroad labor problems in pre-White House days. Photos. Excellent notes replace bibliography.

Truman, Harry S. *Year of Decisions*. Vol. 1 in *Memoirs*. Garden City, N.Y.: Doubleday, 1955. Inimitable Truman, pithy and deceptively straightforward. Good perspectives on the strike wave, the railroad strike, and presidential reactions. Good index. Refreshing and invaluable.

Clifton K. Yearley

Cross-References

The Railway Labor Act Provides for Mediation of Labor Disputes (1926); The Wagner Act Promotes Union Organization (1935); Roosevelt Signs the Fair Labor Standards Act (1938); Roosevelt Signs the Emergency Price Control Act (1942); The Taft-Hartley Act Passes over Truman's Veto (1947).

THE TRUMAN ADMINISTRATION LAUNCHES THE MARSHALL PLAN

CATEGORIES OF EVENT: International business and commerce; government and business
TIME: June 5, 1947
LOCALE: Harvard University, Cambridge, Massachusetts

Through the Marshall Plan, the United States helped resolve European political and economic problems after World War II, greatly aiding European industrial recovery in the process

Principal personages:
HARRY S TRUMAN (1884-1972), the president of the United States, 1945-1953
GEORGE C. MARSHALL (1880-1959), the U.S. secretary of state, 1947-1949
WILLIAM L. CLAYTON (1880-1966), the undersecretary of state for economic affairs
DEAN ACHESON (1893-1971), the secretary of state, 1949-1953, and undersecretary of state, 1945-1947
GEORGE F. KENNAN (b. 1904), a member of the Department of State policy and planning staff
PAUL G. HOFFMAN (1891-1974), a chief Marshall Plan administrator

Summary of Event
The Marshall Plan was officially announced by Secretary of State George C. Marshall in the course of a commencement speech at Harvard

University on June 5, 1947. Although the plan bears the name of its announcer, it had been devised by a team of experts within the administration of President Harry S Truman, including William L. Clayton, George F. Kennan, and Dean Acheson. Marshall's speech was a proposal for a massive aid package for the war-ravaged economies of Europe. The idea behind the aid was that if the United States assisted the European countries, Europe's economic problems would be resolved, leading to political stability. The plan registered as a definite political success but produced fewer results than hoped for in terms of specific American economic objectives.

From a political point of view, it was not easy to persuade the American public to invest about $13 billion in European reconstruction. The United States already had refused to extend massive aid during the two years since the end of World War II. The deteriorating European economic and political situation, coupled with possible further Soviet encroachment in Eastern Europe, led the Truman Administration to assume all the political risks involved in such an aid program.

Europe's situation appeared to be slipping out of control by the spring of 1947. Although the Western European economies had made considerable steps toward recovery between the end of the hostilities and the beginning of 1947, long-term structural problems, particularly with regard to international payments, were far from resolved. The European countries' chief problem consisted of large foreign account deficits and the lack of sufficient gold or gold-convertible currency reserves to cover outstanding foreign debt. These countries found it difficult to buy raw materials and equipment deemed necessary to the recovery process. In addition, unsatisfied consumer demand fueled powerful inflation. Unless the Europeans could obtain large foreign credits, their recovery process would come to a standstill. The United States-sponsored International Monetary Fund (IMF), created in 1944, had extended some of the needed funds, but it was not endowed with much capital. Massive American aid, Marshall Plan proponents argued, would provide the necessary funds to help achieve the most important IMF goal: a multilateral trade and payments system based on convertible currencies and nearly free of governmental impediments such as tariffs.

The international payments problem was coupled with a number of political predicaments. First, there was the problem of Soviet advances in Eastern Europe. The Truman Administration perceived that Stalin had embarked upon a program of Eastern European conquest. Moreover, in the spring of 1947, both the Greeks and the Turks had asked for American economic and military aid, the former to defeat Greek communist guerrillas, the latter to arm themselves against possible Soviet advances toward the

Dardanelles strait. This call for aid had prompted the American president to announce his "Truman Doctrine," which basically stated that the United States would provide economic and military aid to countries threatened by communism. Marshall Plan aid would therefore go hand in hand with the Truman Doctrine, as it would help stabilize the political situation in Europe by giving a boost to the economy. Once standards of living had improved, Europeans would be far less inclined, it was argued, to support communist parties. These anticommunist arguments secured congressional support for Truman's policies.

There was also the so-called "German problem," itself tied to the question of communist containment. It appeared necessary to reinsert Germany into the European community of nations in order to transform it into a Western European democratic bastion against communism. If Germany had been severely punished with the burden of heavy reparations, as after World War I, it would not have been able to rebuild quickly and might have been vulnerable to the Soviets: Stalin might have stood with his Red Army along the Rhine, just across from France. Rebuilding and reinforcing Germany such a short time after the Nazi experience, however, was an extremely difficult political proposition. The Marshall Plan would help resolve that political difficulty by providing Western European countries, particularly Great Britain and France, with funds that the Germans themselves could not provide in the form of reparations. At the same time, Germany would receive aid, though in smaller amounts, and could thus be rebuilt rapidly.

All the above-mentioned European economic and social problems were at the basis of Marshall's commencement speech, which came with a warning: In order to ensure that American aid would be used efficiently, aid beneficiaries should integrate their economies. If the European economies were integrated, Europe would enjoy all the

One of the greatest successes of President Harry S Truman's administration was the Marshall Plan. (Library of Congress)

317

benefits of capital and consumer markets as large as those of the United States. That would eliminate uncompetitive firms while favoring rationalization and regional specialization. Integration would also tie the European countries' economies so tightly as to make old national conflicts disappear. Integration was to help bring Germany and its former enemies, particularly France, closer to each other than they had ever been.

Integration could not happen randomly: It had to be planned. Marshall Plan beneficiaries were soon required to prepare national investment plans that presupposed integration with other European markets. At the same time, intra-European payments would be regulated by accords that would eventually lead to convertible currencies. In the end, the Western European economy would become internationally competitive and able to join the United States in promoting international free trade.

The Marshall Plan was approved by Congress on April 13, 1948, as the European Recovery Program (ERP). It was to be administered by an independent agency, the Economic Cooperation Administration (ECA), headed by Paul G. Hoffman, a businessman who had been president of the Studebaker Automobile Company.

Impact of Event

The Marshall Plan had important effects on the reconstruction of Western Europe, especially from a political point of view, despite the fact that not all the Truman Administration's original goals were achieved. European industry profited greatly. The ERP's clearest success lay in the area of communist containment. Both in France and in Italy, where the Left was very strong at the end of World War II, the Communists were put on the defensive by 1948. Generally, economic hardship that might have aided the cause of communist parties was avoided. Marshall Plan funds were often used to appease political demands: They allowed for smaller tax levies, financial stabilization, relief of unemployment, and much-needed investment in capital equipment. With a strengthening of pro-American centrist forces, the private sector operated in a safer political environment, resulting in higher levels of business confidence.

If the Marshall Plan was a success politically, there are some doubts concerning some of its specific economic goals. It is undeniably true that most Western European countries increased production spectacularly between 1948 and 1951 and became far better able to compete internationally. By 1951, however, the European countries' balance of payments with the dollar area was still in the red, and the United States had to continue to send aid, particularly military aid, after the outbreak of the Korean War.

Moreover, little integration of the Western European economies had been achieved by 1951. Originally American planners had hoped to create a fully integrated single market, perhaps operating under a single currency. By 1951, the European economies were still essentially following national economic development plans. An intra-European payments bloc had been created to simplify the payments mechanism within Western Europe, but this did not lead to European currencies' convertibility, as originally sought by the Americans.

Marshall Plan administrators were only moderately successful in their efforts to influence European countries' economic policies. Western European countries had national agendas that, by and large, they did not abandon in the name of integration or other ERP goals. For example, the British continued with full employment policies, even when that meant withdrawing Great Britain from nearly all American-sponsored intra-European trade and payments integration schemes. In France, authorities did not scale down massive investment plans for economic modernization, even when investment caused inflation, one of the principal economic woes that Marshall Plan officials were attempting to eradicate from Europe.

The German problem itself was resolved more through Franco-German haggling than through the Marshall Plan. After a series of disputes and negotiations, French and German administrations arrived at an accord, the European Coal and Steel Community (ECSC), for integrated Western European control over Ruhr Valley coal and steel. The ECSC dealt with only two commodities and resembled a cartel insofar as it was a market-sharing agreement. The United States accepted this arrangement and helped in the negotiating process, offering Marshall Plan aid to support it. The ECSC, despite its limits and cartel-like features, represented some degree of intra-European economic integration and, more important, marked a rapprochement between France and Germany that planted the seeds of the future European Economic Community.

Western European politics led the Americans to tone down their expectations throughout the 1948-1950 period. In the end, American politicians chose to uphold their political priorities and sacrifice some of the more specific economic goals. It became increasingly apparent that in order for the ERP to succeed, American goals had to be adapted to fit Western Europe's hard political realities.

European industry generally profited from the ERP. Businesses that had experienced difficulties in importing, producing for export, and obtaining credit found that once technologically sound and innovative projects were presented, ERP provisions made available the needed equipment and raw materials, or loans at favorable terms. In some cases, businesses also modernized their outlook through ERP technical assistance and productivity programs. In countries such as West Germany and Great Britain, though less so in France and Italy, American-sponsored non-communist trade unions helped improve industrial relations. Business leaders also cooperated with their governments in devising ERP policy. In part, the effectiveness of business "re-education" programs depended on the fact that the ECA was staffed by many forward-looking American business leaders. Besides Paul Hoffman, these included Thomas K. Finletter of Coudert Brothers; David K. Bruce, a businessman from Baltimore; James D. Zellerbach of the Crown Zellerbach Corporation; and James G. Blaine of Midland Trust Company. These men criticized their European counterparts but also sought to persuade them, at times successfully, about corporate management methods.

Generally, the anti-communist guarantees provided by the United States's presence in Western Europe allayed entrepreneurs' fears and contributed to a more positive investment psychology. By the early 1950's, despite the lack of effective integration or a definitive solution to the payments problems, the private sector was thriving and helping propel Western Europe to high rates of economic growth.

Bibliography

Diebold, William. *Trade and Payments in Western Europe: A Study in Economic Cooperation, 1947-1951.* New York: Harper & Brothers, 1952. One of the best basic studies on Western European efforts to create an intra-European trade and payments system after World War II. Much attention is devoted to the role played by Marshall Plan aid in helping to create that system.

Gimbel, John. *The Origins of the Marshall Plan.* Stanford, Calif.: Stanford University Press, 1976. Directly tackles the difficult question of which goals were considered most important by Truman Administration officials as they devised a policy for the reconstruction of Western Europe. Gimbel takes into account not only economic goals but also strategic ones, with particular regard to the Franco-German settlement.

Hogan, Michael J. *The Marshall Plan: America, Britain, and the Reconstruction of Western Europe, 1947-1952.* Cambridge, Mass.: Cambridge University Press, 1987. Hogan's work is based on extensive documentation found in American and British archives. It poses the question of Marshall Plan success by arguing that the United States sought above all to transplant into Europe a neocorporatist economic model that had emerged in America through New Deal and World War II experiences. Hogan concludes that the Western European countries absorbed much of this model by adapting it to their own political and economic realities.

Milward, Alan S. *The Reconstruction of Western Europe, 1945-1951*. Berkeley: University of California Press, 1984. The most comprehensive study to date concerning the origins of European economic integration. Milward stresses the failures of American initiatives and shows that Marshall Plan aid was used by the Western European countries mainly to carry out their own national agendas.

Wexler, Imanuel. *The Marshall Plan Revisited: The European Recovery Program in Economic Perspective*. Westport, Conn.: Greenwood Press, 1983. A thorough and well-informed inquiry into the economic impact of the Marshall Plan in Europe. Wexler concludes that although not all of Western Europe's economic problems were solved by the ERP, the Marshall Plan was instrumental in assisting Europe to achieve spectacular economic growth.

Chiarella Esposito

Cross-References

The General Agreement on Tariffs and Trade Is Signed (1947); The Agency for International Development Is Established (1961); The United States Suffers Its First Trade Deficit Since 1888 (1971); The North American Free Trade Agreement Goes into Effect (1994).

THE TAFT-HARTLEY ACT PASSES OVER TRUMAN'S VETO

CATEGORY OF EVENT: Labor
TIME: June 23, 1947
LOCALE: Washington, D.C.

Superseding the prolabor Wagner Act, the Taft-Hartley Act invoked federal authority to restore a more popularly acceptable balance of power between management and unions

Principal personages:
HARRY S TRUMAN (1884-1972), a Democratic president who vetoed the Taft-Hartley Act
ROBERT A. TAFT (1889-1953), a leading Republican senator who helped sponsor the act
JOHN L. LEWIS (1880-1969), a United Mine Workers leader

Summary of Event

The Taft-Hartley Act of 1947 represented a national reaction against the presumed excess of power wielded by labor unions in the aftermath of World War II. By 1946, it was widely believed that the labor reforms of Franklin D. Roosevelt's administrations had pushed prolabor legislation too far and had unbalanced the operations of a competitive marketplace. Informed by vocal interest groups, a popular consensus developed around the notion that the existing statutory rules governing collective bargaining ignored the rights of employers, vitiated the rights of individual workers (notably those uninterested in joining unions), and jeopardized the public interest. These opinions were strongly reflected in the dominant mood of the Eightieth Congress, the members of which were overwhelmingly conservative and overwhelmingly Republican.

Specifically, many members of Congress believed that the time had come for amendment of the Norris-LaGuardia Act of 1932, which deprived the federal courts of jurisdiction over most labor disputes, removed unions from subjection to the antitrust legislation of the Sherman Act and the Clayton Act, and ensured unions' freedom to employ the full gamut of their organizing weapons to secure collective bargaining. Similar views extended to operations of the National Labor Relations Act (the Wagner Act) of 1935, which threw the authority of the federal government behind workers' right to select unions of their own choosing and to bargain collectively with employers. Employers, whose businesses were still targets of antitrust legislation, were further constrained by the act's delineation of practices deemed unfair to labor.

Hostility toward labor that manifested itself in Congress also appeared to characterize several dramatic moves by the Democratic administration of President Harry S Truman. Anomalously, through most of his political career Truman had been a reliable ally of organized labor. Truman had won support from the leaders of railroad unions, but these relationships were ruptured abruptly when an irate Truman ordered federal seizure of the railways and threatened to draft striking workers into the armed forces during the nationwide railroad strike of 1946.

The rail strike was only one of a series of labor explosions that the president and the country had had to confront in an uncertain postwar economy. Soaring prices tended to cancel workers' wartime wage gains. Corporate profits were the highest in history, and a massive wave of mergers raised new fears of monopoly. Organized labor's response was to demand higher wages. Some unions, such as John L. Lewis' United Mine Workers (UMW), went further, demanding employer-financed health and welfare benefits. Although employment had reached new heights and the number of work stoppages was modest, crippling strikes erupted between 1945 and 1947 in critical industries including steel, railways, automobiles, electrical goods, rubber, meatpacking, and coal mining. Moreover, these strikes and the threat of others were complicated by shutdowns resulting from union jurisdictional disputes provoked by feuds between the American Federation of Labor (AFL) and the Congress of Industrial Organizations (CIO).

Controlling Congress for the first time in twenty-eight years, the Republican Party, through one of its principal leaders and a presidential hopeful, Senator Robert A. Taft of Ohio, determined to capitalize on an individualistic nation's antipathies toward seemingly strident dictatorial labor leaders and the unions they represented. Taking his cues from a manifesto of the National Association of Manufacturers, Taft became a spokesman for those who sought to curtail what were widely regarded as labor's own unfair practices: secondary boycotts (encouraging others not to trade with a particular business), refusals to bargain or failures to bargain in good faith, violations of contracts, the overt use of coercion against nonunion workers to force them into unions, demands for the closed (or all-union) shop, "featherbedding" (creating jobs or making jobs simpler to add to union membership or benefit members), and jurisdictional strikes. Taft and his fellow Republicans were eager to win political advantage over a Democratic president mired in attempts to deal with a Lewis-led UMW strike and already at odds with labor leaders for what they perceived as Truman's mishandling of the rail strike.

Such was the climate of opinion in which Congress passed the Taft-Hartley Act on June 20, 1947, amending the Norris-LaGuardia Act and the Wagner Act in a number of important ways. Taft-Hartley largely restored employers' freedom to hire and fire workers regardless of union membership. The act consequently severely limited, it if did not entirely void, unions' chances of winning the closed shop. Internal union discipline was impaired by a provision that union members could be dropped from membership only because of nonpayment of dues, thus opening the door to employers' deployment of antiunion provocateurs, spies, and "stool pigeons" within union ranks.

The act further placed under proscription a lengthy list of unfair practices by labor. Vigorous union recruiting measures, particularly during elections to determine workers' choices of bargaining agents, were banned. Union ultimatums to employers were banned, as were union efforts to persuade employers to discriminate in favor of union workers. The checkoff system, whereby employers deducted union dues from workers' wages, was abolished. Under many circumstances, secondary and jurisdictional strikes and boycotts were proscribed, and when they were threatened they could be held in abeyance by court injunctions. Similarly, strikes affecting interstate commerce, which conceivably meant strikes in most industries, were subjected to the delay of eighty-day "cooling off" periods, after which the president could secure a court injunction. Unions were made subject to civil suit for damages to employers' interests, caused by unfair practices.

Especially galling to organized labor was the provision that before the act's administrative agency, the National Labor Relations Board (NLRB), would hear union appeals, union officials were required to take an oath that they neither were communists nor were affiliated with communist organizations. In addition, union files, finances, and the methods by which union officers were elected were thrown open to government scrutiny. Stringent restrictions were imposed on union political activities and political contributions in federal elections.

Siding with labor, whose support he was eager to regain, as well as capitalizing on doubts about the act even among its sponsors, President Truman vetoed the Taft-Hartley Act on June 20, 1947. As Truman probably expected, given the strong votes favoring it in Congress, the measure was passed over his veto, three days later. The act's hundreds of specific provisions covered in twenty pages of fine print thus became the nation's principal labor law.

Impact of Event

President Truman and labor leaders alike condemned the Taft-Hartley Act bitterly. Truman argued that it would sow seeds of discord that would plague the nation's future, that it created an unworkable administrative structure, that it complicated collective bargaining, and that it made no contribution to the resolution of complex labor-management problems. The sentiments of union leaders were summed up by their description of Taft-Hartley as a slave labor bill that threatened to eviscerate their major gains of the preceding fifteen years. Considering the national uproar generated by the act, it was to be expected that it became an important issue in the national elections of 1948 and 1952. More than being an electoral issue, it also became a touchstone for determining one of the bounds between liberals and conservatives, friends of labor and enemies of labor, and champions of business and critics of business.

In the light of the heated debates and dire predictions attending Taft-Hartley's enactment, the subsequent history of the act's operation was markedly placid. With organized labor's support, Truman was reelected in 1948. Strong labor unions continued to grow stronger over the next two decades, with nearly 1.5 million workers becoming union members in the South alone during the 1950's. Unions grew at a slower rate than in the previous decade, but there were many explanations for this in addition to the effects of Taft-Hartley.

Within two years after Taft-Hartley's enactment, it had become clear that both organized labor and employers were managing to live with provisions of the act. Judged by the number of employer appeals to the NLRB about the unfair practices of unions, employers were far less interested in using Taft-Hartley to suppress organized labor than congressional and other political battles had indicated. In 1949, for example, nine-tenths of the appeals filed with the NLRB came from unions rather than from employers.

Union leaders acted swiftly to exploit the Taft-Hartley's gray areas and loopholes. One provision of the act stipulated that workers' refusal to stay on the job because of "abnormally dangerous conditions" did not constitute a strike, so unions claimed dangerous conditions when they wanted workers off the job. Furthermore, since employers could sue unions for violations of Taft-Hartley's no-strike provision, unions simply demanded that new contracts with employers omit the no-strike pledges from the work force. John L. Lewis, whose UMW had been released from federal control on June 30, 1947, negotiated mine operators into acceding to a new contract proviso that miners would work while they were "able and willing."

Lewis was also in the forefront of labor leaders' bitter fight against Taft-Hartley's imposition of a noncommunist oath. A few unions were controlled by communists, but the vast majority were not. Labor leaders were furious that on questions of loyalty they, and not employers, were being singled out. Although a number of unions reluctantly acceded to oath requirements, hoping to placate the NLRB and public opinion, Lewis, a staunch Republican himself, adamantly refused. The NLRB overruled its own general counsel by dropping the oath requirement.

Taft-Hartley's almost universal ban on union political activities, particularly the ban on union political expenditures, was fought by being ignored pending resolution by the nation's courts of the issues involved. The AFL initiated, as a subterfuge, voluntary fund-raising campaigns among union members that were designed to ensure the political defeat of Senator Taft and those politicians who had supported him. As it transpired, a circuit court decision in March, 1948, pronounced the Taft-Hartley ban on political activity unconstitutional. Loopholes were widened when the United Auto Workers (UAW) negotiated contracts exempting it from several of the act's restrictions and several other unions won "no-liability" contracts from employers that removed them from dangers of employer-filed civil suits for unfair practices.

The remainder of 1947 after passage of Taft-Hartley was relatively free of major strikes. Serious stoppages recurred in early 1948, however, providing important challenges to the act. One major stoppage involved the UMW, led by John L. Lewis. When negotiations between Lewis and mine operators over the pending 1949 contract remained unsettled, Lewis, without calling a strike, nevertheless engineered a work slowdown. When operators, in turn, refused to contribute to the UMW welfare fund—as Taft-Hartley permitted them to do—Lewis called a full strike. A federal injunction sanctioned by Taft-Hartley was swiftly issued. Lewis ordered the men back to work, but many refused. Lewis, in company with twenty other UMW officials, subsequently was charged with contempt. A federal district court on March 2, 1950, exonerated the union officials. On March 3, President Truman called upon Congress for authorization to seize the mines and channel their profits into the U.S. Treasury. Within hours, the strike was resolved in a compromise favoring the UMW. There would be six other occasions in 1948 alone in which the president would invoke Taft-Hartley's national emergency provisions to force resolution of strikes, or threats of strikes, that were against the public interest.

Taft-Hartley, on balance, did not bring peace between management and labor. Both sides continued to fault the act, the former because it did too little to curb the monopoly power of unions, the latter because it was excessive and discriminatory in regulating unions. The act did involve the federal government in guiding and controlling certain activities of both employers and unions in discrete ways, a trend strengthened by the Labor-Management Reporting and Disclosure Act of 1959 (the Landrum-Griffin Act).

Bibliography

Cox, Archibald. *Law and the National Labor Policy.* Los Angeles: Institute of Industrial Relations, University of California, 1960. An excellent, readable survey of events and policies leading to Taft-Hartley. Notes and a usable index.

Donovan, Robert J. *Conflict and Crisis: The Presidency of Harry S. Truman, 1945-1948.* New York: W. W. Norton, 1977. A fine, informative book. Chapter 33 is excellent on Truman's reaction to Taft-Hartley. The entire book provides a splendid context for post-1945 labor problems. A few photos, useful chapter notes, and index.

Gregory, Charles O. *Labor and the Law.* 2d rev. ed. New York: W. W. Norton, 1961. An excellent and authoritative survey of the subject. Valuable on the first decade of Taft-Hartley's impact and complications. Some notes, brief bibliography, and good index that includes cases. A fine introduction for lay readers.

Hughes, Jonathan R. T. *American Economy History.* 5th ed. Reading, Mass.: Addison-Wesley, 1998.

Lee, R. Alton. *Truman and Taft-Hartley.* Lexington: University of Kentucky Press, 1966. Scholarly and detailed. A bit turgid, but invaluable. Notes, modest bibliography, and useful index.

Northrup, Herbert R., and Gordon F. Bloom. *Government and Labor: The Role of Government in Union-Management Relations.* Homewood, Ill.: Richard D. Irwin, 1963. Chapters 4 and 5 discuss Taft-Hartley's content, meaning, and implications and provide an appraisal. Detailed and informative. Page notes, chapter bibliographies, table of cases, and name and subject indexes.

Wilcox, Clair. *Public Policies Toward Business.* Homewood, Ill.: Richard D. Irwin, 1966. Strong on businesses' required adaptations to Taft-Hartley. Chapter 32 on government and labor is especially informative on Taft-Hartley as an extension of government's intervention in the economy. Many page notes and brief chapter bibliographies. A valuable synthesis.

Clifton K. Yearley

Cross-References
The Railway Labor Act Provides for Mediation of Labor Disputes (1926); The Norris-LaGuardia Act Adds Strength to Labor Organizations (1932); The Wagner Act Promotes Union Organization (1935); The CIO Begins Unionizing Unskilled Workers (1935); Roosevelt Signs the Fair Labor Standards Act (1938); Truman Orders the Seizure of Railways (1946); The Landrum-Griffin Act Targets Union Corruption (1959).

THE GENERAL AGREEMENT ON TARIFFS AND TRADE IS SIGNED

CATEGORY OF EVENT: International business and commerce
TIME: October 30, 1947
LOCALE: Geneva, Switzerland

The General Agreement on Tariffs and Trade (GATT) set basic rules under which open and nondiscriminatory trade can take place

Principal personages:
CORDELL HULL (1871-1955), the initiator of the idea of GATT; the U.S. secretary of state, 1933-1944
JOHN MAYNARD KEYNES (1883-1946), a British economist and negotiator in wartime talks
JAMES EDWARD MEADE (1907-1995), a British economist and public official, one of the originators of the movement for an international trade organization
LIONEL CHARLES ROBBINS (1898-1984), an economist and public official who represented Great Britain in GATT talks

Summary of Event

On October 30, 1947, representatives of twenty-three countries, meeting in Geneva, Switzerland, signed the General Agreement on Tariffs and Trade (GATT) to reduce trade barriers among signatory nations. GATT was an attempt to combat the rise of worldwide protectionism that had preceded World War II. By providing a set of rules for open and nondiscriminatory trade and a mechanism to implement these rules, GATT sought to create an institutional framework within which international trade could be conducted as stably and predictably as possible.

When the Great Depression set in, the U.S. Congress passed the highly protective Smoot-Hawley Tariff Act in 1930, raising average tariff rates on imports almost 60 percent. Great Britain passed the Import Duties Act in 1932, abandoning its traditional free trade policy. Other countries responded with restrictive import policies in self-defense. The result was a downward spiral in international trade, with the volume of trade in manufactured goods declining by 40 percent by the end of 1932.

The U.S. view on international trade began to change after the Democratic victory in the presidential election in 1932. The new secretary of state, Cordell Hill, strongly favored U.S. leadership in arresting the worldwide protectionist wave. He was convinced that the elimination of trade barriers was the best means of reversing the downward spiral in international trade, which would in turn allow higher standards of living for all countries and promote lasting peace. After several years of his intensive lobbying, the Reciprocal Trade Agreements Act (RTA Act), an amendment to the Smoot-Hawley Act, was passed in 1934. The RTA Act empowered the president, for a period of three years, to initiate trade agreements on the basis of reciprocal tariff reductions. Reductions of U.S. tariffs were limited to 50 percent. The RTA Act was extended several times. The United States concluded agreements with twenty-nine countries on the basis of most-favored-nation treatment before the outbreak of World War II. The idea of negotiating reciprocal tariff reductions, embodied in the RTA Act, was the conceptual basis for GATT. Soon after the United States entered World War II, the Allied nations, particularly the United States and Great Britain, started discussion on postwar trade and monetary issues. The discussion led to the Bretton Woods Conference in July, 1944, at Bretton Woods, New Hampshire. This conference established the charters of the International Monetary Fund and the International Bank for Reconstruction and Development (commonly known as the World Bank) to deal with international monetary issues. It also recognized the need for a comparable institution focusing on trade to complement the monetary institutions.

Negotiations on the form and functions of an International Trade Organization (ITO) were first held on a bilateral basis between the United States and Great Britain. The United States pressed for nondiscrimination, whereby no country is favored over others; Great Britain insisted on continuation of its Imperial Preference, under which British goods receive preferential access to the markets of its former colonies and vice versa. A compromise was reached, and the results of those bilateral negotiations were published in November, 1945, in the Proposals for Expansion of World Trade and Employment. The United States expanded those proposals into a draft charter for the ITO in 1946. The charter was amended in successive conferences from 1946 to 1948 in London, New York, Geneva, and Havana. The final version of the ITO charter, known as the Havana Charter, was drawn up in Havana on March 4, 1948. The charter, which represented a series of agreements among fifty-three countries, never came into effect because most countries, including the United States, failed to ratify it.

At the same time that the United States published the proposals, it invited several countries to participate in negotiations to reduce tariffs and other trade barriers on the basis of principles laid out in the proposals. The United States proposed to integrate all individual treaties into a multilateral treaty. GATT was thus drawn up as a general framework for rights and obligations regarding tariff reductions for twenty-three participating nations. GATT came into being before the Havana Conference but in accordance with the draft charter for the ITO that was currently under discussion. It was originally envisaged as the first of a number of agreements that were to be negotiated under the auspices of the ITO. It was supposed to be a provisional agency that would go out of existence once the ITO was established. The power and the bureaucratic size of the proposed ITO faced strong opposition in the U.S. Congress. Consequently, the Havana Charter was not put before the U.S. Senate for ratification for fear of its defeat. When it was clear that the United States would not ratify the Havana Charter, GATT became by default the underpinning of an international institution, assuming part of the commercial policy role that had been assigned to the ITO.

Technically speaking, GATT is not an organization of which countries become members but a treaty among contracting parties. As a multilateral agreement, GATT has no binding authority over its signatories. When countries agree to GATT, they are expected to commit to three fundamental principles: nondiscrimination, as embodied in the most-favored-nation clause (all countries should be treated equally); a general prohibition of export subsidies (except for agriculture) and import quotas, from which developing countries are exempted; and a requirement that any new tariff be offset by a reduction in other tariffs.

Impact of Event

The agreement itself was without precedent. No agreement had ever been completed before GATT that included more countries, covered more trade, involved more extensive actions, or represented a wider consensus on commercial policy. It provided a promising contrast to the record of failures to liberalize trade that had characterized the years between the two world wars.

Among the twenty-three participating countries, 123 bilateral negotiations occurred. The United States was a party to 22 of them, and the remaining 101 took place among the other members of the group. The signatory nations accounted for more than three-fourths of world trade, and negotiations covered two-thirds of trade among member nations. Tariff was reduced on about fifty thousand items, accounting for about half of world trade. Average tariff rates were cut by about one-third in the United States. By 1950, average tariffs on dutiable imports into the United States had fallen by about 75 percent as compared to Smoot-Hawley levels.

GATT is a remarkable success story of an international organization. Over the years, it has provided the framework for an open trade system and a set of rules for nondiscrimination and settlement of international trade disputes. From 1947 to 1979, seven "rounds" of trade negotiations were completed under GATT auspices: in 1947 (Geneva), 1949 (Annecy, France), 1951 (Torquay, the United Kingdom), 1956 (Geneva), 1960-1961 (Geneva, the "Dillion Round"), 1962-1967 (Geneva, the "Kennedy Round"), and 1973-1979 (Tokyo). An eighth session began in 1986 (the "Uruguay Round") and ended in December, 1993. The tariff reductions in rounds two through five were minimal. The volumes of trade covered by the fourth and fifth rounds were only $2.5 and $4.9 billion. The Kennedy Round (1962-1967) and the Tokyo Round (1973-1979) resulted in significant economic benefits to all major trading nations.

Significant progress toward free trade among market economy (nonsocialist) countries in manufactured and semimanufactured goods was accomplished in the Kennedy Round. The value of trade covered in these negotiations among forty-eight countries was $40 billion. Duties were cut on average by 35 percent spreading over the broadest set of products (sixty thousand) to date, with some cuts made on almost 80 percent of all dutiable imports. By the conclusion of this round, the weighted average tariff rate of the United States was 8.3 percent, that of the original six European Economic Community (EEC) countries was 8.3 percent, that of the United Kingdom was 10.2 percent, and that of Japan was 10.9 percent. Post-Kennedy Round tariffs in industrial countries averaged 8.7 percent. For the first time, an agreement was reached to resolve conflicts over nontariff barriers, particularly elimination of import quotas on almost all nonagricultural products. In some cases, tariffs were completely eliminated, as for tropical food products from developing countries. Developing countries played a minor role in negotiations and were not subject to significant tariff reductions.

The Tokyo Round was negotiated by ninety-nine countries and covered $155 billion in trade. The average tariff cut was about 34 percent. By the conclusion of this round, the weighted average tariff rate on finished and semifinished manufactures of the United States was 4.9 percent, that of EEC countries was 6.0 percent, and that of Japan was 5.4 percent. Post-Tokyo Round tariffs among industrial countries stood at an average of 4.7 percent. The Tokyo Round negotiations resulted in the first comprehensive agreement on reducing nontariff barriers such as quotas. The Tokyo Round failed to reach agreements on a safeguard code and on eliminating heavy restrictions on trade on agricultural products.

The most complex and ambitious round, the Uruguay Round, was launched by ninety countries on September 20, 1986, in Punta del Este, Uruguay. Originally scheduled to be completed by the end of 1990, the Uruguay Round was aimed at the further liberalization and expansion of trade. It sought to extend GATT principles to new sectors (agriculture, services), improve their application to old sectors (textiles, garments), reexamine old issues (safeguard protections), and embrace new issues such as intellectual property, with discussion of copyrights, computer software, and patent protection. By early 1993, no agreement had been reached because of disputes between the European Community and the United States regarding agricultural subsidies. Various compromises resulted in an agreement in December.

As of 1993, GATT was subscribed to by 108 nations that together accounted for 90 percent of world trade. It had emerged as the central forum for multilateral trade negotiations. Nine-tenths of the disputes brought to GATT had been settled satisfactorily. Average tariffs in the industrial countries averaged less than 5 percent, down from an average of 40 percent in 1947. The volume of trade in manufactured goods had multiplied twentyfold.

Despite these successes, the credibility of GATT was undermined by the difficulty of reducing nontariff barriers and exemption of several important sectors from application of GATT principles. In 1989, one-third of world trade, mainly in financial services, agriculture, and textiles and apparel, was not covered. Successful completion of the Uruguay Round was expected to bring many of these sectors under GATT rules and boost world trade by $200 billion a year.

Bibliography

Bhagwati, Jagdish. *The World Trading System at Risk*. Princeton, N.J.: Princeton University Press, 1991. The author is an ardent supporter of GATT. This book contains a collection of his lectures, which make a case for the continuation of GATT-sponsored multilateral trade talks.

Dam, Kenneth W. *The GATT: Law and International Economic Organization*. Chicago: University of Chicago Press, 1970. Excellent discussion of how legal rules have evolved in GATT.

Gardner, Richard N. *Sterling-Dollar Diplomacy: The Origins and the Prospects of Our International Economic Order*. New expanded ed. New York: McGraw-Hill, 1969. Provides complete details of the preparatory work of ITO-GATT.

Hughes, Jonathan R. T. *American Economy History*. 5th ed. Reading, Mass.: Addison-Wesley, 1998.

Jackson, John H. *Restructuring the GATT System*. New York: Council on Foreign Relations Press, 1990. Explores issues relating to future restructuring of GATT. Chapter 1 provides a brief but succinct history of GATT.

_____. *The World Trading System: Law and Policy of International Economic Relations*. Cambridge, Mass.: MIT Press, 1989. An introductory text on trade law and policy within the background of international law, national law, and related disciplines, including economics and political science.

Kock, Karin. *International Trade Policy and the GATT 1947-1967*. Stockholm, Sweden: Almqvist & Wiksell, 1969. A study of the interplay of foreign trade policies of GATT members and their cooperation in GATT.

Tussie, Diana. *The Less Developed Countries and the World Trading System: A Challenge to the GATT*. New York: St. Martin's Press, 1987. Studies GATT from the point of view of less developed countries, with particular focus on how they have been treated by the developed countries in GATT negotiations.

Wilcox, Clair. *A Charter for World Trade*. New York: Macmillan, 1949. An excellent book on the history, provisions, and significance of the Havana Charter. The author represented the United States as chairman of its delegation at the conference in London and vice chairman of its delegations at Geneva and Havana.

Baban Hasnat

Cross-References

The Agency for International Development Is Established (1961); The United States Suffers Its First Trade Deficit Since 1888 (1971); The North American Free Trade Agreement Goes into Effect (1994).

DINERS CLUB BEGINS A NEW INDUSTRY

CATEGORY OF EVENT: Marketing
TIME: 1949
LOCALE: New York, New York

By recognizing the untapped demand for a mobile credit vehicle, the founders of Diners Club turned the idea of credit cards into a viable and profitable industry

Principal personages:

ALFRED BLOOMINGDALE (1916-1982), an unsuccessful film producer and grandson of the founder of the Bloomingdale's stores; one of the founders of Diners Club

FRANCIS X. MCNAMARA (1925-   ), the head of the unsuccessful Hamilton Credit Corporation whose financial difficulties with his company led to the founding of Diners Club

RALPH SNYDER, the attorney of McNamara's Hamilton Credit Corporation, the third founder of Diners Club

Summary of Event

In 1949, three old friends, Alfred Bloomingdale, Francis X. McNamara, and Ralph Snyder, met for lunch at a popular New York restaurant near the Empire State Building. McNamara was the head of an unsuccessful finance company, Hamilton Credit Corporation, that had more than $35,000 in uncollectible receivables.

The conversation turned to McNamara's difficulties in collecting debts. One of McNamara's clients would allow his poor neighbors to use his charge account with local merchants. He would later collect the principal that was charged and also a small fee. Although this sounded like an ingenious entrepreneurial idea, collecting debts from the poor was difficult;

at that time, the gentleman in question owed Hamilton Credit Corporation more than $3,000.

In discussing this concept, the three men found two flaws in the operation of McNamara's customer. First, he was lending to the wrong people: The poor were less likely to pay back their debts. Second, he had to wait until his customers were in an emergency before they would come to him for credit. One of the men remarked that within one mile of where they sat were all the most important New York restaurants, many of which already operated their own credit systems for regular customers. Restaurants seemed to be the ideal market for a more universal credit system.

At the time, large retailers already used "charge plates" to keep track of purchases made on the accounts of their customers. These were metal strips, similar to military dog tags, that were inserted into a machine and copied with carbon paper. The three men discussed the innovative idea of becoming financial intermediaries and issuing these cards to consumers themselves. They conceived of credit as a product to be sold, an end in itself rather than simply a means to an end. The credit card was to become the vehicle for selling such credit. Although there was no precedent for such a company, these entrepreneurs forged ahead with their vision.

They talked to the proprietor of the restaurant at which they were eating and asked him how much he would pay for additional customers. He answered that they were worth 7 percent of their bills. This figure became the set discount rate for use of the card and the means of paying for the Diners Club operation. Yearly fees and interest rates for consumers were introduced later.

At the beginning, the three founders faced a serious problem. Businesses wanted to see a large customer base before they would accept the card, and customers wanted to see a large number of businesses willing to accept the card before they would sign up. Diners Club persevered, convincing many New York City restaurants to accept the card. For a customer base, the company aimed at traveling salespeople who wanted to charge their meals.

Bloomingdale returned to California and started a similar operation in Los Angeles called Dine and Sign. Three months later, as Diners Club began to show a profit, the three men decided to merge, and Diners Club became a nationwide organization. They soon extended their base of operations from restaurants into hotels, retail stores, and other establishments. In 1951, they created a franchise system and went international, extending into Europe.

The first Diners Club cards were more books than cards. Each person who signed up for the card was sent a book describing the places that accepted the card. To publicize new restaurants, a regular publication was issued to consumers.

After eight years of a Diners Club monopoly, other cards, such as Carte Blanche and American Express, entered the market. Other things also changed. The 7 percent set discount rate became variable based on the size of the average purchase at each location. Diners Club also began issuing insurance and gave loans of up to $25,000 on the card.

Credit card operations need a large amount of credit themselves to be able to extend credit to customers. Therefore, as business grew, the three founders of Diners Club found themselves constantly searching for more credit. Early in the business, they used what is referred to as the "float." Since they had offices in both New York and Los Angeles, they paid the New York bills with checks drawn off the Los Angeles account and vice versa. Because checks took a few days to clear, they gained some time before needing money in the accounts. As time progressed, banks became quicker at check clearing, and this avenue of free credit disappeared. As the company grew rapidly, a large influx of capital was necessary. To finance the company, Bloomingdale and Snyder went public. They each held on to 30 percent of the shares, and the other 40 percent were sold. McNamara had already sold his portion of the business to the other partners. As Diners Club became more successful, banks fought for the privilege of lending money to the company, so the difficulty in finding credit disappeared.

Other problems began to arise. Some customers simply did not pay their bills on time. Diners Club also sent unsolicited cards through the mail to increase its customer base, and some of these cards were lost or stolen and then used. No one could be found to hold responsible for these purchases, and Diners Club ended up paying. The practice of sending unsolicited cards later became illegal, insulating the credit card industry from incurring such losses.

The company continued to operate profitably. In 1970, it was purchased by Continental. While under Continental's control, Diners Club became the first card accepted in China. In 1980, the company again was sold, this time to Citibank. It still aimed primarily at the business traveler market, competing primarily with Carte Blanche and American Express. Although it holds a relatively small market share, Diners Club holds a large place in the history of the credit card industry.

Impact of Event

The main impact of the founding of Diners Club was the multibillion dollar global industry that followed. Although Diners Club was the first modern credit card, the concepts underlying this new industry had existed for a long time. Rather than introducing radically new ideas, the founders of Diners Club merely combined already well-known techniques for extending credit and created a new, mobile, credit card.

The Diners Club card influenced the society of the 1950's by crossing product and store lines. This card was universal rather than product- or store-specific. Although many oil companies and retail stores issued their own credit instruments, they were usable only at outlets owned by the issuer. Diners Club introduced the novel idea of a card that could be used at any one of a number of different establishments for a variety of products, from dinner at a restaurant to goods in a retail store.

Innovations in the credit card industry came slowly. Technological advances usually were borrowed from other industries rather than created specifically for credit card usage. For example, neither satellite transmission nor computer authorization codes were invented for the credit card industry but were put to good use by it. The credit card industry thus influenced technology by offering a new outlet for innovative products and methods.

The use of credit cards has become a vital part of many banks' business. Credit card use is seen in a more positive light in the United States than in other countries, and most credit card issuing banks are located there.

In 1952, after two full years of operation, Diners Club showed a profit of $61,222 on sales of $6.2 million. By 1986, 55 percent of all U.S. households held at least one credit card. Charge volume for the big three cards—Visa, Mastercard, and American Express—totaled more than $107 billion. This enormous growth in the credit industry has allowed consumers to purchase more goods and services than they dreamed possible. By allowing consumers to spread their debts over a long period of time but still allowing them to take home what they purchased, credit cards made it possible for consumers to live above their means.

There is a negative side to such purchasing power. Many poorer families purchase more than they can afford to pay for by charging purchases to credit cards. When the bills become due, the families are unable to pay them, and the debt rolls over. Every time the debt is allowed to roll over, interest charges accrue. The debt thus becomes even more difficult to pay off. Banks have attempted to insulate themselves against this by issuing cards only to those consumers above an income cutoff. In the face of increasing competition, however, banks began lowering the limit on income drastically in the 1980's.

The credit card industry has been a peculiarly American development. Since the United States is so large geographically, as the population became more mobile, the personal trust that existed between merchants and their best customers eroded. It was this trust that enabled merchants to extend credit to customers. Customers needed a card that could be used across the nation, and retailers needed a third-party guarantor of the debt. Thus, the advent of the credit card industry affected the ability of consumers to leave their hometowns and still be able to purchase goods and services on credit.

Another impact of the advent of Diners Club, and subsequent credit cards, is the ability of people to cross international borders without the need to carry large amounts of cash to exchange. World travelers found their credit cards accepted at many locations outside their country of origin, making traveling easier.

When Diners Club and its competitors first introduced credit cards, merchants rejected the idea for two reasons. First, they did not wish to pay the 7 percent discount the card required. Second, they thought that the existence of a card that could be used at various establishments weakened their personal relationship with their customers. They soon found that the large increases in sales experienced by retailers who accepted credit cards more than made up for any loss of personalized service. Many customers will pass by a retailer who does not accept their credit card in order to purchase from one who does. This has led to an almost universal acceptance of most major credit cards.

When Alfred Bloomingdale, Francis McNamara, and Ralph Snyder sat down to lunch in 1949, they could not have predicted the size and scope of the multibillion dollar global industry they were about to begin. In the span of less than fifty years, credit cards changed the face of worldwide business and extended buying power to more people.

Bibliography

Bagot, Brian. "Charged Up." *Marketing and Media Decisions* 25 (April, 1990): 76-79. An in-depth comparison of the major credit card companies. Contains a section on Diners Club and discusses how Diners Club compares to the other large credit card companies.

Hall, Carol. "Plastic Binge." *Marketing and Media Decisions* 21 (April, 1986): 117-127. Good article on the state of the credit card industry. Informative chart on the spending patterns of credit card users. Comparison of Diners Club with other major credit cards.

Hendrickson, Robert A. *The Cashless Society.* New York: Dodd, Mead, 1972. Discusses the future of a society that is no longer based on cash. Contains a chapter on the history of credit cards. Although it does contain some valuable information, it is written in a rather speculative, hypothetical manner.

McManus, Kevin. "Wing Tips." *Forbes* 130 (July 5, 1982): 150. When Braniff Airlines went bankrupt, many people were left holding tickets. This article discusses what Diners Club and the other major credit cards did for consumers who had used their cards to purchase Braniff tickets. Good discussion of the responsibilities of card-issuing companies.

Mandell, Lewis. *The Credit Card Industry: A History*. Boston: Twayne, 1990. Discusses the history of the credit card industry, including a complete chapter on the founding of the Diners Club. The first book to focus primarily on the history of credit card usage.

_____. *Credit Card Use in the United States*. Ann Arbor: Institute for Social Research, University of Michigan, 1972. Summarizes data from three nationwide surveys in 1970 and 1971 on specific uses of various cards, attitudes toward credit cards, and the incurrence of debt on credit cards. Contains a full copy of the survey used and data presented in clear, concise tables.

"Playing Your Cards Right." *Consumer Reports* 50 (January, 1985): 47-52. An excellent comparison of all the major credit cards. Concentrates on American Express, Visa, and Mastercard, but also includes data on Diners Club, Carte Blanche, and other smaller retail credit cards.

"Serendipity." *Forbes* 125 (February 4, 1980): 17. Discusses the international aspect of Diners Club. This article is about the entrance of Diners Club into the Chinese market, through Hong Kong. Details the visit of Continental chairman John B. Ricker, Jr., and his subsequent discussions that enabled Diners Club to be the first credit card company to enter the Chinese market.

Sloan, Irving J. *The Law and Legislation of Credit Cards: Use and Misuse*. New York: Oceana, 1987. Although it does not discuss the history of credit cards, this book provides an interesting study of laws that relate to the industry. Contains appendices of specific state laws as well as an overview of federal regulations.

Lewis Mandell
Sarah Holmes

Cross-References

Congress Passes the Consumer Credit Protection Act (1968); Congress Passes the Fair Credit Reporting Act (1970); Congress Prohibits Discrimination in the Granting of Credit (1975); Congress Deregulates Banks and Savings and Loans (1980-1982).

THE FIRST HOMEOWNER'S INSURANCE POLICIES ARE OFFERED

CATEGORY OF EVENT: New products
TIME: September, 1950
LOCALE: Pennsylvania

The booming American economy following World War II forced the traditionally conservative insurance industry to innovate with new concepts such as the homeowner's policy

Principal personages:

JOHN ANTHONY DIEMAND (1886-1974), the president, chairman of the board, and chief executive officer of the Insurance Company of North America, 1941-1964

BRADFORD SMITH, JR. (1901-1988), a senior executive of INA who succeeded Diemand as president and continued his innovative policies

MORGAN BULKELEY BRAINARD (1879-1957), the president of the Aetna Life and Affiliated Companies

WILLIAM ROSS MCCAIN (1878-1972), the president of Aetna (Fire) Insurance Company of Hartford

JESSE W. RANDALL (b. 1884), the president of the Travelers Insurance Company

HAROLD V. SMITH (1889-1962), the president of the Home Insurance Company of New York

Summary of Event

The Insurance Company of North America (INA), a company with a reputation for innovation, made insurance history in 1950 by introducing its famous homeowner's policy. It offered a complete shield of protection for

341

the home, which was most people's single biggest lifetime investment. In offering this new type of policy, INA was responding to changing conditions brought about by World War II and its turbulent aftermath.

When the war ended in 1945, the United States was by far the richest and most powerful nation on earth. It was the only major industrialized nation to escape terrible devastation during the war. The postwar period saw the greatest economic growth the nation had ever experienced. Millions of men returned from military service eager to get married, to find jobs, to have children, and to own their own homes; this was the American Dream.

The federal government had several motives for stimulating home building. For one thing, legislators wanted to reward veterans for the sacrifices they had made for their country. In addition, residential construction was an important element of continuing prosperity because it generated many different kinds of jobs. It created employment not only for carpenters and practitioners of other building trades but also for lumber workers and others whose products and services related to home construction. Once a house was finished and its new residents were ready to move in, they had a need for carpets, drapes, furniture, appliances, and all manner of other home furnishings.

New housing tracts in the developing suburbs created needs for streets, sewers, streetlights, shopping centers, fire and police stations, and schools. At one time, Los Angeles County was adding the equivalent of one entire new school to its public school system every day. All these needs created jobs, and jobs created prosperity. Because so many residents of the new housing tracts were dependent on automobiles for transportation, the phenomenon of the two-car family became commonplace in the United States. This created the greatest boom in automobile manufacturing the country had ever seen.

The federal government made home ownership easy for veterans through the Servicemen's Readjustment Act (G.I. Bill) of 1944, which enabled a veteran to buy a house with no down payment and a very low interest rate on the loan made to purchase the house. Under President Franklin D. Roosevelt's New Deal programs, the government already had made home ownership easier for nonveterans through the Federal Housing Act of 1934, which required low down payments and interest rates only slightly higher than those on GI loans. The Federal National Mortgage Association was set up in 1938 to make government-insured home loans readily salable in secondary markets; this encouraged lenders to make ample funds available for such loans at attractive interest rates. The Internal Revenue Service also encouraged home buying by allowing interest payments to be deducted from gross income before taxes were computed.

For about twenty-five years, from the end of World War II until President Richard Nixon implemented his anti-inflation program in 1971, it was often cheaper to own a house than to rent one. There was also a tremendous resale market for houses, because young families were subject to many vicissitudes. Divorce, job loss, and job transfer were factors that could force a family to sell its home, while promotions and the birth of more children could motivate purchase of larger and better homes. American families were moving into new houses as fast as they could be built.

The entire American landscape changed radically after World War II. Builders created enormous tracts of houses in the suburbs, where land was cheap and easy to build on. Farms, orchards, and grazing land gave way to houses. The term "bedroom community" was coined to describe this new phenomenon of areas consisting mostly of housing, with little business activity. Automobiles made it feasible for young homeowners to commute to jobs in the cities, perhaps also finding entertainment there, then come home to sleep. Major cities across the country were transformed from relatively compact entities into sprawling conglomerations of houses, shops, restaurants, offices, and parking lots. The term "urban sprawl" was coined to describe this new phenomenon.

Businesses of all types competed avidly for the trillions of dollars to be earned from all this activity. The so-called "old-line" insurance companies, such as the Insurance Company of North America (INA), suddenly found themselves confronted by aggressive competitors such as State Farm Insurance Company, Farmers Insurance Company, and Sears Roebuck's successful Allstate Insurance Company.

The old-line companies historically had dealt with independent agents who worked on commission. The new competitors were called "direct writers" because they employed their own agents, who could sell only their company's policies. The newcomers to the insurance business could sell their policies cheaper because they paid their agents lower commissions and had streamlined other aspects of insurance such as claims adjusting. Independent agents hated and feared these cut-rate competitors, contending that they were not truly representing their clients but instead favoring the companies they represented.

In an attempt to remain a step ahead of the competition, the prestigious Insurance Company of North America relied on its greater underwriting expertise to offer innovative new policies, such as its famous homeowner's policy. This type of policy made insurance history when it was introduced in September of 1950. In hindsight, the innovation was of obvious benefit to homeowners, but companies previously had concentrated on selling the various types of coverage included in it as separate policies.

Breaking with tradition, INA introduced the independent insurance agents of America to a new concept, a multiline policy that would cover a homeowner against almost anything that could happen to a house or on a homeowner's property. Because a house was the most valuable purchase the average American would ever make, homeowners wanted assurance that they would not be wiped out by some unforeseen event. A lawsuit not only could strip a homeowner of everything he or she owned but also could cause debt that would take a lifetime to repay.

INA's homeowner's policy offered coverage against damage to the home or its contents caused by fire as well as extended coverage against such forces as lightning, hail, windstorms, explosions, riots and civil commotion, aircraft, land vehicles, and smoke. The policy also included residence theft insurance and provided for legal liability for accidents on the premises and medical care for injuries to visitors. The package policy was about 20 percent cheaper than the total value of all the separate policies that would have to be purchased to obtain the same coverage. It was an immediate success.

Impact of Event

INA's homeowner's policy had a powerful impact on the insurance industry because of the issuer's power and prestige as the largest and oldest company of its kind in the United States. The revolutionary new concept of a multiple-risk policy, to be introduced throughout the country, created a new era in the insurance business. Many other companies were forced to follow INA's leadership to stay competitive. State Farm, Farmers, and Allstate soon had their own policies on the market, along with old-line companies including Aetna and Travelers. Generally speaking, the old-line companies, including INA, were the innovators, while the direct writers followed their leadership but offered lower rates.

Once the precedent had been established of writing so-called "multiple-line" or "multiple-hazard" policies, it was inevitable that INA and its competitors would begin offering other creative insurance packages to consumers. Businesses had long protested against the complicated and expensive insurance needed for protection against all the financial hazards involved in running even a small business. Soon INA and its competitors responded to this complaint by offering comprehensive fire insurance policies as well as tremendously popular comprehensive public liability (CPL) insurance policies.

CPL policies covered a business for injuries sustained by customers on the premises, for injuries or property damage caused by its employees away from the premises, and for all company-owned automobiles and trucks. A business that hired new employees, acquired new properties, or added new motor vehicles to its fleet during the policy period was automatically protected. The insurance premium would be adjusted annually on the basis of an audit.

All these policies made things easier for businesspeople as well as for homeowners. The package policies were created as a result of the demands imposed by an expanding economy of unprecedented proportions, and they helped to encourage further expansion of the economy by generating the confidence people needed to invest their money in real estate and business enterprises. Homeowners no longer needed to lie awake wondering what would happen if a neighbor's child drowned in the home's swimming pool, the family dog attacked the mail carrier, or a visitor fell down the front stairs. A businessperson could feel free to accept the many opportunities for profit that arose in the prosperous economy without having to worry about such petty matters as whether a vacant lot could safely be rented out during December to be used for selling Christmas trees; he or she knew that insurance coverage extended to any conceivable liability hazard not specifically excluded by the business' insurance policy.

The homeowner's policy was also welcomed by banks, savings and loan companies, and other lenders because it offered them protection for their own financial stake in the residential real estate market. Previously, if a homeowner sustained a catastrophic loss not covered by insurance, he or she might be forced to abandon the house, leaving it up to the lender to repossess it. Most homes in America at the time were being purchased on long-term mortgages. GI and Federal Housing Authority (FHA) loans typically were written to be amortized over thirty years, so mortgage holders retained significant stakes in individual homes for many years.

Homeowner's policies helped to accelerate the building boom by providing better protection for the lenders who made home ownership possible. Furthermore, by providing cheaper coverage, they lowered the homeowner's total monthly outlays for principal, interest, taxes, and insurance (PITI), which were usually included in one payment to the mortgage lender. This made it possible for some marginal buyers to own their own homes, adding further fuel to home building and the economy in general.

Other innovations in insurance included new worker's compensation package policies that covered all types of employees under the same policy and automatically covered new employees hired during the policy period. Important in all the insurance innovations of the period was the concept that competitive forces and government intervention were forcing insurance companies to respond to consumers' needs rather than forcing the consumers to respond to the traditionally rigid requirements of the conservative insurance companies.

Insurance agents welcomed the new package policies. They were much easier to sell because they were easier to explain. Agents were relieved of the unpleasant task of apologizing to a client because an unforeseen loss was not covered by any of the single-risk policies the client held.

Insurance became increasingly streamlined and modernized, starting in the 1950's, through the leadership of such American companies as the Insurance Company of North America. Companies found that they had to offer policies and packages that were competitive with those of other companies as consumers became more educated about insurance and learned to shop around for the best price.

Bibliography

"Big Day in Property Insurance." *Business Week*, July 10, 1948, 20-21. Discusses the dramatic impact of the McCarran Act on the insurance industry. Federal antitrust laws became applicable to insurance, creating greater competitiveness in the industry and paving the way for innovative new package coverage such as INA's homeowner's policy.

Carr, William H. A. *Perils, Named and Unnamed: The Story of the Insurance Company of North America*. New York: McGraw-Hill, 1967. A comprehensive history of the Insurance Company of North America as an innovator in the insurance world, with many references to the development and acceptance of its homeowner's policy. The best book-length history of the company, written in an informal style and containing numerous interesting anecdotes. Helpful bibliography.

"INA Ties Itself into a Package." *Business Week*, January 9, 1965, 52-58. Describes how INA was radically restructured to handle package policies more efficiently. Covers such matters as agency relations, underwriting, setting of risk standards, and claims adjusting. Explains how expanding markets forced radical changes in the traditionally conservative insurance industry.

James, Marquis. *Biography of a Business, 1792-1942: Insurance Company of North America*. Indianapolis, Ind.: Bobbs-Merrill, 1942. A corporate history that received critical praise for its scholarship and congenial style.

"160 Years Young." *Newsweek*, April 13, 1953, 78-82. A brief history of, and tribute to, the Insurance Company of North America, emphasizing some of the personalities influential in its development and describing the new competitive conditions in the insurance industry that were a striking part of the booming postwar American economy.

"Packaged Policies Catch On." *Business Week*, September 30, 1950, 100-102. Written shortly after the Insurance Company of North America announced the introduction of its new homeowner's policy. Discusses the reaction of businesspeople, the general public, independent insurance agents, government insurance regulators, and executives of competing insurance companies. An excellent overview.

"The Underwriters: When the Supreme Court Said Insurance Was Commerce, Their World Turned Upside Down." *Fortune* 42 (July, 1950): 77-81, 108-114. An excellent article describing the changes taking place in insurance as a result of recent government rulings. Contains photographs of many of the leading insurance executives of the day. Accurately forecasts the turbulent future of the insurance industry in the United States.

Bill Delaney

Cross-References

Roosevelt Signs the G.I. Bill (1944); Congress Passes the Consumer Credit Protection Act (1968); Congress Passes the Fair Credit Reporting Act (1970); Congress Deregulates Banks and Savings and Loans (1980-1982); Bush Responds to the Savings and Loan Crisis (1989).

THE CELLER-KEFAUVER ACT AMENDS ANTITRUST LEGISLATION

CATEGORY OF EVENT: Monopolies and cartels
TIME: December 29, 1950
LOCALE: Washington, D.C.

By prohibiting certain types of mergers between firms in the same industry, the Celler-Kefauver Act of 1950 led companies to form conglomerates made up of companies in unrelated industries

Principal personages:

EMANUEL CELLER (1888-1981), a New York congressman, coauthor of the act

ESTES KEFAUVER (1903-1963), a senator from Tennessee, coauthor of the act

HARRY S TRUMAN (1884-1972), the U.S. president influential in passage of the act

ROBERT H. BORK (1927-   ), a judge and legal scholar opposed to government enforcement of the act

Summary of Event

The Celler-Kefauver Act of 1950 amended the Clayton Act by closing a loophole that had allowed companies to avoid antitrust suits by acquiring the assets (rather than the stock) of another company. Government enforcement of the Celler-Kefauver Act encouraged companies to seek growth through a strategy of diversification. Thus, the Celler-Kefauver Act contributed to the conglomerate movement of the 1960's.

The roots of the Celler-Kefauver Act can be traced to passage of the Clayton Antitrust Act in 1914. Section II of this law prohibited business firms from acquiring the stock of another company if the resulting merger lessened competition. The Clayton Act, however, made no mention of mergers based on the purchase of another company's assets. During the 1920's, American companies took advantage of this loophole to form mergers based on the acquisition of assets. The Federal Trade Commission (FTC) prosecuted the companies involved in these mergers but, in 1926, the Supreme Court ruled that the Clayton Act did not apply to acquisition of corporate assets. The Court's interpretation made the Clayton Act an ineffective weapon against monopoly.

In 1927, the FTC asked Congress to amend the Clayton Act to close the loophole, but during this prosperous decade Congress lost interest in strict enforcement of the antitrust laws. During the late 1920's and early 1930's, the government downplayed antitrust policy as President Herbert Hoover encouraged corporations to cooperate in a wide range of activities. President Franklin D. Roosevelt granted antitrust exemptions to those companies cooperating with the National Recovery Administration (1933-1935). NRA officials hoped that cooperation in the form of mergers and price controls would lift the nation out of the Great Depression.

During the late 1930's, Roosevelt reversed direction and attempted to silence his critics in big business by supporting a renewed antitrust campaign led by Thurman Arnold, head of the Justice Department's Antitrust Division. Roosevelt also called for the creation of a Temporary National Economic Committee (TNEC) to study the effects of monopoly on the American economy. In its final report, in 1941, the TNEC recommended passage of legislation designed to close the asset loophole. Along with officials in the FTC and the Justice Department, the members of the TNEC formed an activist community committed to strengthening the nation's antimonopoly legislation. Although World War II brought a temporary halt to its activity, this antitrust community pledged to resume its antimonopoly crusade once the war ended.

Several factors sparked a renewed interest in antitrust enforcement in the immediate postwar period. First, a growing number of observers worried that the wartime placement of military contracts with big business had increased the overall level of economic concentration. In December, 1946, The House Small Business Committee's Subcommittee on Monopoly (chaired by Estes Kefauver, a liberal Democrat from Tennessee) issued a report concluding that big business had benefited disproportionately from the wartime boom. The Kefauver report criticized the lackluster wartime performance of the government's antitrust agencies and called for an amendment to the Clayton Act that would close the asset loophole. Meanwhile, the FTC tried to justify its existence by securing passage of stronger antitrust legislation.

The FTC described the weak merger movement of the late 1940's as a grave threat to competition. The FTC enjoyed the support of President Harry S Truman, a longtime advocate of antitrust enforcement. During his presidency, Truman appointed ardent antitrusters to the FTC and secured additional appropriations for the enforcement of antitrust legislation.

At the conclusion of World War II, congressional antitrusters introduced a flurry of bills designed to strengthen the Clayton Antitrust Act. In 1945, Senator Joseph O'Mahoney (D-Wyoming) and Representative Estes Kefauver introduced legislation that would close the asset loophole. Their bills remained in committee, however, and for the next several years they failed in efforts to push their legislation through a Republican-controlled Congress. In 1948, the Democrats secured control of both houses of Congress, thus increasing the likelihood that a major piece of antitrust legislation would become law. During the presidential campaign, Truman had supported legislation to close the assets loophole. He interpreted his victory in the election as a mandate to go forward with strict enforcement of the antitrust law. In 1949, Truman encouraged the chairman of the House Judiciary Committee, Emanuel Celler (D-New York) to go forward with an investigation of monopolies. Celler used his committee hearings as a forum to promote his bill to amend the Clayton Act. As a newly elected senator, Estes Kefauver introduced a companion bill in the Senate. The Celler-Kefauver bills prohibited companies from acquiring the assets of other companies if the resulting mergers substantially lessened competition.

Celler and Kefauver broke with antitrust tradition by emphasizing the alleged evils of bigness per se. In the past, the government had been concerned with the intent behind mergers and their actual effect on competition. The Supreme Court had established a "rule of reason" to govern antitrust cases. According to the Court, antitrust law applied only to unreasonable restraints upon trade. Celler and Kefauver believed that bigness automatically reduced efficiency, dampened innovation, and diminished opportunities for small business. They also argued that big business had given rise to big labor and big government. Ultimately, big business threatened the foundations of American democracy, since an all-powerful state would be required to regulate the nation's monopolies. Celler and Kefauver resorted to Cold War rhetoric, arguing that their legislation would prevent the emergence of a totalitarian state.

The business press feared that the legislation would radically restructure the American economy. Critics of the legislation, led by the United States Chamber of Commerce, believed that existing antitrust laws could prevent the development of monopolies. These opponents also criticized the FTC for exaggerating the extent of the postwar merger movement and for failing to show that mergers actually had lessened competition. Republican conservatives, however, failed to block passage of this legislation. On August 15, the House passed Celler's bill (H.R. 2734) by a vote of 223 to 92. The Senate subsequently passed Kefauver's bill and, on December 29, 1950, President Truman signed it into law.

Impact of Event

The Celler-Kefauver Act of 1950 sent a message to the business community that the federal government would closely examine the effects of any mergers between companies in the same industry. The act also gave the nation's antitrust agencies a powerful new weapon in their campaign against monopoly. The act did not apply, however, to mergers between companies in unrelated industries. Consequently, numerous articles appeared in the business press encouraging companies to seek growth through diversification. Thus, the Celler-Kefauver Act facilitated the conglomerate merger wave of the 1950's and 1960's.

Despite its active role in the passage of the Celler-Kefauver Act, the Truman Administration failed to enforce the law, in large part because the government reduced its antitrust activity in order to secure the cooperation of business during the Korean War. A budget-conscious Congress also reduced funding for the antitrust agencies. Corporate executives nevertheless remained cautious about acquiring competitors, and the number of mergers dropped off in the early 1950's.

Under the administration of President Dwight D. Eisenhower (1953-1961), the Justice Department and the FTC responded to renewed merger activity by acting more aggressively in their prosecution of antitrust cases. In 1955, the attorney general's National Committee to Study the Antitrust Laws issued a report calling for stricter enforcement of antitrust legislation. The report also outlined the government's interpretation of the Celler-Kefauver Act. According to the committee, the government need not prove that a company had intended to lessen competition by acquiring a rival; instead, the government could simply use market share as a measure of competition in an industry. The committee's report did not address the question of conglomerate mergers.

The FTC and the Justice Department followed the guidelines set forth by the attorney general's committee. During the Eisenhower Administration, the two agencies prosecuted more than fifty cases involving alleged violations of the Celler-Kefauver Act. In one important case, brought against the Pillsbury Company, the FTC ruled that the Celler-Kefauver Act allowed the agency to prohibit mergers that lessened competition in regional or local, as opposed to national, markets. The government also brought cases against a number of the nation's largest companies, including Bethlehem Steel, Lever Brothers, Crown Zellerbach, Minute Maid, and Anheuser-Busch. Nearly all of these cases involved mergers within the same industry.

President John F. Kennedy's attorney general continued to charge many companies with violations of the Celler-Kefauver Act. The U.S. Supreme Court approved of the government's strict enforcement of the law. In the landmark *Brown Shoe* case (1962), the Court ruled that the government could halt a merger if there was a chance that it might lessen competition in any region of the country. During the 1960's, the Court continued to consider mergers a threat to competition and, between 1962 and 1970, the nation's highest court decided in favor of the government in all but one of the merger cases.

The hostile environment led companies to avoid mergers within the same industry. Corporate executives began to pursue a strategy of diversification, forming mergers with companies in unrelated fields. Government enforcement of the Celler-Kefauver Act thus indirectly facilitated the massive conglomerate movement of the 1960's. In 1969, President Richard Nixon's attorney general brought antitrust suits against several conglomerates. These companies eventually settled out of court, but the suits brought against them led businesspeople to fear prosecution, and the merger movement finally slowed.

In the early 1970's, the Supreme Court under Chief Justice Warren Burger began deciding against the government in antitrust cases. During this same period, economists and legal scholars also attacked the long-held assumption that mergers necessarily resulted in lessened competition. Led by Robert H. Bork, these scholars argued that mergers often increased efficiency and lowered costs. These critics of the Celler-Kefauver Act preferred to rely upon the market to police mergers. This intellectual climate of opinion influenced policymakers, and the government stopped enforcing the Celler-Kefauver Act. With the threat of government prosecution diminished, the United States witnessed yet another merger movement in the late 1970's and the 1980's.

Bibliography

Bork, Robert H. *The Antitrust Paradox: A Policy at War with Itself.* New York: Basic Books, 1978. A critical study of the American antitrust tradition. In chapter 9, "The Crash of Merger Policy: The *Brown Shoe* Decision," Bork discusses how the Supreme Court's interpretation of the Celler-Kefauver Act has deviated from the original intent of Congress. Assumes some knowledge of antitrust law.

Celler, Emanuel. *You Never Leave Brooklyn: The Autobiography of Emanuel Celler*. New York: J. Day, 1953. Provides insight into the personal and philosophical motivations behind Celler's crusade against big business. Most of the work is devoted to Celler's concern with immigration and other issues.

Fligstein, Neil. *The Transformation of Corporation Control*. Cambridge, Mass.: Harvard University Press, 1990. Shows how antitrust policy has influenced corporate strategy by shifting the emphasis away from control of market share to control of companies in unrelated fields. Chapter 5, "The Emergence of the Celler-Kefauver Act, 1938-1950," explores the legislative history of the act in depth. Chapter 6, "The Impact of the Celler-Kefauver Act, 1948-1980," analyzes the implementation of the act and its effect on merger activity.

Fontenay, Charles L. *Estes Kefauver: A Biography*. Knoxville: University of Tennessee Press, 1980. A balanced account of the career of one of the nation's leading politicians during this period. In part 1, the author discusses Kefauver's relations with Emanuel Celler and other key figures in the antitrust community.

Hughes, Jonathan R. T. *American Economy History*. 5th ed. Reading, Mass.: Addison-Wesley, 1998.

Kovaleff, Theodore Philip. *Business and Government During the Eisenhower Administration: A Study of the Antitrust Policy of the Antitrust Division of the Justice Department*. Athens: Ohio University Press, 1980. A sympathetic account of the government's antitrust policy under President Dwight D. Eisenhower. The author believes that Eisenhower viewed an aggressive antitrust campaign as an alternative to direct government regulation of business.

Peritz, Rudolph J., Jr. *Competition Policy in America, 1888-1992: History, Rhetoric, Law*. New York: Oxford University Press, 1996. History of federal government policies relating to antitrust issues. Includes a substantial bibliography and index.

Jonathan Bean

Cross-References

Champion v. Ames Upholds Federal Powers to Regulate Commerce (1903); The Supreme Court Decides to Break Up Standard Oil (1911); The Federal Trade Commission Is Organized (1914); Congress Passes the Clayton Antitrust Act (1914); Carter Signs the Airline Deregulation Act (1978); Congress Deregulates Banks and Savings and Loans (1980-82); AT&T Agrees to Be Broken Up as Part of an Antitrust Settlement (1982).

CONGRESS CREATES THE SMALL BUSINESS ADMINISTRATION

CATEGORY OF EVENT: Government and business
TIME: July 30, 1953
LOCALE: Washington, D.C.

By ending the Reconstruction Finance Corporation and establishing the Small Business Administration, the federal government tried to ensure that all businesses, not just the well connected, could receive help

Principal personages:
WRIGHT PATMAN (1893-1976), a congressman from Texas, 1929-1974
WILLIAM FULBRIGHT (1905-1995), a senator from Arkansas, 1945-1974
JESSE JONES (1874-1956), a wealthy Texas businessman appointed by Franklin D. Roosevelt in 1933 to head the Reconstruction Finance Corporation

Summary of Event

The Reconstruction Finance Corporation (RFC), established by Congress in January of 1932, was an anti-Depression measure implemented, but little used, during Herbert Hoover's administration. Its original mission was to provide loans to businesses, financial institutions, and railroads, but these powers were later broadened to encompass agriculture and local and state governmental works.

After Franklin D. Roosevelt assumed the presidency in 1933, he installed Jesse Jones, a little-educated, successful, and well-connected businessperson, as the agency's chairperson. In his tenure at the RFC, Jones was involved in the creation of other federal agencies such as the Federal

354

National Mortgage Association, the Export-Import Bank, the Federal Housing Administration, and the Federal Home Loan Bank Board. Jones would later be appointed secretary of commerce.

The RFC was widely respected in the 1930's for its role in aiding businesses and financial institutions. Its influence increased further during World War II, with new subsidiaries and global activities making a substantial contribution to the war's conclusion. The postwar period saw reversal of many of the agency's achievements. The Employment Act of 1946 had as its goals the attainment of full employment, promotion of production, and maintenance of purchasing power. The act acknowledged uncomfortable uncertainties as to what would happen after demobilization. It was thought that after the war, during which the unemployment rate had fallen almost to 1 percent, the rate might spring back to the 9.9 percent of 1941 or even to the 14.6 percent registered in 1940.

Pent-up demand caused by wartime rationing and shifts from consumer to military goods was unleashed after 1945. The main economic problem turned out to be inflation, with a prescription of fiscal restraint. Loans made by the RFC nevertheless rose in the period from 1947 to 1950, from $393 million to $500 million, in the face of Congress' desire to curb lending. Many loans were made to less-than-vital businesses.

Senator William Fulbright, chairman of a subcommittee of the Senate Committee on Banking and Currency, started a probe in 1950 that was the start of the slide of the RFC toward oblivion. A litany of testimony about questionable lending decisions convinced the panel that those with "influence" were more likely to get to the government money trough. Fulbright said the "fixers" were in control, while President Harry S Truman repeatedly said that nothing was amiss. The Republicans used this scandal as a campaign issue in 1952, promising reform and cleanup in Washington. With Dwight D. Eisenhower's victory, the Reconstruction Finance Corporation's demise was imminent.

In May, 1953, the House Committee on Banking and Currency began its hearings on the establishment of the Small Business Administration. The counterpart committee in the Senate commenced its hearings to dismantle the RFC. The Republicans thought that to be certain of support to kill the RFC, they had to offer something in return. The House Small Business Act of 1953 was their vehicle. Its purpose was "to preserve small business institutions and free, competitive enterprise." A new agency, the Small Business Administration (SBA), was to develop a definition of what a small business was, take a census of small businesses' production facilities and decide upon their best utilization, provide technical and general management assistance, develop a procurement program, and develop a lending program.

There was little opposition to the founding of the SBA. The American Bankers Association, the banking industry's trade association, was one of few groups to go on record opposing the SBA. Its premise was that the government should not be involved in business lending of any kind, whether made directly or by a financial institution with a government guarantee. The association did support the dismemberment of the RFC.

The Department of Commerce, though not completely disagreeing with the idea of having an independent small business agency, thought that for economy's sake the proposed activities could be integrated into its own already existing structure. That viewpoint received little sympathy, given the department's own checkered background and the mixed results of entities that had preceded the SBA.

The Smaller War Plants Corporation (SWPC), established in July, 1942, was the first governmental effort to assist small businesses. It provided loans, both directly and in conjunction with private lenders, and assisted in government procurement, obtaining prime contracts or subcontracts for war materials. About 110,000 prime contracts or subcontracts worth about $6 billion were won by small businesses from 1942 to 1945 through the aid of the SWPC. Approximately 5,800 loans totaling more than $500 million were received by small businesses, either through direct lending or with private participation. Production pools involving 2,000 firms and 140,000 workers received $600 million in contracts through the SWPC's efforts.

The SWPC was fairly accomplished in meeting its mission, but it was a temporary agency and was disbanded at the end of the war. The Reconstruction Finance Corporation took over its lending and government procurement functions as well as the authority to sell surplus property. The Department of Commerce and its Office of Small Business assumed all other SWPC functions, including educational efforts.

In 1951, the Small Defense Plants Administration (SDPA) was founded to deal with the urgencies of the war in Korea. It was given similar missions and powers as the earlier SWPC except for lending, which remained with the RFC. Most of its activity was centered in government procurement, assisting firms in receiving somewhat more than $50 million in work. The SDPA was of limited benefit to small businesses because its role was limited to defense work rather than the whole spectrum of business activity.

Congress saw that there was merit in assisting small business, given the success of the SWPC and, to a lesser extent, the SDPA and the early RFC. The RFC, rife with corruption, was headed for extinction. The Department of Commerce did little with its education mandate and, it was widely believed, favored the interests of large corporations over those of independent businesspeople. Congressman Wright Patman thought that giving the new SBA, with its millions of dollars in funding, to the Department of Commerce was like "sending a rabbit for a head of lettuce." The National Federation of Independent Business was also opposed to putting the SBA under the Department of Commerce because of that department's perceived lack of sympathy for small business.

There was thus little support for a new agency within the Department of Commerce. At about the same time, the administration decided to disband the RFC. Originally, this had not been the intent of the House and Senate, since the RFC's authority would have expired on June 30, 1954. A budget deficit was projected for fiscal year 1954, however, and elimination of the RFC, it was thought, would contribute greatly in the reduction of the budget problem.

The original House version of legislation on small business did not have any reference to the RFC. The final bill approved by the Senate in July called for elimination of the RFC by June 30, 1954, and establishment of the Small Business Administration as a temporary agency with a two-year life and a revolving loan fund of $275 million. Eisenhower signed this version on July 30, 1953.

Impact of Event

The impact of small business upon the economy is substantial. If the common employment measure of at least five hundred employees is applied to the approximately twenty million tax returns filed with the Internal Revenue Service in 1990, less than seven thousand firms would be classified as large businesses. Small businesses provided approximately half of all jobs in the 1980's, and a high proportion of new jobs came from that sector. Small businesses provided about one-third of the dollar value of all goods and services supplied to the federal government, and approximately 20 percent of all manufactured goods exported from the United States were provided by firms with fewer than five hundred employees. The SBA has been committed to providing assistance to firms owned by women and members of ethnic minorities. As of 1990, women owned about 30 percent of all businesses, and African Americans owned more than 3 percent of the total.

The SBA has expanded its scope since its start-up in 1953. The fundamental purposes of the SBA are to protect the interests of small business, provide counseling to current or prospective business owners, and assist in government procurement to ensure that small businesses receive a fair share of government contracts and subcontracts. The agency also lends money to small businesses, state and local development companies, and victims of disasters or economic injury. It licenses, regulates, and lends money to small business investment companies. Various specific activities help to achieve these results.

The SBA provides guaranteed or direct loans to firms to acquire assets or as working capital. It can make direct loans to the disabled and to nonprofit agencies employing them, to Vietnam-era and disabled veterans, and to eligible minority contractors. It also lends to exporters. Much of its financial assistance is through a guaranteed loan program, under which loans are actually made by private financial institutions but repayment is guaranteed by the SBA in case of default. Money is also loaned to victims of natural disasters, riots, or other calamitous events to replace or repair property. Direct loans with low interest rates are available to small businesses and agricultural cooperatives hurt by natural disasters. The SBA licenses, regulates, and lends money to small business investment companies. These provide venture capital and other long-term financing to small, high-potential ventures.

The SBA also provides assistance in contracting. It helps make contract bonding available, guaranteeing up to 90 percent of losses under bid, performance, or payment bonds. The SBA also works with other government agencies to increase the amount of federal government work going to small businesses in general and especially to firms owned by women and disadvantaged people.

As part of its business development efforts, the SBA develops educational materials for distribution. It cosponsors workshops and seminars and has developed lists of volunteer businesspeople who provide counseling. These are the Service Corps of Retired Executives (SCORE) and the Active Corps of Executives (ACE). It also sponsors the Small Business Institute (SBI), in which advanced undergraduate or graduate business students work on long-term consulting assignments with local businesspeople. Under the 8(a) program, firms owned by the socially and economically disadvantaged receive loans and federal government work. Under the 7(j) program, these firms receive individual business assistance and consulting.

The SBA's mission has a strong emphasis on women's business ownership. The SBA develops programs to support ownership by women and acts as a liaison with nonfederal business and educational groups to develop women's businesses. It also has initiated a mentoring program in which women who have been in business at least five years provide long-term mentoring to women with one to three years of business experience. The Women's Business Ownership Act of 1988 directed the SBA to develop a long-term education program for female businesspeople. This resulted in the formation of the Women's Network for Entrepreneurial Training (WNET), the first business training program specifically targeted to women. In addition to overseeing this program, the SBA's Office of Women's Business Ownership (OWBO), through the national network of local SBA offices, offers prospective and established female business owners other services, including prebusiness workshops and conferences on obtaining capital, financial and technical information, and access to a national database. Conferences on exporting, government procurement, and how to successfully sell products and services to the federal government are offered to women. Long-term consulting assistance is also available.

The SBA's Office of Veterans Affairs operates as an advocate for assistance to veterans in starting up or in continuing management of existing firms. It reviews existing assistance programs for special consideration for veterans. This office also is a liaison between federal agencies, local and state governments, and other organizations to ensure utilization of all existing programs and to promote the creation of new and more effective ones.

The SBA's Office of Private-Sector Initiatives secures state and local government cooperation to use existing initiatives so as to avoid duplication. It also promotes new ways to increase private-sector involvement to provide assistance to the SBA in meeting its goals. The Small Business Innovation Research Program sponsors projects that spark technological innovation, directs federal government research to small businesses, and increases commercialization of governmental research and development efforts.

Small Business Development Centers (SBDCs), usually associated with a college or university, provide individual shorter-term counseling using students, faculty, or other staff members. The SBDC system is sometimes likened to the agricultural Cooperative Extension Service which, upon its creation in 1914, disseminated information about the most modern farming methods through county offices. The Small Business Development Center Act of 1980 empowered the Office of Small Business Development Centers and established criteria for the selection of centers not only at the more traditional sites at colleges and universities but also at state and local governmental locations and private and nonprofit organizations.

In general, the SBA acts as an advocate of small business at all levels of government and in the private sector. It coordinates with other agencies to increase small business participation in international trade as well as promoting domestic business development. The SBA provides its services either at no charge or at a nominal charge. Numerous regional offices around the United States help make SBA services available to everyone. Though few data are available on the SBA's impact, its services undoubtedly have helped many businesses increase their likelihood of success.

Bibliography

Blackford, Mansel G., and Austin K. Kerr. *Business Enterprise in American History.* 2d ed. Boston: Houghton Mifflin, 1990. Provides a concise coverage of the history of the American business firm and the evolution of government-business relations, from colonial times to the present.

Dwyer, Christopher. *The Small Business Administration.* New York: Chelsea House, 1991. A short, nontechnical overview of the SBA's current activities.

Hughes, Jonathan R. T. *American Economy History.* 5th ed. Reading, Mass.: Addison-Wesley, 1998.

Parris, Addison W. *The Small Business Administration.* New York: Frederick A. Praeger, 1968. A comprehensive history of the SBA from 1953 to 1968. A readable summary of the events that caused the demise of the Reconstruction Finance Corporation and the formation of the SBA. Does provide some detail, but a reader interested in any specific subject will require supplementary material. Includes the text of the Small Business Act of 1953 in an appendix.

U.S. Congress. House. Committee on Banking and Currency. *Creation of Small Business Administration.* 83d Congress. Washington, D.C.: Government Printing Office, 1953. Includes transcripts of hearings that led to the creation of the SBA.

U.S. Congress. Senate. Banking and Currency Committee. *Study of the Reconstruction Finance Corporation Hearings.* 81st Congress. Washington, D.C.: Government Printing Office, 1950. Detailed recounting of the governmental investigation leading to the dismantling of the RFC.

U.S. Small Business Administration. *The State of Small Business: A Report of the President Transmitted to the Congress 1987.* Washington, D.C.: Government Printing Office, 1987. Yearly report on small business compiled by the SBA and released by the president. Includes both a narrative and statistics. An excellent source for data on small business.

John R. Tate

Cross-References

The U.S. Government Creates the Department of Commerce and Labor (1903); The Supreme Court Strikes Down a Maximum Hours Law (1905); The Supreme Court Rules Against Minimum Wage Laws (1923); The National Industrial Recovery Act Is Passed (1933); The Civil Rights Act Prohibits Discrimination in Employment (1964).

EISENHOWER BEGINS THE FOOD FOR PEACE PROGRAM

CATEGORY OF EVENT: International business and commerce
TIME: July 10, 1954
LOCALE: Washington, D.C.

Public Law 480 allowed the U.S. Department of Agriculture to buy surplus agricultural commodities and use them for donation abroad, for barter, or for sale for native currency.

Principal personages:

EZRA TAFT BENSON (1899-1994), the secretary of agriculture during the Eisenhower Administration

JOHN FOSTER DULLES (1888-1959), the secretary of state for seven years during the Eisenhower Administration

DON PAARLBERG (1911-   ), an assistant secretary of agriculture under Benson

CLARENCE FRANCIS (1888-1985), a special adviser to Eisenhower on disposal of agricultural surpluses

CLARENCE RANDALL (1891-1967), a special assistant to Eisenhower on foreign economic policy

WILLIAM S. HILL (1886-1972), a congressman from Colorado who introduced the legislation that subsequently became Public Law 480

Summary of Event

The Agricultural Trade Development and Assistance Act of 1954, commonly known as Public Law 480 or the "Food for Peace" program, provides for surplus U.S. farm commodities to be sold for foreign currencies and used as donations and barter goods. The objectives of PL 480, as stated by

One of the greatest controversies that Dwight D. Eisenhower faced during his first term as president was the question of farm subsidies. (Library of Congress)

Congress, are to promote economic stability for American agriculture, to expand international trade in agricultural commodities, to encourage the economic development of friendly countries, and to promote the collective strength of the free world.

A variety of factors led to the passage of this legislation. Food and peace have long been closely linked in the minds of Americans. Many times in the aftermath of war, food from U.S. farms has aided in the rehabilitation of ravaged areas. In addition, from a political standpoint food has often been used as a lever to achieve political goals and objectives.

In the 1940's and 1950's, a domestic agricultural problem developed. Incomes from food production in the United States did not permit American farmers to live on a scale comparable to that of people in other occupations. In order to boost farm incomes, the government agreed to buy certain products that could not be sold on the open market above a specified price. Between February, 1952, and February, 1956, the stocks of the Commodity Credit Corporation (CCC, the governmental agency charged with stockpiling surplus agricultural goods) in inventory as well as pledged against outstanding loans and purchase agreements increased almost fivefold, from less than $2 billion to $9.1 billion. Most of this buildup took place during 1952 and 1953, when annual increases in the stockpiles of 70 and 100 percent were registered. This problem of surplus government stocks was exacerbated by scientific technology. Farm productivity during this same period had increased significantly as a result of better products to control weeds, plant diseases, insects, and parasites, combined with developments in plant and livestock genetics and improved farm machinery.

An additional factor was important in the subsequent passage of PL 480. American farm exports had been declining during the early 1950's. Factors in this decline included a reduction in American economic aid to Western Europe (which had been quite high under the Marshall Plan following

World War II), the fact that agricultural production and protectionism were recovering in Western Europe, scarcity of the dollar in importing countries, domestic price supports that set American commodity prices above world levels, and American export controls that limited trade with the Soviet Union and its allies. As the repercussions of the decline in exports and the growth of surplus stocks rolled across the farm economy, farm spokespeople began demanding that the government act to stabilize farm income. President Dwight D. Eisenhower's administration was faced with the task of dealing with these multiple problems.

In the summer and fall of 1953, three groups began wrestling with program proposals for agricultural policy: the U.S. Department of Agriculture, the Commission on Foreign Economic Policy, and an interdepartmental committee on the surplus. In the summer of 1953, the U.S. Department of Agriculture surveyed three national farm groups—the American Farm Bureau, the Grange, and the National Farmer's Union—regarding farm income stability and trade versus aid, among other things. Overwhelming support was shown for a "two-price" plan for agricultural commodities. Such a scheme would support a high domestic price for the percentage of a commodity normally marketed in the United States and would allow the remainder (ostensibly exported) to be sold at the world price. Thus, the mood in the country was to continue farm income support.

The Commission on Foreign Economic Policy was chaired by Clarence Randall, special assistant to President Eisenhower on foreign economic policy. The seventeen-member group was composed of agribusiness representatives, prominent agricultural economists, five U.S. senators, and five U.S. congressmen. Agricultural policy was only part of the foreign economic policy reviewed by the commission. The commission issued a report on January 23, 1954, that included a five-page section on agricultural policy. The section on agriculture elicited written dissents from eight of the seventeen members. The report argued that "a dynamic foreign economic policy as it relates to agriculture cannot be built out of a maze of restrictive devices such as inflexible price-support programs which result in fixed prices, open or concealed export subsidies, . . . and state trading." It recommended the complete "elimination of such devices as a part of, or supplement to, our own agricultural policy."

This obviously went against the wishes of American farmers. The Department of Agriculture was effective in nullifying the report's agricultural recommendations by insisting that any inconsistencies between the report and President Eisenhower's January state of the union message be resolved in favor of the latter, in which Eisenhower had supported price supports on farm commodities.

Meanwhile, the interdepartmental committee on the surplus had been working on legislation. This study group had been Secretary of Agriculture Ezra Taft Benson's idea. He had persuaded President Eisenhower to establish it at the subcabinet level. After several meetings, on December 14, 1953, this committee had in hand the first draft of an administration surplus disposal bill. Despite President Eisenhower's call for fast action, the committee could not agree on a final draft bill. Stumbling blocks included disputes concerning which commodities to include, who would have administrative authority, and to what extent the private sector should be involved.

While the administration squabbled, the House of Representatives began considering various surplus disposal bills. As the spring of 1954 wore on, some sixty bills were introduced into Congress. This flurry of activity spurred the interdepartmental committee to compromise. A compromise draft was introduced by Representative William S. Hill of Colorado. It was discussed by the House Agriculture Committee on June 3, reported out, debated for two days by the House as a Committee of the Whole, and passed on June 16. Following rapid Senate action, the conference committee made some adjustments. The bill was agreed to by both houses, and Eisenhower signed it into law on July 10.

Impact of Event

As passed, Public Law 480 had three titles. Title I authorized sales of surplus agricultural commodities for foreign currency to "friendly" nations, identified as any countries other than the Soviet Union and those under the influence of the world Communist movement. Commodities were to move through private channels to the extent possible. Foreign currencies acquired in trade were to be used for market development, stockpile purchases, military procurement, debt payments, educational exchanges, new loans, and aid to friendly countries not part of the trades.

Title II provided for grants of surplus agricultural commodities to friendly nations to meet emergency situations. Title III authorized the donation of surplus food for domestic distribution and for distribution to needy persons overseas through nonprofit relief agencies. In addition, Title III allowed for the barter of surplus agricultural commodities for strategic and other materials produced abroad.

As written, the legislation did not assign administrative responsibility. Thus, President Eisenhower still had to decide which agency or agencies would administer the various titles. After considerable bureaucratic wrangling, Eisenhower issued Executive Order 10560 on September 9, 1954. This order gave the Department of Agriculture Title I authority, the Foreign

Operations Administration (FOA) authority for Title II, and the Department of State the function of negotiating and entering into agreements. The budget office received allocation authority for foreign currencies, and the Treasury Department was to regulate the purchase, custody, deposit, transfer, and sale of currencies. The Office of Defense Mobilization received authority for stockpile purchases, the Department of Defense the military procurement authority, and other various agencies authority for other foreign currency uses.

The executive order and accompanying documents also formalized the position of the interdepartmental committee that had been working for nearly a year. Known now as the Interagency Committee on Agricultural Surplus Disposal (ICASD), it was to continue to formulate policy under the chairmanship of Clarence Francis. Francis was brought into this position from the chairmanship of General Foods. Actual direction of the surplus disposal operation was to be handled by an Interagency Staff Committee on Agricultural Surplus Disposal (ISC), composed of one representative from each agency in the ICASD. William Lodwick, a Foreign Agriculture Service (FAS) official, was appointed as both administrator of FAS and chairman of the ISC.

During the first two years of operation, PL 480 was broadened to include feed grains and to authorize the use of federal funds to pay the costs of ocean transportation and consumer packaging. During late 1958, the Department of Agriculture developed a message that the president sent to Congress on January 29, 1959. As part of this communication, Secretary Benson inserted a "Food for Peace" section in which Eisenhower announced that he was setting steps in motion to explore, with other surplus-producing nations, means of utilizing agricultural surpluses in the interest of reinforcing peace and the well-being of friendly peoples throughout the world.

Title IV of PL 480 was enacted on September 21, 1959. It provides for long-term supply of U.S. agricultural commodities and sales on a credit basis to assist in the development of the economies of friendly nations. The program is of particular help to countries that "graduate" from Title I foreign currency purchasing to dollar purchasing.

By early 1960, the original PL 480 program had been modified and extended several times. The Eisenhower Administration wanted to heighten public awareness of accomplishments under the program. On April 13, 1960, Eisenhower designated Don Paarlberg as the Food for Peace coordinator. Previously, Paarlberg had been an assistant secretary of agriculture and had worked with the PL 480 program as a member of the White House staff.

The first, and least controversial, consequence of PL 480 has been the effect on food consumption in recipient countries. The diets of many thousands of people have been improved as a result of this program. There is some concern that the program has not facilitated economic development to the extent hoped for.

The effect around which there exists the most controversy and the most confusion regards the impact of PL 480 on producers and production in the recipient countries. One view holds that the surplus disposal operations of the United States have generally hurt producers in the recipient countries and, more important, have acted to remove the incentive to increase total production in those countries. In this view, the program has acted to perpetuate food shortages. An opposing view holds that PL 480 shipments have been administered in such a way as not to hurt the producers involved; through the beneficial effects on capital formation, they have acted to increase agricultural production above what it could have been without the program.

Two titles were added to the program, which became known as "Food for Progress." Title V is the "Farmer to Farmer Program." It provides for a minimum of 0.2 percent of total PL 480 funds to assist farmers and agribusiness operations in developing countries by transferring knowledge of farming methods from U.S. farmers, agriculturalists, land-grant universities, private agribusinesses, and nonprofit farm organizations to farms and agribusinesses in developing and middle-income countries and emerging democracies. Title VI authorizes certain activities for the reduction of debts of Latin American and Caribbean countries. In 1989, agricultural exports under PL 480 included $722 million under Title I and $469 million under Title II. This dollar volume was 3 percent of total agricultural exports. After 40 percent of the surplus commodity shipments, by value, were wheat.

Bibliography

Baldwin, David A. *Economic Development and American Foreign Policy: 1943-62*. Chicago: University of Chicago Press, 1966. Discusses a variety of approaches the United States has taken to economic development in foreign countries. Contains numerous references to PL 480 but no in-depth discussion.

_____. *Foreign Aid and American Foreign Policy*. New York: Frederick A. Praeger, 1966. This text is a documentary analysis of American foreign policy and aid. It presents the facts in a straightforward manner with little editorializing. Much of the book is dedicated to congressional hearings. One chapter is devoted to agriculture and foreign aid.

Peterson, Trudy Huskamp. *Agricultural Exports, Farm Income, and the*

Eisenhower Administration. Lincoln: University of Nebraska Press, 1979. This is an excellent source on the background and implementation of PL 480. The author painstakingly researched the subject. Well documented with notes and bibliographic material. Quite detailed.

Tontz, Robert L., ed. *Foreign Agricultural Trade: Selected Readings.* Ames: Iowa State University Press, 1966. Has an entire section on trade programs, including Food for Peace shipments. The majority of the sections were written by well-known agricultural economists and are short and to the point.

U.S. Department of Agriculture. *Agricultural Statistics, 1991.* Washington, D.C.: U.S. Government Printing Office, 1991. Contains statistics on exports of agricultural commodities under specified government-financed programs, including PL 480. Similar volumes are produced annually.

John C. Foltz

Cross-References

Congress Passes the Agricultural Marketing Act (1929); The Truman Administration Launches the Marshall Plan (1947); The Agency for International Development Is Established (1961).

THE AFL AND CIO MERGE

CATEGORY OF EVENT: Labor
TIME: December 5, 1955
LOCALE: New York, New York

The American Federation of Labor and the Congress of Industrial Organizations reunited to cope with major union problems and a changing business and political environment

Principal personages:
GEORGE MEANY (1894-1980), the AFL president who aided the merger with the CIO and served as the first president of the AFL-CIO
PHILIP MURRAY (1886-1952), a CIO president who contributed to the merger
JOHN L. LEWIS (1880-1969), a CIO president and leader of the United Mine Workers
WALTER REUTHER (1907-1970), a leader of the United Auto Workers and an AFL-CIO president
SIDNEY HILLMAN (1887-1946), a leader of the CIO's political arm
JIMMY HOFFA (1913-1975), a Teamsters Union president whose corruption caused major labor problems

Summary of Event
Led by the fiery leader of the United Mine Workers Union, John L. Lewis, nearly a million members of the American Federation of Labor (AFL) were suspended by the AFL in 1935 and were expelled officially in 1938. This massive division within the ranks of organized labor, leading to formation of the rival Congress of Industrial Organizations (CIO), was destined to last for two decades. Debate continues over whether the split was inevitable. Labor leaders such as David Dubinsky, who headed the ladies' garment workers, along with labor historians such as Philip Taft and many politicians including President Franklin D. Roosevelt, believed the

separation within the ranks of organized labor to be unfortunate as well as unnecessary. Given the tumults and uncertainties that characterized the labor scene after the CIO's ejection from its parent organization, these perspectives were shared widely throughout the nation's business community and the general public.

Personality and generational conflicts undoubtedly fueled the causes of division. Lewis allied with David Dubinsky and Philip Murray, for example, against AFL president William Green and AFL officials such as William Hutcheson, John Frey, and Matthew Woll. Questionable actions of

Samuel Gompers, one of the founders of the AFL. (Library of Congress)

the AFL's executive committee in its handling of dissidents also led to divisiveness. The split in labor's ranks sprang from profound differences in attitudes and philosophy and from differing visions of labor's future.

The AFL, the largest, most enduring, and most successful of American labor organizations, had won its way to prominence by adhering to the principles of its founders, most notably those of Samuel Gompers, the AFL president from 1886 until his death in 1924. Carried forward diligently by Gompers' successor, William Green, the AFL was built around the unionization of skilled workers. It stood for craft organization and craft autonomy. Mills, factories, and plants, with few exceptions, were unionized according to the trades of their skilled workers. That is, the AFL's affiliated unions exercised jurisdiction over members working in specific crafts. A given factory thus could have several trade unions. The internal affairs of each trade's union were virtually invulnerable to interference from AFL officials.

The CIO's leaders, on the other hand, were committed to industrial unionism, or the organization of all workers in a given plant or industry, irrespective of skills, into one comprehensive union. The rationale for this approach grew from awareness of dramatic changes in American society and in the workplace that had manifested themselves by the mid-1930's. Lewis and other CIO leaders lamented the fact that, for the most part, semiskilled and unskilled workers lay beyond either the interest or the respect of most AFL leaders. These workers constituted large and growing parts of the workforce in mass-production industries.

After furious battles against major industries during the last half of the 1930's, reflected in the media almost daily, the CIO's achievements were registered in its membership. By 1938, the CIO had more than 4 million members, while the AFL had 3.4 million. The CIO had grown by successfully targeting workers in mass-production industries and by winning cost-of-living increases, guaranteed annual wages, job security, and unemployment payments, as well as welfare and benefit plans. The AFL grew by adopting many CIO attitudes and objectives and by responding positively to CIO competition.

By the end of the 1940's, however, each organization had long been suffering the penalties of division, including erosive losses from duplication of effort. In addition, the national disposition toward unions had grown less tolerant, partly as a result of crippling strikes between 1945 and 1948. The political climate had therefore become less friendly. Legislative and judicial victories, moreover, had begun diminishing after the late 1930's. An unmistakable anti-union trend was evident in the U.S. Supreme Court's 1939 decision pronouncing sit-down strikes illegal in the Fanstock Steel case and subsequent federal court decisions upholding employers by fining union leaders for violations of the Sherman Antitrust Act. Although the Labor-Management Relations Act of 1947 (the Taft-Hartley Act) proved not to be the slave labor bill that union leaders feared it would be, it still invoked authority to curb the seemingly engorged power of union leaders and to shift the legal balance toward employers. Public confidence in and respect for union leadership were shaken further by exposures of Communist influences in several unions and by federal revelations of union racketeering and corruption, most notoriously in the Teamsters Union.

These factors registered as declining union membership and quickened the drive toward reunification of the AFL and the CIO. President Roosevelt had urged a reunification as early as 1934. The deaths in 1952 of Philip Murray, who had succeeded John L. Lewis as head of the CIO, and of AFL president William Green brought new leadership to both organizations. The brilliantly successful organizer of the auto workers, Walter Reuther, took command of the CIO, while the steady, forceful George Meany became president of the AFL. With the initiative for negotiations in their hands, a stalled unity committee was reactivated.

The range of divisive issues was soon narrowed. Reuther, no longer willing to have labor identified with Communist influences, previously had purged Communists from his own unions. He insisted that they be expelled from the AFL. Despite the AFL's traditional sanctification of craft autonomy, Meany undertook a cleansing of the AFL, even though by implication it meant the beginning of centralized control within the organization. Similarly, both organizations, having confirmed by National Labor Relations Board (NLRB) statistics that their mutual membership raids and jurisdictional battles were costly and ineffective, consented to abandon them. Sixty-five AFL and twenty-nine CIO unions pledged in June, 1954, to abandon raids. With other practical and emotional complaints eased by the unity committee, a formal agreement to merge was consummated in February, 1955. The agreement was ratified on December 5 of that year.

Reunification signalled agreement within the AFL-CIO to recognize both craft and industrial unionism. All unions previously holding charters from either the AFL or the CIO were eligible to join the AFL-CIO. George Meany and Walter Reuther respectively assumed the presidency and vice-presidency of the union, and posts on the executive council were divided according to the relative sizes of the former federations' memberships. Assets were pooled. The AFL-CIO at its founding was the free world's largest labor organization, encompassing sixteen million workers.

Impact of Event

In the decades following the 1955 merger, the AFL-CIO bargained with rapidly changing and unprecedentedly powerful corporations and managements. An acceleration of the corporate drive toward automation, management's steady upgrading of skills required for employment, corporate mergers, and the rise of conglomerates and of multinationals with team-managed technostructures all confronted the AFL-CIO with new managerial attitudes and strategies. At the same time, manufacturing industries, the traditional source of union strength, declined in importance. Union membership soon showed both a numerical decline and a decline as a proportion of the workforce.

Although less susceptible to measurement, the effects of a generational change among labor leaders were important to the evolving fortunes of the AFL-CIO. The combative and colorful union leaders of the early years were replaced by less charismatic officials. Teamsters leader Jimmy Hoffa certainly contributed color to the labor arena, but his actions led the AFL-CIO to expel the Teamsters in 1957. One concomitant of the generational transition was a loss of union morale. As some labor experts noted, this was attributable to AFL-CIO unions concentrating too heavily on job security rather than on job creation, as well as to what Walter Reuther decried as the AFL-CIO's complacency and lack of drive and vision.

The tactics of conglomerates often involved the closing of unprofitable plants, the pursuit of mergers that blurred workers' rights, and the capricious handling of union welfare, benefit, and pension funds. The AFL-CIO initiated coordinated bargaining in response. By the 1970's, the federation had formed eighty coordinated bargaining committees charged with negotiating for workers employed by conglomerates.

There were other manifestations of pressure against AFL-CIO unions by many of the country's major corporations. Labor historians have pointed to General Electric's (GE) employee relations policies of the late 1960's and early 1970's as examples of managerial strategies designed to preclude further union gains and erode existing positions. These policies were named for a vice-president of GE's affiliated companies, Lemuel Boulware, who was responsible for reviewing labor relations. "Boulwareism" focused on persistent advertising and merchandising tactics to undermine unions and resulted in one-time, "take-it-or-leave-it" GE offers at the bargaining table. The consequence was a series of battles, some conducted under provisions of the Taft-Hartley Act before the National Labor Relations Board, and some in the courts. The highlight of the battles was a 102-day strike against the nation's fourth largest corporation, involving 147,000 workers from thirteen unions. By spending nearly two million dollars to counter Boulware's intensive public relations campaigns, the AFL-CIO cut so markedly into GE's earnings that the company chose to give in to most union demands.

Boulwareism was one manifestation of what some observers regarded as a 1960's crisis in industrial relations, characterized by management's hardened attitudes. Many large corporations reputedly believed that their attempts to achieve better employee relations, and thereby to improve worker efficiency, had failed. Nothing remained, therefore, except to destroy gains made by unions since the mid-1930's and to regain at the bargaining table the same measure of managerial authority that management had won politically with passage of the Taft-Hartley Act and the Landrum-Griffin Act.

Some observers attributed the crisis in labor relations less to labor-management conflict than to labor-management collusion. Daniel Bell argued that the age of genuine collective bargaining as an instrument of economic and social justice was ending. Economist and public servant John Kenneth Galbraith interpreted collective bargaining as a joint exercise of "countervailing power," by labor and management. Bell and others saw it as their jointly administered manipulation of inflation at the general public's expense. Evidence for this thesis was drawn, for example, from events occurring in the steel industry, among others. Leaders of unions and management agreed to publicize phony threats of strikes or to call brief token strikes to raise wages and benefits for the unions; the increased costs were used to justify higher prices for products. The maneuvering, Bell and others said, contributed to persistent inflation.

Other experts explained the crisis of labor-management relations differently. Crisis was explicable as a transition stage. Union-management collusion, resistance to technological change, complacency, low morale, inflationary pressures, political and governmental interference in the affairs of capital and labor, and the runaway legalism attending passage of major labor-management legislation (including the Wagner Act, the Taft-Hartley Act, and the Landrum-Griffin Act) were nothing new when viewed in historical perspective. The genuine crises of major strikes and national disruptions lay well behind. Strike activity was low, and the industrial scene increasingly could be characterized by its placidity. Government officials closely monitored the affairs of the AFL-CIO and independent unions, as well as those of corporations. Collective bargaining, in some respects, moved from the unilateral and bilateral settings prevailing from the mid-1930's through the early 1960's to a trilateral and more complex phase, with government as a player in the game. This new phase of industrial relations involved careful consideration of the effects of an increasingly internationalized economy, of foreign competition, and of the public welfare.

In 1990, the AFL-CIO reported a membership of 14.1 million. Its representation of the total workforce had declined to 19 percent. Crippling national strikes lay decades behind, and work stoppages resulted in a loss of only .02 percent of potential working time. The AFL-CIO and constituent unions had grown into an era of conciliation.

Bibliography

Brooks, Thomas R. *Toil and Trouble: A History of American Labor*. 2d ed. New York: Delacorte Press, 1971. Colorful and interesting reading. An instructive prolabor account. Chapters 12 through 25 concern the era from the 1930's to 1970. No notes or bibliography.

Galbraith, John Kenneth. *The New Industrial State*. Boston: Houghton Mifflin, 1967. Eloquently describes changes in American economic life that furnished the context for the AFL-CIO merger and its aftermath. Few notes. Good index.

Goldberg, Arthur J. *AFL-CIO, Labor United*. New York: McGraw-Hill, 1956. Interesting contemporary assessment of the merger. The author is a former CIO counsel, later a U.S. Supreme Court justice.

Jacoby, Daniel *Laboring for Freedom: A New Look at the History of Labor in America*. Armonk, N.Y.: M. E. Sharpe, 1998.

Kerr, Clark. *Labor and Management in Industrial Society*. Garden City,

N.Y.: Anchor Books, 1964. Expert, balanced, and informative. Notes and select bibliography. A useful and reflective work.

Preis, Art. *Labor's Giant Step: Twenty Years of the CIO*. New York: Pathfinder Press, 1972. The author's provocative view of "American class struggle" as seen through the CIO. Chapters 36-39 deal with the merger. Brief notes on sources.

Taft, Philip. *The A.F. of L. from the Death of Gompers to the Merger*. New York: Harper & Brothers, 1959. Standard and authoritative. Clear but colorless scholarship. Valuable index.

Clifton K. Yearley

Cross-References

The Wagner Act Promotes Union Organization (1935); The CIO Begins Unionizing Unskilled Workers (1935); Roosevelt Signs the Fair Labor Standards Act (1938); The Taft-Hartley Act Passes over Truman's Veto (1947); The Landrum-Griffin Act Targets Union Corruption (1959); Firms Begin Replacing Skilled Laborers with Automatic Tools (1960's).

CONGRESS SETS STANDARDS FOR CHEMICAL ADDITIVES IN FOOD

CATEGORY OF EVENT: Consumer affairs
TIME: 1958
LOCALE: Washington, D.C.

Following extensive debate about the long-term impact of food additives on public health, the Delaney Amendment to the Food, Drug, and Cosmetic Act required safety clearance for food additives

Principal personages:
GEORGE P. LARRICK (1901-1968), a commissioner of the Food and Drug Administration
JAMES J. DELANEY (1901-1987), a congressman from New York
ANTON JULIUS CARSON, a faculty member at the University of Chicago

Summary of Event
The use of chemical additives in food products as flavoring, as preservatives, or as part of packaging grew rapidly during the 1940's. The long-term impact of these chemicals on public health, however, remained largely unknown. This period also witnessed a substantial increase in the agricultural use of commercial pesticides such as DDT; again, it was unclear whether the pesticides used in production of raw agricultural goods caused any harm. Given the enormous public health implications of these issues, the U.S. House of Representatives formed a select committee to investigate the use of chemicals in foods in June, 1950. Until March, 1952, this committee (also known as the Delaney Committee, headed by James J.

Delaney, representative from New York) held extensive hearings on the impact of chemical additives and pesticides in products intended for human consumption. Findings from these hearings were published later in four volumes focused on fertilizers, cosmetics, food, and fluoridation. The volume devoted to food recommended that chemicals intended to be used with foods should be tested carefully before such use to ensure safety. Although this recommendation was not acted upon by Congress immediately, it provided a basis for the Food Additives Amendment of 1958.

Chemical food additives can perform a wide variety of functions. Depending on the specific food product considered, additives serve to increase the acidity or alkalinity levels, preserve or age, increase or decrease water retention characteristics, enhance color or flavor appeal, and prevent spattering of cooking fats. Preservatives have been used widely to avoid or minimize the growth of microbes in foods over time. Antimycotic agents such as acetic acid and calcium propionate are employed to fight the growth of mold and other bacteria in bread; similarly, benzoic acid inhibits bacterial growth in pickles and fruit juices. Sulfur dioxide is a popular preservative for dried fruits. Antioxidants are often used in lard, crackers, and soup bases. Another class of additives, called sequestrants, is used to retain the color, flavor, or texture of many products. Emulsifiers (such as lecithin, monoglycerides, diglycerides, and dioctyl sodium sulfosucinate) are added to food products to improve their texture or other physical characteristics: for example, enhancing the whipping attribute in frozen desserts or facilitating the dissolution of hot chocolate in cold milk. Finally, other chemicals known as stabilizers, thickeners, buffers, and neutralizers are added to food products for a variety of purposes.

The Food, Drug, and Cosmetic Act, enacted in 1938, prohibited the presence of harmful or poisonous substances in food products. This provision was largely ineffective in practice because it did not require premarket clearance of food additives; it mandated premarket clearance only for new drugs and coal tar dyes. The Food and Drug Administration (FDA) had to bear the burden of proof to show that a given chemical food additive was harmful after it had been introduced in a product. Establishing such proof was difficult and time-consuming. A major flaw in the regulatory framework during the 1950's was that as long as such proof was not established, even suspect food additives could be used legally in products available to the public.

The Delaney Amendment of 1958 corrected this flaw by mandating premarket clearance of chemical additives that were not generally recognized as safe (GRAS). That is, if qualified scientists and experts believed that a given substance could be added safely to food products, the substance could be classified under the GRAS category and thereby exempted from the premarket clearance requirement. The inclusion of a new food additive under GRAS could be justified on the basis of scientific data; for food additives already in use before January 1, 1958, such justification could stem from prior safe-use experience in food products.

The Delaney Amendment mandated the submission to the FDA of certain details concerning any new food additive—the formula depicting its chemical composition, a description of proposed usage characteristics, the procedure used for its manufacture, and the manner in which its presence in food products could be detected accurately at the expected levels of use. In addition, the prospective user of the new additive was required to furnish evidence that the additive accomplished the intended effects on food and that the degree of additive usage was not higher than necessary to achieve these effects. More important, the user had to provide data documenting the safety of the proposed food additive. This evidence took the form of studies in which varying amounts of the additive were included in the intakes of at least two species of animals. Finally, even if the FDA approved the usage of a newly proposed food additive, it could limit the additive's usage by specifying tolerances. Tolerances are commonly determined through animal feeding tests. These tests of an additive may show, for example, that a 1 percent residue of the chemical has no adverse effect. A pharmacologist in charge then may arbitrarily divide by one hundred and say that .01 percent is safe for humans. Tolerances rest on the tenuous assumption that small doses of poisonous chemicals are harmless even if ingested over a long period of time; therefore, it is possible that tolerances lend acceptability to additives that are inherently dangerous to public health.

During the congressional hearings on the Delaney Amendment, two issues caused significant debate. The first controversy centered on the "Delaney anticancer clause," which declared that no food additive could be considered safe if it was found to induce cancer in humans or animals. This clause was opposed by several experts and even by the FDA, on the grounds that it was not in line with scientific judgment. For example, several individuals called into question the wisdom of banning the limited human consumption of food additives merely because they induced cancer in some animals. Others thought that it was inappropriate to focus on a specific disease (cancer) while establishing legislative standards. These objectives notwithstanding, the Delaney anticancer clause was incorporated into the 1958 amendment as signed into law.

The second issue involved sustained lobbying efforts by the food and chemical industries for the inclusion of a "grandfather clause," a provision specifically exempting all chemical additives in use at that time from the mandatory testing requirement. Delaney strongly objected to this plea because the grandfather clause would render almost 150 chemical additives automatically acceptable without any rigorous scientific evidence on their safety. Although industry representatives argued that the food additives in use qualified for exemption because of their past record of safety during prolonged use, it was unclear what constituted an acceptable definition of prolonged use for each additive. Some chemical food additives may require as long as twenty years before their cumulative health impact can be assessed. Furthermore, several chemical additives had been declared as unsafe only after they were used in food products for several years. For example, Anton Julius Carson, a medical expert from the University of Chicago, had testified before the Delaney Committee about the harmful effects of hydrofluoric acid and mineral oil, food additives that had been added routinely to beer and popcorn, respectively, for several years. Delaney also questioned the value of mandating public protection against new food additives through elaborate testing when "old" additives that were untested for safety were permitted in food products consumed by the public.

The grandfather clause was not incorporated into the 1958 amendment despite sustained efforts from the food and chemical industries. These industries, however, won other notable concessions. First, through a series of legislative measures, Congress gave the industry substantial time (until December, 1965) to finish safety evaluations of specific chemicals already in use. Second, the amendment did not incorporate the FDA viewpoint that chemical food additives should not only be harmless to humans but also must possess some functional value; the motivation was to discourage the use of additives that, while not considered unsafe, did not serve any useful purpose to consumers.

Both Delaney and George P. Larrick, the FDA commissioner, vehemently argued for the functional value provision. Larrick defined functional value as stemming from any characteristic of the food additive that directly benefited consumers by enhancing convenience or indirectly benefited consumers during the process of product distribution. Further, he provided several examples in which chemical additives had been added to food products only because it was profitable or convenient for the industry to do so, and not because they served any consumer interest: the use of boric acid to preserve codfish and whole eggs in an attempt to conceal poor manufacturing or storage practices; the reliance on fluorine chemicals in alcoholic beverages such as wine and beer to curb fermentation, a result better accomplished through pasteurization; the inclusion of monochloracetic acid in carbonated beverages as a substitute for proper sanitation practices; and the addition of salicylates in shrimp sauce to inhibit decomposition processes triggered by poor manufacturing or holding practices. Larrick argued in vain that the safe but unnecessary use of chemical additives should not be a prerogative of the food industry.

Impact of Event

The 1958 amendment played a major role in promoting long-term public health primarily because of two features. It extended the premarket clearance requirement to food additives and prohibited the addition to foods of any chemicals shown to be animal carcinogens (substances that cause cancer in animals).

To appreciate the impact of the Food Additives Amendment, it is useful to study its interpretation and enforcement over the years. The anticancer clause applies to both direct and indirect food additives. The latter comprise chemicals that migrate into food from food packaging material. In addition, more than one hundred drugs used in food-producing animals are subject to the clause.

Three important practical issues arise from the clause. First, although it appears to categorically prohibit the addition of carcinogenic chemicals to foods, there appears to be considerable leeway in deciding whether a substance is carcinogenic. As one example, there was an intense debate as to whether saccharin is carcinogenic. Other fairly common additives are the subject of the same question. Second, a proviso in the clause specifically exempts carcinogenic food and animal drugs added to the feed of food-producing animals. That is, if chemical additives in animal feed do not harm the animal and do not leave any residue on the edible parts of the animal (intended for human consumption), such additives are exempt from the scope of the clause. Finally, no chemical food additive is strictly free from all carcinogens. Certain carcinogens such as lead and halogenated compounds contaminate all chemicals, including food additives, at minute levels. Moreover, subsequent to the 1958 amendment, it has become technologically feasible to analyze chemical substances at extremely low trace levels, measurable in parts per million or parts per billion. For these reasons, the FDA developed a constituent policy in March, 1982, that states that a food additive can include carcinogens as long as the degree of risk associated with the extent of the carcinogenic presence is acceptably low. This is in keeping with the spirit of the 1958 amendment, although it is a reversal of the letter of the Delaney clause. In defining what constitutes an acceptably low standard, the FDA has used an upper limit of one case of cancer following the exposure of a million people to a food additive.

In the early 1980's, several bills introduced in Congress contained language that would have revised the food safety legislation that had prevailed for several decades. These bills—S. 1938 and H.R. 4121 in 1983, S. 2512 in the 99th Congress, S. 2875 and H.R. 4739 in the 100th Congress, and S. 722 and H.R. 1725 in the 101st Congress—called for revisions of the Delaney clause to avoid the ban of a carcinogenic additive if scientific evidence suggests that the human risks involved under intended conditions of use are negligible. None of the bills passed.

Bibliography

Flamm, W. G. "Food-borne Carcinogens." In *Chemical Safety Regulation and Compliance*, edited by Freddy Homburger and Judith K. Marquis. Basel, Switzerland: S. Karger, 1985. Discusses this class of carcinogens.

Kleinfeld, Vincent A., and Alan H. Kaplan. *Federal Food, Drug, and Cosmetic Act: Judicial and Adminstrative Record 1961-1964*. Chicago: Commerce Clearing House, 1965. This book belongs to the Food Law Institute Series and is a useful source of information on laws related to food and drugs. It contains the text of the Food, Drug, and Cosmetic Act and its amendments as well as the details of legislative and judicial activities initiated in connection with the Federal Food, Drug, and Cosmetic Act between 1961 and 1964.

Kokoski, C. J. "Regulatory Food Additive Toxicology." In *Chemical Safety Regulation and Compliance*, edited by Freddy Homburger and Judith K. Marquis. Basel, Switzerland: S. Karger, 1985. Discusses testing methods for food additives.

Mooney, Booth. *The Hidden Assassins*. Chicago: Follett, 1966. Provides an informative overview of the hearings conducted by the Delaney Committee and describes how these hearings led to the 1958 Food Additives (Delaney) Amendment.

Skinner, K. "Scientific Change and the Evolution of Regulation." In *Chemical Safety Regulation and Compliance*, edited by Freddy Homburger and Judith K. Marquis. Basel, Switzerland: S. Karger, 1985. Describes how advances in science have affected regulation and testing.

U.S. Congress. House. Committee on Interstate and Foreign Commerce. Subcommittee on Public Health and Environment. *A Brief Legislative History of the Food, Drug, and Cosmetic Act*. Washington, D.C.: U.S. Government Printing Office, 1974. Presents a comprehensive account of the historical circumstances that led to the Food, Drug, and Cosmetic Act of 1938. Also discusses the circumstances surrounding the formation of the Delaney Committee and how this committee's findings eventually led to the 1958 Food Additives Amendment. Several other amendments to the act are also discussed.

Siva Balasubramanian

Cross-References

Congress Passes the Pure Food and Drug Act (1906); Nader's *Unsafe at Any Speed* Launches a Consumer Movement (1965); Congress Passes the Consumer Credit Protection Act (1968); The United States Bans Cyclamates from Consumer Markets (1969); The Banning of DDT Signals New Environmental Awareness (1969); Nixon Signs the Consumer Product Safety Act (1972).

THE LANDRUM-GRIFFIN ACT TARGETS UNION CORRUPTION

CATEGORY OF EVENT: Labor
TIME: September 14, 1959
LOCALE: Washington, D.C.

By regulating union elections, requiring disclosures, establishing a bill of rights for members, and eliminating "hot cargo" clauses, the Landrum-Griffin Act attempted to reduce union corruption

Principal personages:

PHILIP M. LANDRUM (1907-1990), a Democratic representative from Georgia, cosponsor of the Landrum-Griffin bill

ROBERT P. GRIFFIN (1923-   ), a Republican congressman from Michigan, cosponsor of the Landrum-Griffin bill

JOHN F. KENNEDY (1917-1963), a Democratic senator from Massachusetts, subsequently the thirty-fifth president of the United States

SAM ERVIN (1896-1985), a Democratic senator from North Carolina, cosponsor of the Kennedy-Ervin bill

GEORGE MEANY (1894-1980), the president of the AFL-CIO

JOHN L. MCCLELLAN (1896-1977), a Democratic senator from Arkansas

GRAHAM ARTHUR BARDEN (1896-1967), a Democratic congressman from North Carolina, chairman of the House Committee on Education and Labor

BARRY GOLDWATER (1909-1998), a Republican senator from Arizona, sponsor of the administration's reform bill

DWIGHT D. EISENHOWER (1890-1969), the thirty-fourth president of the United States

SAM RAYBURN (1882-1961), a Democratic congressman from Texas, Speaker of the House in the eighty-sixth Congress

Summary of Event

On September 14, 1959, in response to revelations of corrupt labor practices during hearings of Senator John L. McClellan's Committee on Improper Activities in Labor-Management Affairs, President Dwight D. Eisenhower signed the Labor-Management Reporting and Disclosure Act of 1959, popularly known as the Landrum-Griffin Act. The McClellan Committee had focused much of its investigation on the Teamsters Union and its president-elect, James R. "Jimmy" Hoffa. The American Federation of Labor-Congress of Industrial Organizations (AFL-CIO) had responded to the adverse publicity by expelling the Teamsters and other unions from its ranks. In addition, the McClellan Committee's recommendations in favor of legislation to regulate benefit funds and to ensure union democracy received widespread public support. In 1958, Congress passed the Welfare and Pension Plans Disclosure Act to regulate benefit funds. The public anticipated further legislative action in 1959.

There were several labor bills before the Senate in 1959, the most important of which were the Kennedy-Ervin bill, successor to the Kennedy-Ives bill of 1958, and the Goldwater bill, which reflected the Eisenhower Administration's interests. Both bills contained provisions requiring regulation of and reporting and disclosure of financial information by trusteeships, which had been misused by national unions to assume control of dissident locals.

The AFL-CIO and its president, George Meany, backed the Kennedy-Ervin bill, subsequently called the Kennedy bill. Management groups such as the National Association of Manufacturers and the Secondary Boycott Committee of the United States Chamber of Commerce objected to several provisions in the Kennedy bill that were favorable to unions. The management groups argued that Congress should place unions under antitrust laws and curb their use of secondary boycotts. In a secondary boycott, a union involved in a labor dispute with one employer brings pressure to bear on a second employer, which may be a customer of the first, to encourage the second employer to refrain from purchasing the first's products or otherwise doing business with the first. More than one hundred conservative amendments, including more than seventy by Senator Barry Goldwater, were introduced on the floor of the Senate.

The most important of the proposed amendments was Senator McClellan's "bill of rights for union members." In response to an impassioned speech, McClellan's amendment passed the Senate by one vote. The Senate subsequently softened the amendment when it was realized that McClellan's bill of rights inadvertently opened union membership to black workers. The labor movement was stunned by the antilabor amendment's passage, because congressional Democrats had won a substantial majority in 1958. Labor believed that Congress would inevitably support its interests.

A bipartisan group proposed a compromise between conservative and labor interests that saved the Kennedy bill by including the McClellan amendment. Ultimately, to the AFL-CIO's chagrin, the Kennedy bill, including the McClellan amendment, passed the Senate. Labor faced setbacks in the House of Representatives as well, and its intransigence with respect to the compromise bill resulted in the ultimate passage of the Landrum-Griffin bill, which was even more antagonistic to labor's interests than was the Kennedy bill. The House Committee on Education and Labor, chaired by Representative Graham Arthur Barden, reported a revised version of the Kennedy bill in spite of intensive lobbying by the AFL-CIO. George Meany became embroiled in an argument about it with Sam Rayburn, Speaker of the House, and wrote a letter to all members of Congress stating the AFL-CIO's opposition to the committee's bill. Only four days after the committee voted to report its version of the bill, committee members Philip M. Landrum and Robert P. Griffin introduced their bill, which was backed by management groups and the Eisenhower Administration.

The Landrum-Griffin bill, the committee's bill, and a bill supported by the AFL-CIO all had similar anticrime provisions. The chief differences among them concerned economic issues unrelated to crime in unions. The Landrum-Griffin bill had stronger provisions with respect to organizational picketing, secondary boycotts, and "hot cargo" clauses than did the other bills. Under hot cargo clauses, an employer agrees not to handle the goods of nonunion employers.

Lobbying was intense. President Eisenhower made a television appearance in support of the Landrum-Griffin bill. Management lobbyists broadcast and publicized the Armstrong Cork Company's television play *The Sound of Violence*, which depicted union corruption.

The labor movement was divided about reform. The Teamsters and the United Mine Workers opposed any legislation, the United Auto Workers favored strict legislation, the construction unions were ambivalent, and the AFL-CIO supported mild legislation. Despite the divisions, which weakened the labor movement's lobbying efforts, the Senate-House Conference Committee softened some of the bill's provisions, for example by offering special provisions to unions in the construction and garment industries.

As passed, the Landrum-Griffin Act had two distinct objectives: first, to regulate unions and end corruption, and second, to tighten the proscription of secondary boycotts contained in the Taft-Hartley Act of 1947. The act's first six titles concern corruption. Title I, the bill of rights, guarantees members' rights to vote in union elections, to sue their unions, to run for union office, and to speak openly. It prohibits increases in dues except by secret ballot or appropriate procedures at the national level.

Title II requires unions to adopt constitutions and to file annual financial reports and disclosures of officers' assets with the secretary of labor. It also requires that unions report on qualifications for union membership, procedures for the calling of elections, and disciplinary procedures.

Title III regulates trusteeships. It requires that a report be filed with the secretary of labor within thirty days of the imposition of a trusteeship. Title IV regulates the election of union officers and requires that elections be held by secret ballot or by convention not less often than once every five years.

Title V imposes fiduciary standards; that is, it declares that every union officer is a trustee who is open to suit by union members in case of unethical conduct. It establishes bonding requirements for union officers and prohibits loans in excess of $2,000 by unions to their officers or employees. It also prohibits communists and individuals convicted of a crime within the last five years from holding union office. Title VI illegalizes picketing for the personal enrichment of union officers.

Title VII, the most controversial portion of the act, proscribes secondary boycotts and hot cargo clauses. It proscribes organizational picketing when the employer has previously recognized another union, when the union has not petitioned the National Labor Relations Board for an election within thirty days, or when there has been a union election within the preceding year. More favorable to union interests, it permits strikers who have walked off the job for economic reasons to vote in union elections.

Impact of Event

The Landrum-Griffin Act was a harbinger of a long decline in the labor movement's political and organizational power. Its economic provisions, which received much of the lobbyists' and politicians' (but not the public's) attention in 1959, may have been more important than its provisions on labor racketeering. There were tangible results from the act's anticrime rules. Fifty-four unions revised their constitutions to comply with the act, and by 1970 the Department of Labor's Office of Labor-Management and Welfare-Pension Reports was processing thousands of complaints under the Landrum-Griffin Act each year. More than 90 percent were found to be lacking in merit or were settled voluntarily. Indictments for embezzlement and other offenses under the act proceeded at a rate of at least seventy per year from the 1960's through the 1980's. Furthermore, the Department of Labor supervised a number of court-ordered elections and oversaw national and international elections in which officers of the Steelworkers, Electrical Workers, and Teamsters were removed or defeated by opposition candidates. In addition, the number of trusteeships of locals fell by 60 percent from five hundred to two hundred per year, subsequent to the act's passage.

For most working people, the act's availability of law suits against union officers in court is impractical to use for financial reasons. The costs of bringing suit are out of most workers' reach. Furthermore, some observers have noted that the Department of Labor has been reluctant to bring suits on behalf of individuals who have been denied the right to a fair election and that this reluctance undermines the act. Ronald G. Goldstock, director of a task force on organized crime in New York State, argued that the Department of Labor should be relieved of responsibility for enforcing Landrum-Griffin and that attorneys' fees should be more readily available to plaintiffs. Although it is difficult to measure the act's effects on rates of crime and racketeering, Goldstock provided extensive documentation of continued criminal influences in unions thirty years after the Landrum-Griffin Act was passed. Criminal laws with respect to embezzlement, racketeering, and violence in unions existed prior to Landrum-Griffin and continue to exist under state criminal codes.

Few observers believe that union democracy has increased dramatically as a result of the act. There is little evidence to suggest that membership participation in internal affairs has appreciably increased. Despite its conservative impetus, some labor analysts see it as reaffirming federal policies that fundamentally support collective bargaining and labor unions.

The law's impact on existing unions may not have been as great as its impact on the establishment of new unions. For example, the law had scant effect on the Teamsters. The union merely followed the act's election procedures and rewrote its hot cargo clause in 1961 to emphasize the individual worker's right to refuse to handle hot cargo. The 1961 Teamster's contract disingenuously included a section emphasizing the need for employers to deliver goods subject to secondary boycotts and waiving the union's jurisdiction in case of a secondary boycott, although the courts rejected this ruse. It was not until the late 1980's that the federal government took aggressive action against the Teamsters.

The act's symbolic and practical effects on the union movement's political power and ability to organize may have been most significant. When Landrum-Griffin was passed, the American labor movement was at its historical peak of political influence and power. Even with a Democratic Senate and House, however, it could not command the votes necessary to pass the Kennedy-Ervin or Shelley bills, the crime bills it supported. Furthermore, the act's prohibitions on aggressive organizational picketing, secondary boycotts, and hot cargo clauses may have contributed to the subsequent decline in union membership from nearly 32 percent of the nonagricultural labor force in 1959 to about 16 percent in 1990.

Bibliography

Chamberlain, Neil W., and James W. Kuhn. *Collective Bargaining.* 3d ed. New York: McGraw-Hill, 1986. An excellent introduction to the concepts and ideas behind collective bargaining. The authors argue that in the historical context of the development of labor law, both the Taft-Hartley Act and the Landrum-Griffin Act can be viewed to have affirmed that labor unions are essential.

Goldstock, Ronald G. *Corruption and Racketeering in the New York City Construction Industry: Final Report to Governor Mario M. Cuomo.* New York: New York University Press, 1990. A 233-page report of interest to students of organized crime and corrupt labor practices. Published more than thirty years after Landrum-Griffin was passed, it provides detail on continuing pervasive corruption in New York City's construction unions. Argues that Landrum-Griffin has failed and recommends specific reforms.

Gould, William B. *A Primer on American Labor Law.* Cambridge, Mass.: MIT Press, 1986. A 260-page book of interest to lay readers. Offers an overview of U.S. labor law and describes the Landrum-Griffin Act in its legal context.

Hutchinson, John. *The Imperfect Union: A History of Corruption in American Trade Unions.* New York: Dutton, 1970. Analyzes the history of labor racketeering and corruption in several industries. Argues that the Landrum-Griffin Act has been moderately successful.

Jacoby, Daniel. *Laboring for Freedom: A New Look at the History of Labor in America.* Armonk, N.Y.: M. E. Sharpe, 1998.

James, R. C., and E. D. James. *Hoffa and the Teamsters.* Princeton, N.J.: D. Van Nostrand, 1965. A 430-page classic describes two university professors' ninety-day field study of Hoffa. Of interest to general readers. Includes discussions of practices that led to the Landrum-Griffin Act and an analysis of the Teamsters Union's reaction.

Katz, H. C., and T. A. Kochan. *An Introduction to Collective Bargaining and Industrial Relations.* New York: McGraw-Hill, 1992. Well-written introduction to the general subject of industrial relations by two leading scholars in the field.

McAdams, Alan K. *Power and Politics in Labor Legislation.* New York: Columbia University Press, 1964. This 346-page book analyzes the legislative background and history of the Labor-Management Reporting and Disclosure Act of 1959. Valuable for its information about the political context in which Landrum-Griffin was passed and its step-by-step analysis of the law's development in Congress.

National Labor Relations Board. *Legislative History of the Labor-Management Reporting and Disclosure Act of 1959, Volumes I and II.* Washington, D.C.: U.S. Government Printing Office, 1959. A 1,926-page reference work containing documents concerning the Landrum-Griffin Act. Volume 1 includes early drafts, including drafts of related bills and conference committee reports. Volume 2 includes the congressional debate and a comparison of the Taft-Hartley Act of 1947 with amendments made by the Landrum-Griffin Act.

Summer, Clyde W., et al. *Union Democracy and Landrum-Griffin.* New York: Association for Union Democracy, 1986. Includes a good description of the Landrum-Griffin Act.

Mitchell Langbert

Cross-References

The Wagner Act Promotes Union Organization (1935); The Taft-Hartley Act Passes over Truman's Veto (1947); Hoffa Negotiates a National Trucking Agreement (1964); Nader's *Unsafe at Any Speed* Launches a Consumer Movement (1965).

FIRMS BEGIN REPLACING SKILLED LABORERS WITH AUTOMATIC TOOLS

CATEGORIES OF EVENT: Manufacturing and labor
TIME: The 1960's
LOCALE: The United States and other industrialized countries

By adding programmable control devices to machines used in manufacturing, industry was able to retain much of the flexibility provided by skilled workers while automating production

Principal personages:
JOHN PARSONS (1908-1969), the designer of the Cardamatic milling system and father of numerical control
GORDON BROWN (1907-   ), the director of the MIT servomechanisms laboratory
WILLIAM PEASE, the director of the MIT numerical control project

Summary of Event
Numerical control (N/C) is a form of general-purpose machinery control that uses digital computers and programs in the manufacture of items formerly made using general-purpose equipment under the control of skilled operators. The development of this technology in the 1950's provided manufacturing management in the 1960's with the opportunity to increase control over manufacturing operations by replacing a class of skilled laborers with machines. Previously, these skilled workers had been irreplaceable.

Significant social and technical factors were behind the development of N/C technology. Among these factors were a hazardous work environment in manufacturing. Between 1940 and 1945, according to one estimate, eighty-eight thousand workers were killed and more than eleven million were injured as a result of industrial accidents, eleven times the total U.S. casualties in combat during World War II. Second, labor unrest and disruption of work by strikes motivated management to find technology to replace workers. The end of World War II marked the beginning of the greatest industrial crisis in American history, industrial relations expert Neil W. Chamberlain has written. The years 1945 and 1946 saw the biggest strike wave in the history of a capitalist country. Between 1945 and 1955, there were more than forty-three thousand strikes, idling some twenty-seven million workers. A third factor in the development of N/C technology was a shortage of skilled machinists. As early as 1947, the Bureau of Labor Statistics had warned that the pool of skilled machinists was drying up. A 1952 study verified this assertion and named retirement, reduced immigration from Europe, and a shortage of apprenticeships as the causes. Fourth, the military was developing aircraft and missiles that required extremely tight tolerances and advanced machining skills to produce. Finally, management had a desire for greater control of manufacturing processes in order to achieve technical and economic objectives.

In the environment outlined above, it is not surprising that labor replacement technologies were of great interest to industrialists. Wide use of automation technology in industry began with "continuous flow" processes, in which elements of a product are combined continuously. By the 1950's, the first industrial operations to be controlled by analog computers appeared in the electrical power and petroleum refinery industries. At Texaco's Port Arthur refinery, production went under full digital computer control in 1959. A year later, Monsanto went to digital computer control at its Louisiana ammonia plant, as did B. F. Goodrich at its vinyl plastic facility in Calvert, Kentucky. Soon, steel rolling mills, blast furnaces, and various chemical processing plants around the United States went under full computer control. Companies such as International Business Machines and Honeywell began to design computer systems specifically for manufacturing operations in the 1950's. By 1964, there were approximately one hundred systems operational, or on order, in the petroleum refining industry alone. This technology, however, was special-purpose in nature and only effective in replacing unskilled workers performing extremely repetitive tasks.

The greater challenge in replacing labor with machines was the development of a means of nonhuman control of general-purpose equipment that currently required skilled operators. The challenge of automating machine tools was how to render a general-purpose machine tool (such as a lathe or drill press) self-acting, or acting automatically according to prespecified instructions without human intervention. Adding to the challenge was the desire to retain versatility, which was required for short-run production and small batch jobs. Essentially, this was a problem of programmable automation, of temporarily transforming a universal machine into a special-purpose machine through the use of variable programs. With programmable automation, a change in the product being manufactured required only a switch in programs rather than reliance upon machinists to retool or adjust the configuration of the machine itself. Programmable automation would not simply render automatic operation flexible; it would also give management more direct control over the machinery of production and undermine the power of machinists on the shop floor.

A variety of approaches to programmable automation were considered. These included record-playback or motional control (with a machine recording the movements of a human worker and then playing them back), tracer control, plugboard controls, and numerical control (N/C). The N/C technique ultimately became the industry standard by meeting the challenge of automating general-purpose machine tools and providing management with greater control of production. With both record-playback control and N/C, the motional information required to manufacture a part was stored on a permanent medium, such as paper tape or magnetic tape. In this way, the record-playback system served to enhance or multiply a machinist's value; this may have contributed to management's lack of complete satisfaction with this approach. With N/C, however, the need for machinists' skills was reduced. The motions of the machine tool required to produce a particular part were described in detail mathematically, corresponding to the blueprint specifications for the part, and were recorded as numerical information. The entire process of producing a part, including the skill of the machinist, was reduced to formal, abstract description. That description was then translated (usually by a computer) into commands to activate machine controls. Numerical control was an abstract synthesizer of skill, circumventing the need for the machinist; an N/C tool acted as an "automatic machinist."

The widely recognized father of numerical control is John Parsons. Parsons was a machinist who was in search of a means of manufacturing a particular type of wing for the Air Force. His initial designs used extensive hand computations and made use of drilling equipment that was automated, by use of commands recorded on tape, to make specified parts by drilling holes tangent to the surface of the part to be manufactured. The remaining excess material was then to be sanded down in order to bring the part into specification.

In June, 1949, Parsons was awarded a contract by the Air Force to develop an "automatic contour cutting machine" that would be controlled by punched cards or tape and would be capable of making contour cuts, or cutting rounded shapes such as those found in an aircraft wing. In the pursuit of this business, Parsons subcontracted with the servomechanisms laboratory at the Massachusetts Institute of Technology (MIT) for a portion of the development. Ultimately, the MIT lab adopted and successfully developed a continuous path contour cutting approach beyond the scope of Parsons' expertise and funding. The lab took over the development of N/C technology with funding from the Air Force that endured until 1959.

Impact of Event

The development of N/C technology has been referred to as the greatest innovation in manufacturing since the assembly line. In the late 1950's and early 1960's, expectations for numerical control were high. Industry experts predicted sales growth of 50 percent per year for N/C systems. Others referred to the inevitability of automation. Willard F. Rockwell, chairman of North American Rockwell Corporation, linked numerical control with nuclear power and space flight as the three great developments of the contemporary generation.

The early expectations were too high. As late as 1973, *American Machinist* reported that N/C machines represented less than 1 percent of all machine tools in use and perhaps several percent of overall industry capacity. This was despite the doubling of the number of N/C machines in the previous five years and a tenfold increase in the previous ten years. The concentration of these systems was in the machine tool industry itself as well as in the aircraft and aircraft engine industries. Diffusion of the technology was slower than commonly anticipated.

Part of the difficulty with the diffusion of N/C technology was its economic justification. Previous methods for justifying equipment purchases and previous methods for determining the cost of parts did not fit the new technology well. Programming the new equipment was another problem: Machinists were not programmers, and programmers were limited in number and lacked understanding of machining practices. Finally, the equipment developed initially was quite sophisticated, with control of five axes of movement, and offered more than many manufacturers required or were willing to pay for. As a consequence, many early adoptions of the technology were motivated by blind faith in the technology, fear of getting left behind, or faith in the advantages of automated machinery over labor rather than strict cost-benefit evaluations.

N/C technology did provide industry with "islands of automation," and there have been notable successes in its use. Since the development of N/C technology, advances in other areas of automation have taken place. The N/C approach has been improved by incremental advances, beginning with computerized numerical control (CNC). CNC eliminates the need for tape as a means of programming and control. A programmable control unit with its own memory is housed on the machine tool itself. Direct numerical control (DNC) was the next incremental advance. This allowed a host computer to control one or more N/C machines directly. Flexible manufacturing systems (FMS) have been developed, utilizing group technology to identify a set of items that can be made with some combination of N/C, CNC, and DNC machines within a completely automated manufacturing cell. Finally, computer integrated manufacturing links a variety of computerized automation technologies (including FMS, DNC, CNC, N/C, computer-aided design, computer-aided manufacturing, automated material handling systems, and manufacturing planning and control systems) in a common centralized manufacturing computing system with shared data access. As the "islands of automation" become integrated to greater degrees, and as organizational structures and operational systems change to reflect the changes in technology, manufacturers are beginning to experience some synergy in the automation technologies they employ. A devotion to technological solutions to manufacturing problems is part of American industrial society, and N/C technology remains an integral part of the American concept of modern manufacturing technology.

It should be noted that a "people" revolution also took place in American industry. The "total quality" revolution of the 1980's brought with it a dedication to employees and to employee involvement as the primary means of process improvement. This philosophy and approach is at odds with the wholesale replacement of labor by machines and technology. By the early 1990's, the pendulum had swung to the side of process improvement via employee involvement. It is likely that both the technological revolution and the people revolution will come to be recognized as vital elements in the development of modern manufacturing processes.

Bibliography

Chase, Richard B., and Nicholas J. Aquilano. *Production and Operations Management: A Life Cycle Approach*. 6th ed. Homewood, Ill.: Irwin, 1992. This text is widely used in courses surveying the function of operations management. Chapter 3, "Product Design and Process Selection—Manufacturing," is the most directly applicable to this topic. The authors focus almost exclusively on the technologies, rather than including labor reduction considerations. Productivity and competitiveness issues are discussed more directly elsewhere in the text.

Gaither, Norman. *Production and Operations Management*. 5th ed. Fort Worth, Tex.: Dryden Press-Harcourt Brace Jovanovich, 1992. Chapter 5 of this basic text deals with production technology. This chapter discusses types of automation, automated production systems, factories of the future, and decision-making issues related to automation in manufacturing and services.

Greene, James H., ed. *Production and Inventory Control Handbook.* 2d ed. New York: McGraw-Hill, 1987. This exhaustive reference work is the authoritative publication of the American Production and Inventory Control Society. Chapter 20, "Computers in Manufacturing," is particularly relevant to modern automation technologies. Robotics, computer-aided design, computer-aided manufacturing, group technology, flexible manufacturing systems, cellular manufacturing, and information systems are discussed.

Jacoby, Daniel. *Laboring for Freedom: A New Look at the History of Labor in America.* Armonk, N.Y.: M. E. Sharpe, 1998.

Krajewski, Lee J., and Larry P. Ritzman. *Operations Management: Strategy and Analysis.* 3d ed. Reading, Mass: Addison-Wesley, 1992. Chapter 6 discusses technology management as applied to both the service and manufacturing sectors. Part of the emphasis in this chapter is linking technologies with strategic choices. The chapter covers such topics as electronic data interchange, office automation, and managing technological change.

Noble, David F. *Forces of Production: A Social History of Automation.* New York: Oxford University Press, 1986. An extremely thorough treatment of the development of automation from the perspective of technological history. The author notes the social factors that influenced the choices made in determining the form that automation technologies would take. An underlying theme in the book is the impact of technology on the labor/management conflict.

Schonberger, Richard J., and Edward M. Knod, Jr. *Operations Management: Improving Customer Service.* 4th ed. Homewood, Ill.: Irwin, 1991. Chapter 3, "Product, Service, and Process Planning," focuses on the selection of process technologies. The chapter describes alternatives for automation and emphasizes the way in which human potential is influenced by automation.

Mark D. Hanna

Cross-References

Ford Implements Assembly Line Production (1913); American Firms Adopt Japanese Manufacturing Techniques (1980's); CAD/CAM Revolutionizes Engineering and Manufacturing (1980's); Electronic Technology Creates the Possibility of Telecommuting (1980's).

THE U.S. SERVICE ECONOMY EMERGES

CATEGORIES OF EVENT: New products and labor
TIME: The 1960's
LOCALE: The United States

In the aftermath of World War II, the United States economy evolved from one based on manufacturing to one based on services

Principal personages:
RAY KROC (1902-1984), the entrepreneur responsible for the success of McDonald's
STEVEN JOBS (1955-   ), a founder of Apple Computer
STEPHEN WOZNIAK (1950-   ), a founder of Apple Computer
WALT DISNEY (1901-1966), the founder of Walt Disney studios, the products of which provided the basis for theme parks
KEMMONS WILSON (1913-   ), the founder of the Holiday Inn motel chain

Summary of Event

American manufacturing, emergent after the victory of Republican policies in the Civil War and symbolized by the smokestack, came to dominate the world's economy, especially in the period after World War I. Big industry benefited from ample supplies of fuel and iron as well as from the protection of oceans and tariffs that stymied competition. Industry focused on the conquest of time and space, meaning railroads and later automobiles. After World War II, the development of a mass market based on consumer culture meant more factories, long production runs, well-paid labor, a higher standard of living, and abundant consumer goods.

By 1990, however, the census reported that more than 73 percent of Americans worked in the service sector. More than 70 percent of gross national product (GNP) came from services and from the production of intangibles such as entertainment, education, health care, hospitality, and financial services. The symbols of progress were no longer smokestacks but computers, films, hospitals, and universities. Service industry factories look more like universities than like the industrial complexes of the early twentieth century that foreigners came to admire and copy.

How and why has this transformation occurred? No single dramatic event or product marked the emergence of services. The advent of the service economy can be tied neither to introduction of the mainframe computer after World War II nor to the rise of the personal computer in the early 1980's, though both facilitated the standardization and hence expansion of services. Nor is it linked directly to the television set, which took mass culture from the theater to the home, or to the first McDonald's restaurant. Most of the services provided in the service economy had been provided for decades or longer. Professionals such as doctors, lawyers, and accountants had existed for centuries, as had colleges, restaurants, and hotels. It is useful to see the contemporary dominance of services as a culmination of a series of patterns that converged after World War II.

Part of the shift to a service economy in the United States came from the movement of manufacturing abroad, particularly to Latin America and the Far East, where labor cost far less than in the United States. Thus, for example, Japan came to dominate electrical appliances in the 1950's and 1960's. Later, as Japanese labor costs rose, the country moved to high tech consumer electronic goods and captured about one-fourth of the American automobile market. Japan built its initial cost advantage into a reputation for solid performance in technology and quality. It is a good example of another country undergoing adaptation. Asia became a primary source of clothing for the mass market by employing low-wage workers. Important in nurturing America's service economy have been labor-saving technological changes that have not only increased manufacturing output but also created new jobs in the service sector for technicians and repair people.

The postindustrial impetus toward services has come in part from the changing demographics of the United States, particularly from the largest population explosion in the history of the United States, the baby boom. Born between 1945 and 1964, the baby boom group became the best-educated and most affluent population segment ever. Affluence came both from education and training and from the first major movement of women into business. The advent of the two-career family was impetus for the conversion to a service economy. As far as services involve hiring others to do things that people used to do for themselves, the two-career family has, by dint of increased disposable income and lack of disposable time, generated a flourishing service economy performing tasks from day-care to cooking.

The proliferation of services has also stemmed in part from government activities, especially the deregulation of the 1980's, which brought competition into services. In financial services, for example, the Depository Institutions Deregulation and Monetary Control Act of 1980 began erasing the distinctions between commercial banks, savings and loan associations, and credit unions. These organizations became more visible, more competitive, and consequently market driven. They opened more branches in attempts to reach more customers, and thus needed more employees. Airline expansion stemmed from similar causes. Airlines used to fly when and where they were allowed by the Civil Aeronautics Board; now they fly wherever they can make money. Some competed through lower prices, but many offered improved service, which meant more workers. Expansions of schedules added jobs. Court decisions and Federal Trade Commission regulations also helped bring services to prominence. For example, lawyers never advertised before 1978. Restrained by traditions reinforced by law, legal professionals "advertised" most commonly by running for office. The decision by the Supreme Court in *Bates v. State Bar of Arizona* (1979) permitted lawyers to advertise. The legal profession expanded tremendously, but cause may be difficult to untangle from effect. Law schools had ever-larger classes, so that nearly half of all attorneys practicing in 1990 had graduated after 1980. It is possible that the market demanded these attorneys but also possible that the new attorneys needed to advertise to create a market.

Perhaps the greatest changes in the nature of services have been their standardization and automation. Service-oriented businesses could grow from local firms serving local (sometimes protected) markets to global companies serving the world once they standardized. Traditionally, services are considered to have four properties that distinguish them from goods: they are intangible, heterogeneous (that is, they vary from producer to producer, and even a single producer may not be consistent), produced and consumed simultaneously (the creation of the haircut is when the hair is cut), and perishable. Given these traditional distinctions between services and goods, the lack of proprietary technology (all airlines can clothe employees in designer uniforms and serve drinks in flight), and short channels of distribution in services, the emergence of national and American firms serving worldwide customers can be viewed as nothing short of a major, if not revolutionary, industrial shift.

In a sense, services grew because of the use of information technology to conquer time and space. Probably no single breakthrough has aided establishment of a national network of services more than has the computer, for it enabled what were once personal services to be conducted at a distance. Computer linkages, for example, made possible multisite and multinational operations in transportation and leisure that were previously possible only locally and on a small scale. Even the National Park Service has campground reservations listed through Ticketron, so people around the country can easily guarantee reservations. Similarly, the automatic teller machine has enabled financial service institutions to break down geographical and time barriers, making it convenient to perform more banking transactions. Although a teller is not directly involved, each transaction does create work.

One major mechanism for the expansion of services has been the franchise, which has erased geographical barriers. From hotels to restaurants, from hairdressers to muffler shops, the "McDonaldization" of America—the national provision of standardized services—is well under way. Franchises have erased geographical barriers, replicating successful local businesses on a national scale. They have simultaneously depersonalized many industries that still require personal contact between service provider and customer. McDonald's has become the largest-volume chain in most of the countries it serves, including Japan, by turning to a production-line approach to deliver consistent quality everywhere. Franchising also provided a relatively inexpensive and less risky means for entrepreneurs to get started, prompting more start-ups. Buyers know what they are getting when they purchase a franchise and do not have to invent a new product.

Impact of Event

A location that may exemplify the shift from agriculture to industry, then to services, is Bloomington-Normal, Illinois. The twin cities typify the origins of many American urban areas as commercial and political centers rising out of farmlands. The arrival of the railroads in the 1860's fostered the development of local businesses that served a national market, as well as allowing distribution of goods from across the country in the local market. One of the biggest businesses was the railroad itself. This opening of markets made a national name in the 1880's for Dr. Wakefield, a producer of pharmaceutical nostrums (one of the earliest branded and nationally distributed consumer goods), and in the 1920's for the Williams Oil-o-Matic, a low-pressure oil furnace that boasted of making Bloomington the cleanest city in the United States.

Following World War II, however, railroad traffic declined to the point at which the railroads closed the repair yards that were the region's largest single employer. Although townspeople worried that the changing economic base presaged economic decline, what followed instead was the burgeoning of services. Two of the largest employers were State Farm Insurance, begun to serve farmers in need of automobile coverage in 1922 and eventually America's largest property and casualty insurance company, and Illinois State Normal University, a small state college built in 1857 to train teachers. It grew from an enrollment of three thousand in 1959 to nearly twenty thousand a decade later, as baby boomers sought an education. Although these two businesses predate the service revolution, their growth coincided with it. Furthermore, by 1963, more than 40 percent of the major companies in the area were less than twenty years old, indicating that new companies were forming in the new environment. In short, what happened to Bloomington-Normal was a major shift from agriculture to manufacturing, then from industry to services. This occurred elsewhere in America, and on the same scale. Other countries have followed.

In 1900, less than 20 percent of the American workforce was employed in white-collar jobs, while more than 30 percent derived primary income from farming. By 1960, nearly half of the workforce was white collar, while fewer than 6 million of the 74 million workers made their living from farming. By 1989, only 3 million of the 117 million workers derived their income from farming; 30 million held managerial and professional positions; 51 million claimed income from technical support and traditional service jobs in health care, food service, and household maintenance; and only 18 million were classified as manufacturing personnel.

The dominance of service in the American economy has made a major difference in the way Americans work and live. For example, most central cities have declined in population, while suburban areas have grown as workers no longer need to be near manufacturing centers. Service businesses tend to be "flatter," with fewer levels of management than manufacturing organizations. This is a response to the simultaneous production and consumption of the service and allows service firms to be more responsive. In the early 1990's, manufacturing became more like service industries by providing more customized products on shorter deadlines. Customers have learned to expect high levels of service, whether from service firms or from manufacturers.

Bibliography

Bateson, John E. G. *Managing Services Marketing: Text and Readings.* 2d ed. Fort Worth, Tex.: Dryden Press, 1991. Most of the textbooks on managing or marketing services are compilations of readings. This contains an excellent selection of articles that illustrate the problems of managing service industries. Some readings are geared toward advanced M.B.A. students and will stretch the average undergraduate.

Berry, Leonard L., and A. Parasuraman. *Marketing Services: Competing*

Through Quality. New York: Free Press, 1991. Berry and Parasuraman are leaders in exploring the nature of services and particularly in defining quality services. This book distills many of their previous articles and advances an integrative framework in chapter 1 that ties together much of the previous literature.

Hartley, Robert F. *Marketing Successes, Historical to Present Day: What We Can Learn.* 2d ed. New York: John Wiley & Sons, 1990. No student of marketing history should miss Hartley's volumes on successes and failures. This volume describes Penney's, the supermarket (King Kullen as pioneer), Korvette, McDonald's, Kmart, Hyatt Legal Services, and Apple Computer, among others. Although there is little depth, the articles are well written, and the stories are quite engaging.

Peters, Thomas J., and Robert H. Waterman, Jr. *In Search of Excellence: Lessons from America's Best-Run Companies.* New York: Harper and Row, 1982. This is the best-selling business book of all time. Although somewhat dated, it provides an interesting framework for evaluating successful companies. Readable and understandable, it highlights some service companies such as McDonald's and Disney.

Ritzer, George. *The McDonaldization of Society: An Investigation into the Changing Character of Contemporary Social Life.* Newbury Park, Calif.: Pine Forge Press, 1993. Ritzer is a sociologist who views the "McDonaldization" of society with a great deal of skepticism, as enshrining homogeneity and mediocrity at the expense of variety, individualism, and excitement.

Worthy, James C. *Shaping an American Institution: Robert F. Wood and Sears, Roebuck.* Urbana: University of Illinois Press, 1984. Worthy, a professor of management, served from 1938 to 1961 with Sears, Roebuck. He explains how and why Sears succeeded.

Zemke, Ron, with Dick Schaaf. *The Service Edge: 101 Companies That Profit from Customer Care.* New York: New American Library, 1989. Although this book is largely anecdotal, it is readable and insightful. The examples range from Chicken Soup, a day-care center in Minneapolis, to such well-known giants as Wal-Mart and American Airlines. Half the book deals with principles, the other half with companies, arranged by industry.

Frederick B. Hoyt

Cross-References

Carter Signs the Airline Deregulation Act (1978); American Firms Adopt Japanese Manufacturing Techniques (1980's); Electronic Technology Creates the Possibility of Telecommuting (1980's); Congress Deregulates Banks and Savings and Loans (1980-1982); IBM Introduces Its Personal Computer (1981); A Home Shopping Service Is Offered on Cable Television (1985).

THE AGENCY FOR INTERNATIONAL DEVELOPMENT IS ESTABLISHED

CATEGORIES OF EVENT: International business and commerce; government and business
TIME: November 3, 1961
LOCALE: Washington, D.C.

The Agency for International Development coordinated U.S. foreign assistance programs and expanded private sector investments in developing countries

Principal personages:
JOHN F. KENNEDY (1917-1963), the president of the United States, 1961-1963
EVERETT M. DIRKSEN (1896-1969), a Republican senator from Illinois
ALLEN J. ELLENDER (1890-1972), a Democratic senator from Louisiana
HARRY F. BYRD (1887-1966), a Democratic senator from Virginia
BOURKE B. HICKENLOOPER (1896-1971), a Republican senator from Iowa

Summary of Event

The Agency for International Development (AID) provided the framework for central coordination of U.S. foreign assistance programs. As a quasi-autonomous agency within the Department of State, AID symbolized the institutional consolidation of foreign assistance as a tool in U.S. foreign policy. AID provided the bureaucratic pivot for the apportionment and delivery of benefits under the Foreign Assistance Act of 1961 and for the containment of communism abroad.

Congress passed the Foreign Assistance Act (Public Law 87-195) to promote the foreign policy, security, and general welfare of the United States, and to assist the less-developed areas of the world in achieving self-reliance and economic development. On the basis of the act and the recommendations of the presidential task force on foreign economic assistance, AID came into existence by Executive Order 10973 of November 3, 1961.

The creation of AID a was milestone in American foreign assistance, which began as a stopgap measure and gradually acquired institutional permanence as a tool of economic diplomacy. The earliest offer of U.S. foreign assistance was in 1778, under Article I of the Treaty of Alliance, by which the United States agreed to render assistance to France in a war with England. A recognizable framework of global assistance did not emerge until after World War II. The Truman Doctrine conditioned U.S. bilateral and multilateral assistance in the postwar era.

Prior to the establishment of AID, foreign assistance passed through multiple agencies established on the basis of postwar exigencies. These agencies included the Economic Cooperation Administration (1948), the Technical Cooperation Administration (1950), the Mutual Security Agency (1951), and the Foreign Operations Adminstration (1953). In 1955, the International Cooperation Administration (ICA) was established by Executive Order 10610 as a quasi-independent agency in the Department of State. In 1957, the Mutual Security Act authorized the Development Loan Fund (DLF), which became a corporation in 1958.

The creation of AID in 1961 underscored the transitory nature of its predecessors and brought stability to the programming and implementation of assistance. Congress abolished the ICA. Its functions, together with the DLF program, were inherited by AID. In 1962, AID assumed responsibility, in cooperation with the Department of Agriculture, for the Food for Peace program under the Agricultural Trade Development and Assistance Act (Public Law 480) of 1954. AID also consulted with other aid-providing agencies, including multilateral agencies, the Peace Corps, the Department of Defense, and the Export-Import Bank. AID's development loan committee included the chairman of the Export-Import Bank so that lending policies would be coordinated.

The act of 1961, much like the Act for International Development of 1950, responded to what President John F. Kennedy saw as a special moment in history by providing assistance to developing nations in their quest for self-reliance, economic growth, and political stability. Unlike previous instruments, however, the act deemphasized military assistance in favor of country-specific needs, long-range planning, self-help, and multilateral involvement in the developing countries.

The administrative structure of AID, based on recommendations of the presidential task force, departed significantly from previous arrangements. Four regional bureaus, headed by assistant administrators, were created for Latin America, Europe and Africa, the Near East and South Asia, and the Far East. The regional administrators worked in cooperation with mission directors and ambassadors in the beneficiary countries. A range of specialized offices and advisory groups provided depth and definition to programs. The basic resources for assistance included development loans, grants and technical cooperation, supportive assistance, contingency funds, food, surplus government stockpiles of materials, and private-sector resources. AID's priority shifted to long-term development assistance, including support for the Alliance for Progress, formed in 1961 to improve the quality of life in Latin America through loans, grants, and technical cooperation.

The premise for assistance remained fairly consistent over the years. U.S. policy requires beneficiaries of development assistance to show progress toward self-reliance or the capacity to reach that point. Program loans, which may cover payments for imports, appropriately strengthen private-sector efforts and governmental initiatives. Project loans cover specific capital projects from design to completion. Development assistance has been based on a recipient country's ability to mobilize available resources, both domestic and external.

Development grants and technical cooperation provide specialist and other technical support and do not substitute for development loans. Generally, grants and technical cooperation have gone toward the development of education, agricultural extension, health service, sanitation, and general welfare. As with other programs, assistance is based on the strategic interests of the United States, including the impact of aid on the domestic economy. AID will consider whether a country has alternative sources of assistance. Developing nations have received bilateral and multilateral assistance from other sources, including the European Organization for Economic Cooperation and Development (OECD), through its Development Assistance Committee.

Supportive assistance provides loans and grants for internal security, defense, capital expenditure for relief, and projects that contribute to economic growth or political stability. The military aspect ordinarily involves the Department of Defense. AID's Economic Support Fund supports countries and areas unable to meet the specific criteria for development assistance. The support is based on the strategic and foreign policy interests of the United States and often is a preliminary step toward an offer of long-term assistance.

Impact of Event

Foreign assistance programs provided a platform for the expansion of U.S. private direct investment in developing areas. AID encouraged and nurtured private-sector participation in long-term assistance projects and worked to harmonize business goals with the developmental aspirations of the beneficiary countries. AID's policies steered developing economies toward long-term growth, self-reliance, and the traditions of Western capitalism.

Because development assistance involved the monitoring of programs and projects in recipient countries, foreign assistance provided a vehicle for the achievement of foreign policy objectives. The programs supported efforts of policymakers to integrate precapitalist economics into the free enterprise system. The effort, however, was at a cost to private U.S. investors, whose assets in foreign countries became the target of expropriation in the 1960's and 1970's.

In developing areas, the sudden influx of foreign investment and aid elicited nationalistic sentiments and reactions. Between 1961 and 1975, there were 260 reported cases of investment disputes arising from the expropriation of U.S. private investments in Africa, Asia, Latin America, and the Middle East. Third World economic nationalism led to capital disinvestments as well as efforts among the capital exporters to establish a regulatory mechanism for the protection of foreign investments. In 1969, Congress authorized the establishment of the Overseas Private Investment Corporation for the purpose of providing investment guarantees and other services to business proprietors in developing countries.

AID, on its part, provided a package of incentives and investment guarantees to investors, including subsidies for feasibility surveys, dollar loans, local currency (Cooley) loans under Public Law 480, and investment guarantees. A specific-risk guarantee covered such risks as the inconvertibility of foreign currencies, confiscation, expropriation, or loss of investment resulting from war or insurgency. Extended-risk guarantees protected investments from political and unusual investment risks. The incentives contributed to the expansion of private-sector participation in foreign development. The Office of Development Finance and Private Enterprise prepared entrepreneurs for foreign investment. The Development Loan Committee, headed by AID's administrator, formulated lending policies and standards for profitable investment. The office worked with AID's regional bureaus to promote trade and investment.

Because aid was tied to trade, U.S. domestic exports and industrial capacities expanded with foreign assistance. Under the programs, beneficiary countries purchased capital goods and services from U.S. sources except when technical or other factors necessitated otherwise. In the 1980's, however, AID increasingly nudged beneficiary countries toward self-reliance by encouraging and sustaining local productivity and private-sector enterprises. AID supported the privatization of state-owned enterprises in developing countries.

AID afforded American investors the opportunity to expand abroad. More than any other nation, the United States provided developing nations with the capital base for economic growth. In the fiscal year of 1962, the transitional period, Congress appropriated a total of $4.515 billion in assistance, including $600 million for Latin America. In 1961, bilateral assistance to developing areas from France, Germany, the United Kingdom, Japan, Belgium, Italy, Portugal, Canada, and The Netherlands combined amounted to $1.986 billion in loans and grants. By 1985, the value of U.S. bilateral assistance exceeded $12 billion.

The Development Fund for Africa has tackled food deficit and development barriers on the continent. Under Titles II and III of Public Law 480, surplus stockpiles of food were applied, with significant success, to relief and economic assistance in the developing areas. AID's administrator has coordinated international disaster assistance. AID programming has enhanced the status of women abroad. The Office of Women in Development, which implements the mandate of Congress for inclusion of women in the development process, ensured that programs of assistance gave both urban and rural women ways of participating in the economic development process. Housing programs have supported urban development and housing investments in Latin America, Asia, and other developing areas. In the 1970's, rural development projects expanded. The agency developed schemes for commercial home ownership for medium-to low-income families.

In spite of criticism of AID as a pork-barrel agency and dispenser of charity with strings attached, the agency has been a crucial contributor to the economics of international development and the dissemination of U.S. business traditions abroad. Of crucial importance is the fact that aid appropriations give Congress a measurable influence and oversight in the conduct of foreign policy and the direction of U.S. private investments overseas.

Within the U.S. domestic economy, AID's development mission has adopted affirmative action policies in favor of enterprises owned by women and members of other disadvantaged groups. Under the Gray Amendment of 1984, as amended in 1990 and 1991, Congress set aside 10 percent of AID's primary and subsidiary contracts for small or disadvantaged U.S. firms and for qualified educational and voluntary organizations. AID's

Office of Small and Disadvantaged Business Utilization worked with the Small Business Administration and other agencies to optimize the involvement of "minority" firms in direct-contract programs.

Bibliography

Chilcote, Ronald H., and Joel C. Edelstein, eds. *Latin America: The Struggle with Dependency and Beyond.* Cambridge, Mass.: Schenkman, 1974. The analyses are thought provoking and show the extent of problems to be overcome by Latin American states in their search for economic stability.

Cohen, Stephen D. *The Making of United States International Economic Policy.* New York: Praeger, 1977. Provides in-depth analysis of factors and considerations that have shaped U.S. foreign economic policy over the years.

Duignan, Peter, and L. H. Gann. *The United States and Africa: A History.* New York: Cambridge University Press, 1984. See chapter 22 for a summary and insightful discussion of U.S. economic and other assistance to Africa, including aid.

Parrini, Carl P. *Heir to Empire: United States Economic Diplomacy, 1916-1923.* Pittsburgh: University of Pittsburgh Press, 1969. Offers good background reading and excellent perspectives on early application of economic resources to diplomatic goals.

Tendler, Judith. *Inside Foreign Aid.* Baltimore: Johns Hopkins University Press, 1975. Useful analysis. Helpful in understanding the scope and implications of economic and development assistance, as conditioned by politics and national interest.

Thorp, Willard L. *The Reality of Foreign Aid.* New York: Praeger, 1971. Sheds light on the benefits and burden of foreign assistance for the donor and the beneficiary.

Todaro, Michael P. *Economic Development in the Third World.* 4th ed. New York: Longman, 1989. Identifies and discusses the patterns and problems of economic development in developing areas, including global efforts to meet the challenges and prospects of development in the Third World.

Wennergren, E. Boyd, et al. *The United States and World Poverty.* Cabin John, Md.: Seven Locks Press, 1989. Contains useful discussions and quantitative data on global growth patterns, including income distribution, agricultural output, and food supply.

Satch Ejike

Cross-References

The Truman Administration Launches the Marshall Plan (1947); The General Agreement on Tariffs and Trade Is Signed (1947); Eisenhower Begins the Food for Peace Program (1954); Mexico Renegotiates Debt to U.S. Banks (1989); The North American Free Trade Agreement Goes into Effect (1994).

CONGRESS PASSES THE EQUAL PAY ACT

CATEGORY OF EVENT: Labor
TIME: 1963
LOCALE: Washington, D.C.

The Equal Pay Act attempted to bring equity to the setting of wages for women, bringing them to equality with men's wages for identical work

Principal personages:
JOHN F. KENNEDY (1917-1963), the U.S. president who launched the Equal Pay Act
WAYNE MORSE (1900-1974), a 1940's congressional advocate of equal pay for women
CLAUDE PEPPER (1900-1989), a 1940's supporter of equal pay
ELEANOR HOLMES NORTON (1938-   ), the chair of the Equal Employment Opportunity Commission in the 1970's
MILLICENT GARRETT FAWCETT (1847-1929), a feminist and advocate of equal pay
LYNDON B. JOHNSON (1908-1973), the president of the United States, 1963-1969; a strong supporter of equal rights

Summary of Event
Late in the spring of 1963, the Equal Pay Act was signed into law by President John F. Kennedy. The president had lent his support to the bill in 1962. In about 150 words, the act placed a federal ban on the payment of unequal wages to women and men who performed the same work. The proposed wording of the bill called for equal pay for "work of comparable quantity and quality," a concept of "comparable worth" that remained in debate into the 1990's and one that was excised before the act's passage.

The act ended one phase of a long struggle and opened a fresh phase that presidents, Congress, and the federal courts would continue to define for the next thirty years.

Agitation for equal pay for men and women had a venerable history. In opposition to the prevailing wisdom of leading political economists and contrary to the practices of nearly all businesses, a number of British feminists, notably Dame Millicent Garrett Fawcett and Eleanor F. Rathbone, championed versions of "equal pay for equal work" during the late nineteenth and early twentieth centuries. In

Feminist leader Millicent Fawcett. (Library of Congress)

the United States, incorporating the demands of American feminists that dated from the 1840's, the National Labor Union took up the cry in 1867. Most change, however, resulted from the varied impacts of the Great Depression and from the experiences attending American involvement in World War I and World War II. During the wars, millions of women occupied jobs previously dominated by men. It was during war years that policymakers nationally began grappling with the issues presented by equal pay reform and the broader problems of gender discrimination in the workplace.

Michigan and Montana, for example, enacted equal pay laws in 1919, and several industrial states followed suit between 1942 and 1945, with the active backing of substantial elements of organized labor and of management. Skeptical observers concluded that widening acceptance of equal pay principles resulted from an assumption that there would be full male employment. There was no doubt that the federal government actively worked to implement equal pay. This was true particularly of the War Labor Board, which through its General Order #16 in 1945 authorized equal pay for women and men doing work of comparable quality and quantity under the same or similar conditions. In many firms where women replaced men during wartime, equalization of wage rates did occur.

Wartime advances toward equal pay gave way, however, to two subsequent decades of almost no progress, in regard not only to equal pay but also to other forms of gender discrimination in the workplace. By 1962, amid general social unrest centered on eradicating the worst abuses of racial discrimination and expanding a whole range of civil rights, the originally reluctant Kennedy Administration was prepared to move forward.

Politically, the positions of the president and Congress were strengthened by vast increases in the employment of women, who accounted for one-third of the workforce in 1960, and by changes in the lives of American women. More women were divorced, and more were dependent on their own earnings to maintain themselves or their families. There also was a strong national demand for greater social justice. The fact that by the early 1960's twenty-six states and a number of cities had passed equal pay acts reflected these popular sentiments. Legislatively, equal pay laws were no longer novelties. There was little opposition, consequently, when the equal pay bill was introduced to the House of Representatives, and scarcely any debate in the Senate. Labor unions, eager to shield male workers from lower-paid female competition, lent their support to wage equalization as a step toward job security. Employers seemed unaware of or unconcerned with what in many ways appeared to be a piece of noninterventionist legislation that, in any event, would prove difficult to apply to the distinctive conditions prevailing among millions of employers.

Certain characteristics distinguishing female employment were incontrovertible. Scores of statistical studies plotted across wide as well as discrete segments of the economy indicated that women's earnings, on average, typically were 60 percent of men's. The disparity was overwhelmingly clear for jobs in which women performed the same tasks and bore essentially the same responsibilities as did men. In addition, studies of the workforce confirmed that women were heavily segregated in specific and relatively low paying positions such as those in nursing, teaching, service, and secretarial fields. These facts provided the salient rationale for passage of the Equal Pay Act. What the act sought to achieve was wages for women equal to wages earned by men doing the same or similar work. A source of subsequent, vigorous, and persistent complaint for the future was that the act had nothing to declare about equal wages for women performing different work requiring equivalent skill and training, that is, engaged in work of "comparable worth."

Impact of Event

Pressed to passage by the administration of President Lyndon B. Johnson, the 1964 Civil Rights Act furnished the judicial testing ground for the legality of the Equal Pay Act and various forms of discrimination in employment practices and procedures as well as in the workplace itself. Federal authority to correct employment discrimination, including discrimination in regard to wages, derived chiefly from expansive judicial interpretations of the "commerce clause" of the U.S. Constitution (article I, section 8, clause 3). The wording of Title VII of the Civil Rights Act represented a comprehensive step by federal authorities toward establishing equal employment opportunity. It prohibited employment discrimination on the basis of race, color, religion, and national origins, and for the first time in any civil rights act it named sex as a basis on which employers could not discriminate.

As viewed by women's rights advocates and many other civil libertarians, this represented a remarkable accomplishment. Ruth Bader Ginsburg, a distinguished attorney who joined the U.S. Supreme Court in 1993, noted that in the past the Supreme Court had uniformly refused to alter sexually discriminatory practices. Thus women legally had been prevented from serving on juries and barred from many occupations, from law to bartending. Furthermore, despite the considerable gains made for civil liberties during the 1950's and 1960's, almost nothing had been achieved at the national level to equalize women's employment opportunities. Indeed, from the 1860's until 1971, gender discrimination was implicitly sanctioned by the Constitution.

After 1969, with the ascent of Warren Burger to the Chief Justiceship of the United States, sex barriers to equal employment opportunity began crumbling before the impact of fresh Court decisions. The campaign for equal pay for women that had last manifested vigor during the 1940's showed signs of revival, thanks to initiatives by congressmen such as Wayne Morse of Oregon and Claude Pepper of Florida. Legislators were under the lash of the National Committee on Equal Pay, the National Organization for Women, trade unions, and proponents of the Equal Rights Amendment. The opinions of these groups not only created new legislative mandates but also likely influenced the direction taken by the Burger Court. In any event, the Burger Court recognized that, like race, sex had been a source of pervasive and often subtle discrimination.

Proof that this was the Court's general perception came in the first of its gender discrimination cases based on Title VII of the 1964 Civil Rights Act. *Phillips v. Martin Marietta Corporation* was decided unanimously on January 25, 1971. Ida Phillips began her suit in a federal district court in Florida, claiming that the Martin Marietta Corporation had denied her employment because of her sex. Specifically, Martin Marietta had refused her job application on the grounds that it was not accepting any applications from women with preschool-age children. When Phillips applied to Martin

Marietta, the company routinely employed men with preschool-age children. In addition, of the applicants who filed for the position sought by Phillips, more than 75 percent were women, and 80 percent of those hired for the job of assembly trainee had been women. No argument was made that Martin Marietta had shown a bias against women as such. Accordingly, the district court decided in favor of Martin Marietta. The case was then called before the Supreme Court on a writ of certiorari, an order by a higher court to review the finding of a lower court.

In the *Phillips* case, the Burger Court ruled that an employer willing to hire fathers of preschool-age children, but not mothers, was guilty of sex discrimination under section 703(a) of the 1964 Civil Rights Act. A Court majority thought that only if the existence of conflicting familial obligations was more relevant to job performance for a woman than for a man could it decide otherwise. That would have called for evidence showing that "a bona fide occupational qualification reasonably necessary" to the normal operation of a business was involved. Such evidence was not before the Court. As a result of the Court's interpretation of the antidiscrimination provisions of Title VII in the *Phillips* case, the relatively weak employment discrimination provisions of the Equal Pay Act appeared to have been significantly strengthened.

The intent of Congress in passing the Equal Pay Act, as summarized by members of the House of Representatives' Special Subcommittee on Labor, was that men and women doing the same job under the same working conditions would receive the same pay. Subsequent to the *Phillips* decision, the courts stuck closely to effecting congressional intent and eschewed arguments that would have allowed comparisons of jobs that were different but required similar levels of effort, skill, and responsibility.

By the 1980's, however, the battle for pay equity for women had been transformed into a struggle for payment to women on the basis of a difficult to define and controversial concept, that of comparable worth. Champions of pay equity believed that men and women should draw the same pay for the same work. Comparable worth advocates went further. Noting that women were segregated into certain occupations that on average paid less than occupations employing primarily men, they called for rethinking and reevaluating traditional ideas about the labor market. They pointed out the fact that traditionally female occupations such as nurse and librarian required more education, training, skill, and responsibility than many higher paying male-dominated jobs and objected to this inequity.

At the close of the 1980's, there were signs of progress. Federal legislation and that on local levels, along with judicial decisions, had made gender-based employment discrimination illegal. In addition, more than half of the American workforce was composed of women. Actions by the American Federation of State, County, and Municipal Employees, to cite one example, had raised women's wages in the City of Los Angeles by placing wages of female secretaries, clerks, and librarians in line with the salaries of male gardeners, truck drivers, garage attendants, and maintenance personnel.

Nevertheless, observers and many detailed public and private studies confirmed that a majority of working women filled jobs in occupations that were 75 percent female and that women held 80 percent of American service jobs, traditionally low on the pay scale. Ample evidence also indicated that full-time female employees earned only about 60 percent of the wages earned by full-time male employees. In addition, studies in several states showed that about 70 percent of state employees in the highest paying jobs were male. Many scholarly observers and civil libertarians agreed that the working woman's situation was in substantial part a result of sex discrimination.

Bibliography

Fogel, Walter. *The Equal Pay Act*. New York: Praeger, 1984. A clear, informative, and critical survey of the origins and operations of the Equal Pay Act, with special reference to its influences on the comparable worth movement. Fogel questions whether social reform legislation, as opposed to market forces, works well.

Ginsburg, Ruth Bader. "The Burger Court's Grappling with Sex Discrimination." In *The Burger Court*, edited by Vincent Blasi. New Haven, Conn.: Yale University Press, 1983. Crisp analysis of the subject. Gives high marks to the Burger Court's decisions in sex discrimination. Contains profiles of Burger Court justices.

Hutner, Frances C. *Equal Pay for Comparable Worth: The Working Woman's Issue of the Eighties*. New York: Praeger, 1986. A fine comparative survey of pay equity and comparable worth in the United States, France, Canada, and Australia. Shows that costs of implementing comparable worth have been lower than feared by employers. Intelligent advocacy.

Kelley, Rita Mae, and Jane Bayer, eds. *Comparable Worth, Pay Equity, and Public Policy*. New York: Greenwood Press, 1988. Superb, clear, and informative essays. A splendid survey of these subjects by a variety of experts who are balanced advocates of equity.

Kessler-Harris, Alice. *A Woman's Wage*. Lexington: The University Press of Kentucky, 1990. A clear, useful historical survey of pay equity, with emphasis on social consequences.

Clifton K. Yearley

Cross-References

Roosevelt Signs the Fair Labor Standards Act (1938); The Civil Rights Act Prohibits Discrimination in Employment (1964); The Supreme Court Orders the End of Discrimination in Hiring (1971); The Pregnancy Discrimination Act Extends Employment Rights (1978); *Firefighters v. Stotts* Upholds Seniority Systems (1984).

GPU ANNOUNCES PLANS FOR A COMMERCIAL NUCLEAR REACTOR

CATEGORY OF EVENT: New products
TIME: December 12, 1963
LOCALE: New York, New York

General Public Utilities Corporation, the parent company of Jersey Central Power and Light, announced plans to construct the first commercial nuclear reactor to generate electricity

Principal personages:

CHESTER HOLIFIELD (1903-1995), a congressman from California; the vice chairman of the Joint Committee on Atomic Energy

DWIGHT D. EISENHOWER (1890-1969), the president of the United States, 1953-1961

EDWARD W. MOREHOUSE (1896-1974), a vice president of General Public Utilities Corporation, in charge of the firm's evaluation of applications of nuclear energy

HYMAN RICKOVER (1900-1986), the head of the U.S. Navy's nuclear development program

LOUIS H. RODDIS, JR. (1918-1991), a member of the U.S. Navy's Nuclear Ship Propulsion Program and president of Pennsylvania Electric Company

LEWIS L. STRAUSS (1896-1974), the chairman of the Atomic Energy Commission, 1953-1958

Summary of Event

On December 12, 1963, General Public Utilities Corporation (GPU), a utility holding company with operating properties in New Jersey and

Pennsylvania, announced the company's plan to build a nuclear generating plant in Oyster Creek, New Jersey. The plant was designed to produce electricity for Jersey Central Power and Light, a GPU subsidiary serving customers in the central portion of the state. The commercial nuclear generating facility was generally regarded as the first to be wholly privately financed. GPU's announcement was greeted with approbation by President Lyndon B. Johnson, who declared, "it appears that the long promised day of economical nuclear power is close at hand."

The Argonne National Laboratory in Illinois became the site of the first breeder reactor in the United States in 1951. (Argonne National Laboratory)

The GPU announcement was the part of the saga of nuclear power that began with the dropping of the atomic bomb on Hiroshima and Nagasaki in 1945. The creation of the atomic bomb was wholly a product of governmental research. Initially, all thought concerning nuclear power was focused on how to keep the secret of atomic weaponry from spreading to other nations. It was in the light of this preoccupation that the first legislation dealing with atomic energy, the Atomic Energy Act of 1946, required that the U.S. government retain ownership and control of all atomic facilities.

The act created a new government organization to control all the government's atomic activities, the Atomic Energy Commission (AEC). The government owned a variety of atomic installations and controlled all research into possible applications of atomic power, although much of the research and development was done through contracts with private companies, notably General Electric (GE) and Westinghouse, each of which had its own atomic laboratory. Further, the government retained ownership of all nuclear material.

Pressure was already building, however, to find a peaceful use for this powerful new energy source. The creation of the AEC led to a new congressional committee, the Joint Committee on Atomic Energy, to oversee the work of the new commission. The committee, and particularly its vice chairman, Congressman Chester Holifield of California, was a strong voice for finding peaceful applications. The congressional agenda pushed the Atomic Energy Commission in the direction of seeking nonexplosive uses for atomic energy.

The first step in the long process of adapting atomic energy for use in the generation of electricity was the formation, in 1949, of an Ad Hoc Advisory Committee on Cooperation between the Electric Power Industry and the Atomic Energy Commission. The chairman of the commission was Philip Sporn, a utility economist and the president of American Gas and Electric Corporation (later to become the American Electric Power System); the other two members were Edward W. Morehouse, also a utility economist and vice president of General Public Utilities Corporation, and Walton Seymour, another utility economist and director of the Power and Programs office of the Department of the Interior.

The members of the committee received security clearances that enabled them to visit all the major atomic installations of the government except that at Los Alamos, New Mexico, which was wholly dedicated to weapons production. They consulted scientists at Argonne Laboratories, at Oak Ridge Laboratories (assigned the mission of leading the AEC's research efforts into industrial applications of atomic power), Brookhaven Laboratories, Hanford (concerned primarily with the enrichment of uranium), the Knolls Atomic Power Laboratory (a GE facility dedicated to contract research for the AEC), and the Bettis Laboratory (a Westinghouse facility comparable to Knolls).

Extensive consultation by the committee members with AEC scientists convinced them that the potential for civilian and commercial application existed. At the same time, much would need to be done in the way of research into a safe reactor form that could be produced at a cost competitive with fossil fuels. The chief advantage of nuclear generation would turn out to be the small size of its fuel compared to coal, making possible immense savings in fuel transportation costs.

A major factor in the evolution of civilian nuclear power was the interest of the U.S. Navy, under the leadership of Admiral Hyman Rickover, in the development of small nuclear "engines" that could propel naval vessels, particularly submarines. Rickover assembled a group of scientists and engineers, including Louis H. Roddis, Jr., later to become an active participant in the GPU decision-making process as president of Pennsylvania Electric Company, a GPU subsidiary. In late 1947, intensive research efforts were begun in search of a suitable format for an atomic power plant for naval, especially submarine, use.

These efforts bore fruit in 1953, when a prototype submarine-propulsion reactor was successfully tested at the National Reactor Test Station in Idaho Falls, Idaho. This reactor led directly to the propulsion units for submarines. This reactor also led directly to the pressurized-water and boiling-water reactors that became the predominant form of nuclear power plant for electricity generation in the United States.

The Joint Committee on Atomic Energy seized on these developments as confirmation of its belief that a major effort directed toward the development of nuclear power reactors was justified. It pressured the Atomic Energy Commission to make a formal commitment to research dedicated to developing suitable forms for nuclear power generation. The administration of President Dwight D. Eisenhower, himself an advocate of the peaceful use of atomic power, strongly supported this agenda, which it labeled "atoms for peace."

Because there was concern on the part of the public about the safety of nuclear power, much of the research focused on safe operation. The problem was one of controlling nuclear fission so that only enough of a chain reaction occurred to keep the process going. Research focused on the safety factor rapidly led researchers to conclude that the safest design was either the pressurized-water reactor or the boiling-water reactor. In both types, the water used as a coolant quickly turned to steam and shut down the reaction.

It was clear that the legislation passed by Congress in 1946 was too constraining to permit effective development of a nuclear power industry, especially one predominantly in private hands, as President Eisenhower's administration ardently desired. Accordingly, the Atomic Energy Act of 1946 was replaced by a new Atomic Energy Act in 1954. This act authorized the licensing of private nuclear facilities by the AEC and permitted the AEC to furnish the nuclear fuels for such facilities, though the government retained ownership of the fuels. Armed with this enlarged authority, the AEC's chairman, Lewis L. Strauss, created a demonstration reactor program, under which the AEC welcomed proposals for the construction of demonstration reactors on the part of private utilities. The utilities would finance, or at least contribute to, the capital costs, but the AEC would provide funds for research, development, and evaluation, and would also provide the nuclear fuel.

A number of small-scale plants were built under this program. The first was a plant at Shippingport, in western Pennsylvania. The power generated there was supplied to Duquesne Light Company. Another early plant was commissioned by a consortium of New England utilities called Yankee Electric; it built a plant at Rowe, in western Massachusetts, that operated successfully for more than thirty years. All these plants were, however, of modest dimensions. They did provide the basis for cost studies that led to defining a goal of the utility industry of costs less than four cents for each ten kilowatt-hours generated.

Intensive studies were carried out by both industry and the government to determine the costs of nuclear power generation. The basic question was how the cost of nuclear generation compared with that of coal-based power. All utilities performed cost studies, but among those most intensively studying costs were the officials of GPU. GPU's operating plants had access to Pennsylvania coal, so the competitive factor was intense. The decision to go ahead with the Oyster Creek facility was based on the belief that the company could produce electricity below the cost of four cents per ten kilowatt-hours.

Equally decisive was the successful negotiation with General Electric for a turnkey price for the Oyster Creek plant of $76.6 million. GE was able to offer such a proposition because it was a major producer of turbines and generators for utilities and eager to get in on the potentially profitable field of building nuclear power plants. In the early 1960's, electricity use was increasing at a steady rate of about 3 percent per year, so GE could foresee a large demand for new electrical generating facilities. By signing on with Jersey Central for the construction of the Oyster Creek facility, GE opened for itself a potentially highly lucrative business, even though the early turnkey plants were probably constructed at a loss.

Impact of Event

The immediate impact of GPU's announcement of the Oyster Creek project was the decision, on the part of eleven privately owned utilities, to embark on their own nuclear construction programs. By 1975, fifty-three civilian nuclear power plants had received operating licenses, and an additional sixty-three plant-construction licenses had been issued by the AEC. At that time, applications were pending for an additional seventy-four construction permits. In a short period of time, the American utility industry had made a major commitment to nuclear power.

One of the conditions for the adoption of nuclear power cited by the Ad Hoc Committee on Cooperation Between the Electric Power Industry and the Atomic Energy Commission had been met: Standardized designs and a sufficient number of orders brought the capital costs down to a point at which nuclear power constituted an attractive investment on the part of the utility industry. Oyster Creek was built for a cost of $138 per kilowatt, a price that made a nuclear plant highly competitive with coal.

The coal industry was galvanized by the announcement of the Oyster Creek facility. At the time of the announcement, the coal industry promptly indicated that, had it been aware of the announcement in advance, it would have offered a better price to the utility. In fact, faced with growing nuclear competition, the coal industry was driven to introduce numerous structural improvements, particularly new coal-cutting machinery, that enabled output per hour of labor in mines to double over the forthcoming five years.

The emergence of civilian nuclear power as a reality gave a great boost to the government's business of uranium enrichment. Pressurized-water reactors and light-water reactors require enriched uranium for successful operation. The government's plants that had been enriching uranium for the production of plutonium for use in weapons now had a much larger demand for their services. The question surfaced of whether the government should continue to own all the uranium fuel. In 1964, the Private Fuels Ownership Act was passed by Congress. The act required the AEC to terminate its existing practice of leasing nuclear fuel to private utilities and abolished the ban on private ownership of nuclear fuel. The AEC would continue to provide enrichment services for a fee, but utilities would own the fuel they used. The government continued to buy back the plutonium that was a by-product of the operation of nuclear power reactors.

Another important legislative action had already been taken in 1957, when the Price-Anderson Act was passed by Congress. The insurance industry had made clear that it would provide insurance against a catastrophic accident only up to a limit that the utility industry found to be inadequate coverage. The government agreed to provide backup insurance beyond the $60 million the insurance industry was ready to commit. The act was originally intended to last ten years, but in 1965, in anticipation of the operation of private nuclear generating plants, it was extended for another ten years, with the inclusion of a "no-fault" clause permitting immediate indemnification of anyone injured.

It was clear that a major portion of the government's role in the field of civilian nuclear energy would be licensing and regulation. This entailed several reorganizations of the AEC, resulting finally in its replacement by the Energy Research and Development Administration (which later became the Department of Energy) in 1974. The regulatory role was spun off to the Nuclear Regulatory Commission, the job of which it was to oversee the nuclear power industry.

The Oyster Creek facility went on line in 1968. Its original rated capacity was 550 megawatts, but following a "run-in" or "stretch" period, as it was known in the industry, it was able to increase its capacity to 640 megawatts. That was the largest capacity contemplated when Oyster Creek was announced, but within a few years technology had advanced to the point at which thousand-megawatt plants were being ordered.

Oyster Creek was the beginning of a whole new technology, one that has since spread to much of the industrialized world. The promise of a technology that could provide power at a cost below that of fossil fuels in most parts of the world was irresistible; Oyster Creek demonstrated its practicality. Safety and environmental issues, however, mitigated against widespread use.

Bibliography

Atomic Industrial Forum. *Atomforum 64: Proceedings Atomic Industrial Forum 1964 Annual Conference*. New York: Author, 1965. Contains speeches by Louis H. Roddis, Jr., and Chester Holifield, both celebrating the bright future for civilian nuclear power.

Dawson, Frank G. *Nuclear Power: Development and Management of a Technology*. Seattle: University of Washington Press, 1976. A clear presentation of the stages in the development of nuclear power as a workable commercial technology. Contains a reasonably clear explanation of technical factors.

Mullenbach, Philip. *Civilian Nuclear Power: Economic Issues and Policy Formation*. New York: Twentieth Century Fund, 1963. A critical review by a former Atomic Energy Commission economist of the decisions leading to the development of civilian nuclear power. Mullenbach argues that many of the decisions were made on strategic rather than economic grounds.

Roddis, Louis H., Jr., and Daniel K. Park. "Nuclear Energy and the Electric Power Industry: Before and After Oyster Creek." In *Innovation and Achievement in the Public Interest*, edited by Ward Morehouse and Nancy Morehouse Gordon. Croton-on-Hudson, N.Y.: Wayward Press, 1966. This account of the events leading up to the Oyster Creek project, together with some discussion of its consequences, is the most concise and informative story of the Oyster Creek facility.

U.S. Atomic Energy Commission. *Civilian Nuclear Power: Current Status and Future Technical and Economic Potential of Light Water Reactors*.

Washington, D.C.: Government Printing Office, 1968. This publication appeared just as the Atomic Energy Commission was winding down its research on light water reactors, on the ground that they had become a "proven" technology. Contains a list of civilian nuclear plants in operation and planned, as of 1968.

Nancy M. Gordon

Cross-References

The Environmental Protection Agency Is Created (1970); The United States Plans to Cut Dependence on Foreign Oil (1974); The Alaskan Oil Pipeline Opens (1977); The Three Mile Island Accident Prompts Reforms in Nuclear Power (1979).

HOFFA NEGOTIATES A NATIONAL TRUCKING AGREEMENT

CATEGORY OF EVENT: Labor
TIME: January 16, 1964
LOCALE: Chicago, Illinois

Jimmy Hoffa negotiated a National Master Freight Agreement consolidating his own power and that of his Teamsters Union

Principal personages:
JIMMY HOFFA (1913-1975), the brilliant, powerful, and corrupt leader of the Teamsters from 1957 to 1964
ROBERT F. KENNEDY (1925-1968), a principal investigator and prosecutor of Hoffa and corrupt Teamsters
FRANK E. FITZSIMMONS (1908-1981), a top Teamster official who succeeded Hoffa
JOHN L. MCCLELLAN (1896-1977), the chairman of Senate committees that investigated Hoffa and the Teamsters from 1957 to 1961
DANIEL J. TOBIN (1875-1955), an honest Teamster president who led a largely decentralized union for forty-five years
CLARK R. MOLLENHOFF (1921-1991), a Pulitzer Prize-winning journalist who helped expose Hoffa's corrupt Teamster empire

Summary of Event

On behalf of the International Brotherhood of Teamsters, Chauffeurs, Warehousemen, and Helpers of America (IBT), union president James R. "Jimmy" Hoffa signed the National Master Freight Agreement (NMFA) in Chicago, Illinois, on January 16, 1964. Labor experts, Teamster dissidents, and even many state and national officials who would later comment that

Hoffa's sensational disappearance (and probable murder) in 1975 was the best thing that could have happened to American trade unionism agree that the NMFA represented, from Hoffa's perspective as well as from those of many Teamsters, his finest achievement. It was the first agreement to cover the trucking industry nationwide.

The NMFA and its successive versions brought contractual uniformity to the wages, hours, and working conditions of 30 percent of the Teamster's 1964 members, encompassing 450,000 intercity (or "over-the-road") truckers and local carters. Despite local unions' resistance to it in the San Francisco Bay area, in New York City, and in northern New Jersey, as well as qualifications to it in the form of regional supplements and local riders, the agreement paved the way for standardization of the wages and contracts of the rest of the membership. For Hoffa, the agreement, which was renegotiable every third year, consolidated his political position within the IBT and made him the chief collective bargainer for the nation's largest trade union. Given Hoffa's profound knowledge of the industries with which he dealt, his domineering personality, his exploitation of underworld and political alliances, and his unbridled ruthlessness, it bestowed unprecedented power upon him within the IBT at the same time that it gave the IBT unprecedented power within the American labor movement.

Hoffa always generously acknowledged that if the attainment of a national agreement was his, the vision was that of Farrell Dobbs, a far-sighted union leader in the Depression years and an obscure presidential candidate in early 1960's. In the mid-1930's, Dobbs, a Minnesota Trotsky-ite and leader of the Minneapolis Teamsters, successfully reached out to organize and integrate the much-despised and hard-pressed truck drivers of the Midwest into the North Central District Drivers Council, soon designated as the Central States Drivers Council (CSDC). Originally embracing thirteen local unions in the Dakotas, Minnesota, upper Michigan, Iowa, and Wisconsin, the CSDC under Dobbs's guidance swiftly expanded to encompass forty-six locals. The tough young Hoffa was introduced to Dobbs late in the 1930's by Red O'Laughlin, a Detroit teamster and friend of longtime Teamster president Daniel J. Tobin.

Insofar as Hoffa espoused any political ideology, it was borrowed from Dobbs's own, namely that the American economy was fated to endure cycles of depression and faced ultimate failure. Dobbs believed that trade unions ought to contribute to revolutionary change. At the peak of a promising union career, Dobbs abandoned unionism, later to lead the Socialist Workers Party. He imparted a number of invaluable lessons, some strategic, some tactical, to young Hoffa.

Foremost was Dobbs's insistence on establishing centralized areawide collective bargaining mechanisms through which to acquire uniformity in wages, hours, and working conditions for "over-the-road" truckers. Dobbs believed such centralization was mandated by the nature of the trucking industry, one characterized by ease of entry, low capital requirements, and tens of thousands of intensely competitive operators. In such circumstances, individual operators had little opportunity to pass increased costs to consumers through price hikes. They could lower their basic costs, principally labor, only by undercutting wages, increasing hours of work, or moving operations to low-wage areas. Dobbs believed that the harmful effects of this competition could be mitigated if uniformities were brought to the drivers' wages, hours, and working conditions. Under common conditions, operators could raise their prices together and more readily pass their cost increases to consumers without traditional price wars, wage cuts, or changes of base.

Tactically, Hoffa became a master of Dobbs's techniques of leverage, or of using an employer or situation the union controlled to organize or to negotiate successfully with employers or other unions. Hoffa maximized advantages inherent in labor reform laws of the 1930's. The federal Norris-LaGuardia Act of 1932, for example, contrary to the previous half century of antilabor legislation emanating from all levels of government, legalized organizing campaigns conducted by means of picketing and secondary boycotts. The National Labor Relations Act of 1935 (Wagner Act) appended the principle of employee self-determination, permitting workers—under procedures stipulated by the National Labor Relations Board (NLRB), the quasi-judicial monitor of the act—to select or reject, by secret ballot vote, unions attempting to represent them.

Labor reforms, in short, legalized certain types of economic coercion peculiar to the needs of a vigorous labor movement. To the leverages legally available, Hoffa and his cohorts added their preferred efforts to impose organization from the top down. They invoked their own forms of coercion, from questionable contract clauses to tertiary boycotts, beatings, and bombings. The sweeping centralization afforded by the NMFA, linked to the clout of the IBT and to a personality such as Hoffa's, gave Hoffa and his union vast power.

Impact of Event

Several immediate consequences resulted from Hoffa's centralization of Teamster authority in his own hands by virtue of the NMFA, within a union historically characterized by its decentralization and the substantial autonomy of its locals. Union membership had risen to 1.7 million by 1964 from 1.4 million in 1957, when Hoffa became Teamster president. By the time

Hoffa left the union presidency for prison in 1967, three years after the first NMFA, the Teamsters had gained 300,000 members, only a minority of whom were truckers. Unionization had been extended, for example, to warehousemen, chauffeurs, bakers, and confectionery workers. In addition, as the Teamsters' chief collective bargaining agent, Hoffa redrafted and shrewdly reinterpreted the union constitution to funnel the all-important, and politically exploitable, grievance procedures into his own office. Furthermore, but of vital importance. Hoffa extended and intensified his power over the Teamsters' Central and Southern States Pension Fund (CSSPF).

Despite the fact that Hoffa had become the Teamsters' principal leader by 1954, three years prior to his election to the union's presidency, he lagged far behind other major labor leaders in developing pension funds and in recognizing their economic and political potentials. Union-negotiated pensions had been pioneered a decade earlier, during 1944 and 1945, by the International Ladies' Garment Workers Union, whose initiatives were swiftly followed by the International Brotherhood of Electrical Workers and by John L. Lewis on behalf of his United Mine Workers (UMW). The UMW's defection from the American Federation of Labor-Congress of Industrial Organizations (AFL-CIO) forced the AFL-CIO leadership to respond with their own pension plan. In the light of favorable rulings by the NLRB and several judicial decisions, other major unions were soon pursuing similar courses.

Hoffa clearly was aware of how to deploy the funds of local union treasuries and welfare trusts to buttress his personal empire, but he did not negotiate the Teamsters' CSSPF, his first pension fund, until January, 1955. Thereafter, however, with characteristic astuteness, he learned to manipulate CSSPF moneys by grasping personal authority over their dispersal and investment and made these decisions his principal preoccupation.

There was much to preoccupy him, for successive NMFA Teamster contracts with employers stipulated ever-rising employer contributions to the CSSPF. The $2 per week that employers paid for each employee in 1955 rose to $4 by 1960 and to $7 in 1964. By 1965, $6 million in such contributions flowed into the CSSPF monthly. The fund's total value for the union's 1.7 million workers had soared to $200 million. By 1967, the U.S. attorney general's office and the nation's courts had handed down 200 individual indictments against Teamsters and their allies, winning 125 convictions related mainly to Hoffa's and other Teamster officials' illegal uses of CSSPF funds. The ability to exploit the power inherent in this immense fund stemmed from Hoffa's ability, thanks to this control over successive NMFA contracts, to control the Teamsters' collective bargaining.

Hoffa's unprecedented labor empire and the many threats it posed were brought to the general public's attention rather dramatically on several fronts. The menace of the IBT was already painfully evident to both union and nonunion workers, as well as to employers and employer representatives, who were victims of the Teamsters' ostracization, intimidation, beatings, shootings, and bombings. Pulitzer Prize-winning journalist Clark R. Mollenhoff was among the first at the national level to expose Hoffa's tentacles of power. He informed and advised congressional and other federal officials as they investigated Hoffa's union.

Public awareness was more broadly awakened by the persistent investigations of the McClellan committee (officially the U.S. Senate Select Committee on Improper Activities in the Labor or Management Field). Under the direction of Senator John L. McClellan, an Arkansas Democrat, the committee began hearings on January 30, 1957. Within two years, McClellan's committee was able to bring eighty-two charges against Hoffa alone and to provide a political launching pad for the impressive investigative talents of Robert F. Kennedy, who would pursue Hoffa and other suspected labor racketeers after becoming the U.S. attorney general. To these activities should be added a nationwide televised speech by President Dwight D. Eisenhower calling for strong legislation designed to curb union excesses and racketeering.

Legislative response came even as McClellan's hearings proceeded. The Labor-Management Reporting and Disclosure Act (the Landrum-Griffin Act) of 1959, despite its sweeping title, was understood to be aimed chiefly at Hoffa and his Teamsters. The IBT possessed the economic capability to bring America's most vital form of transport to a halt, paralyzing the nation's economic life and thereby its well-being. Congress wanted some reins to be put on such a powerful union. Even with restraints in force and while under indictment, Hoffa was able to negotiate the NMFA.

The labor reform legislation enacted between 1932 and the mid-1940's—in spirit mostly trusting and permissive by past comparisons—was altered by modifications following the lines of the Taft-Hartley Act of 1947. Sober questions were raised concerning how much union power the national welfare could tolerate and whether union "monopolies" ought to be subject to the full force of the country's antitrust laws. Hoffa's consolidation of power through the NMFA brought further concerns as well as achieving the practical purpose of standardizing the working conditions of truckers and ending some of the competition among them.

Bibliography

Franco, Joseph, with Richard Hammer. *Hoffa's Man: The Rise and Fall of Jimmy Hoffa as Witnessed by His Strongest Arm.* New York: Prentice-

Hall Press, 1987. Candid and colorful. Written by a voluble Hoffa admirer and organizer whose background of violence is characteristic of Hoffa's associates, many of whom are depicted here. Photos, excellent index.

Hoffa, James Riddle. *The Trials of Jimmy Hoffa: An Autobiography.* Chicago: Henry Regnery, 1970. Interesting, if self-serving. Politicians, judges, journalists, and others not "connected" with Hoffa are presented as wrong or confused. No reference features. To be read for balance and some color.

Jacoby, Daniel. *Laboring for Freedom: A New Look at the History of Labor in America.* Armonk, N.Y.: M. E. Sharpe, 1998.

James, Ralph C., and Estelle Dinerstein James. *Hoffa and the Teamsters.* Princeton, N.J.: D. Van Nostrand, 1965. An invaluable and unique inside scholarly study based on ninety days of close association with Hoffa in action and broad access to Teamster files. Admiring of Hoffa's intelligence and abilities, but objectively raises serious questions about his use of power and money. Clearly written. Chapter notes, glossary, and good index.

Moldea, Dan E. *The Hoffa Wars: Teamsters, Rebels, Politicians, and the Mob.* New York: Paddington Press, 1978. Exciting reading. The book began as a working thesis and became the author's project for the National Broadcasting Company in the mid-1970's. Detailed and informative insights into both Hoffa's connections and his decline. Photos, brief chapter notes, excellent index. Updates aspects of Mollenhoff's work.

Mollenhoff, Clark Raymond. *Tentacles of Power: The Story of Jimmy Hoffa.* Cleveland: World Publishing Company, 1965. Superb reporting that earned the author a Pulitzer Prize. Relies heavily on Mollenhoff's investigations and McClellan Committee testimony. An exciting, informative, and frightening read. Photos, notes, brief appendix, but no index. Outstanding objective damnation of Hoffa's abuses of power.

Clifton K. Yearley

Cross-References

The Norris-LaGuardia Act Adds Strength to Labor Organizations (1932); The Wagner Act Promotes Union Organization (1935); The Taft-Hartley Act Passes over Truman's Veto (1947); The AFL and CIO Merge (1955); The Landrum-Griffin Act Targets Union Corruption (1959).

THE KENNEDY-JOHNSON TAX CUTS STIMULATE THE U.S. ECONOMY

CATEGORY OF EVENT: Government and business
TIME: February 26, 1964
LOCALE: Washington, D.C.

On February 26, 1964, President Lyndon B. Johnson signed the Revenue Act of 1964, which was the first deliberate attempt to stimulate the United States economy by reducing taxes

Principal personages:
JOHN F. KENNEDY (1917-1963), the president of the United States at the time the tax cut was sent to Congress
LYNDON B. JOHNSON (1908-1973), the president of the United States at the time the tax cut was enacted
JOHN MAYNARD KEYNES (1883-1946), an economist who favored the use of government policy to control business cycles and manage the economy
WILBUR MILLS (1909-1992), the chairman of the House Ways and Means Committee when the tax cut was under consideration
WALTER W. HELLER (1915-1987), the chairman of the Council of Economic Advisers under Kennedy and Johnson
CLARENCE DOUGLAS DILLON (1909-1992), the secretary of the treasury under Kennedy and Johnson

Summary of Event

In the early 1960's, the U.S. economy was experiencing problems in many areas. These problems included recurring recessions, high rates of unemployment, excess productive capacity, inadequate profits, and lack of business investment. Because of the sluggishness of the economy, the federal budget ran a deficit, an unusual occurrence in peacetime. The country had experienced five recessions since the end of World War II. The annual economic growth rate was down to 3 percent, and unemployment was above 6 percent. For 1963, President John F. Kennedy originally projected a $500 million surplus, but as a result of the stagnating economy, a $9 billion deficit was projected by mid-year.

Walter Heller, chairman of the Council of Economic Advisers, was a key proponent of a tax cut. He believed that the structure of high tax rates, which dated back to World War II, was acting as a brake on the economy. Whenever the economy went into an expansion, the high tax rates slowed it down.

What Kennedy proposed was a tax bill that contained both a tax cut and tax reform. The original proposal was for a $13.6 billion reduction in taxes. Key reforms included an end to the dividend credit exclusion and changes in deductions for charitable contributions, home mortgage interest, and casualty losses. For corporations, he proposed both a reduction in rates and changes in the tax payment dates that in effect speeded up the receipt of corporate tax payments. The focus was on helping small business by reducing the corporate tax rate from 30 percent to 22 percent on the first $25,000 of corporate income. The surtax on earnings in excess of $25,000 would be 30 percent, later reduced to 28 percent.

Capital gains tax rates would be reduced from 25 percent to 19.5 percent. The required holding period for an asset would change from six months to a year. Executives with restricted stock option plans would not be able to use capital gains rates. A big change was proposed in the treatment of real estate tax shelters. Investors had been using accelerated depreciation methods and then selling properties for a profit. Under the proposed change, part of the gain would be taxed as ordinary income rather than as capital gains, which were taxed at lower rates. This caused concern among Realtors, who argued that the tax advantage had been built into real estate prices and that an increase in taxes would deflate prices in the real estate market.

Business was cool to the Kennedy Administration for two major reasons. After the Bay of Pigs invasion, the government paid ransom to Cuba to release American prisoners. Since government funds could not legally be used for ransom, corporate donations were solicited. Companies with large government contracts or with pending hearings were particularly hard hit for contributions. In addition, in the spring of 1962, Kennedy had pressured the steel industry to reduce its proposed price increases.

Overall, businesspeople and workers were concerned about the power of government and how its use affected business in both positive and negative ways. There was not as much concern about the size of government, with business accepting the necessity of a large federal bureaucracy. In one example of a challenge to the government's use of power, the administration was charged with pressuring aerospace firms and other large contractors to accept union shop clauses, which mandated union membership for company workers.

The investment community favored the idea of the tax cut but was cautious about what might happen to the bill as it made its way through Congress. Wall Street liked the planned corporate tax reduction but was concerned about budget deficits and the potential for inflation. American business as a whole initially opposed the plan because of concern about the effect that financing the deficit would have on the credit markets and interest rates.

The proposed tax cuts primarily benefited lower income groups. Business advocates argued that spending by the lower income groups would not be sufficient to stimulate the economy. Business liked the cut in corporate tax rates and the decrease in rates for the upper tax brackets but was concerned about the acceleration of corporate tax payments.

The proposal also called for a reduction in the oil depletion allowance. In addition, foreign tax credits would be limited. Companies would be prohibited from using foreign development costs to offset U.S. taxable income. These changes would hit the oil and gas industries hard, and industry leaders predicted a substantial decrease in domestic drilling.

The home building industry was concerned about the proposed reduction in the mortgage interest deduction, as were homeowners. The auto industry, on the other hand, favored the tax cut, seeing a potential increase in the number of two- and three-car homes as the tax cut would likely encourage car purchases. Federal Reserve Board chairman William C. Martin, Jr., clearly favored the tax cut and indicated that he would not let interest rates rise if the tax cut passed.

Goals of the tax cut were to achieve economic growth of 4.5 percent per year and to bring unemployment down from 5.8 percent to 4 percent. By April, 1963, the unemployment rate was 6 percent. There was concern over the impending entrance of the baby boom generation into the workforce and the need for significant job expansion to meet that challenge. There was equal concern about the loss of jobs resulting from automation. The Council of Economic Advisers estimated that two million new jobs would be needed each year to offset jobs lost to automation. Walter Heller estimated that the tax cut would create two to three million new jobs. At first, Kennedy tried to boost the economy by increasing government spending, but concern over the resulting deficits caused him to turn instead to the use of the tax cut strategy.

As the bill made its way through Congress, many of the tax reform items were dropped. Capital gains rates stayed at 25 percent. Individual marginal tax rates were cut from 91 percent to 70 percent for the highest tax brackets. Long-term capital gains rules would apply after only six months. A one-time tax exemption was offered for the sale of a personal residence. Stock options held for more than three years would still qualify for capital gains treatment. No change was made to the deductibility of mortgage interest. Changes were made to the deductibility of casualty losses, charitable contributions, and sick pay. There was a new increased standard deduction.

At the time of President Kennedy's assassination, the tax bill had not yet passed the Senate. President Lyndon B. Johnson supported the tax cut and was opposed to increased government spending as a way to stimulate the economy. Johnson was perceived to be more friendly to the business community.

In the Senate, the Long Amendment extended the benefits of the investment credit and added leased equipment to the list of qualified investments. Real estate tax shelters held for less than ten years were taxed at a higher rate. In the final version of the bill, few of the original tax reform items remained. On February 26, 1964, President Johnson signed the Revenue Act of 1964. It had taken thirteen months for the bill to pass Congress.

Impact of Event

The Revenue Act of 1964 cut taxes by $11.6 billion, with individuals receiving $9.2 billion and corporations receiving $2.4 billion. There was a major reduction for people with annual incomes below $3,000; they would no longer pay taxes. Tax cuts for individuals slightly favored the higher income brackets. The 15 percent of taxpayers at the highest brackets benefited from a 40 percent reduction in their taxes. The remaining 85 percent of taxpayers received 60 percent of the benefit. In total, an estimated 90 percent of taxpayers received some benefit from the tax cut.

The impact was felt immediately because of prompt changing of payroll withholding rates, which pumped an additional $800 million into the economy monthly. That additional money would prompt extra purchases and lead to a chain reaction of increased economic activity. It was expected that the Gross National Product would increase by $30 billion. The hope was that investment spending would increase as firms saw that investment was profitable because of the increased consumer spending.

Concerns of business after the tax cut focused on inflation. Productivity was rising 2.6 percent per year in the nonfarm sector and 6.1 percent in the farm sector. Unions pushed for wage increases to match productivity increases. There was concern that increased costs would create an inflationary spiral.

There was also concern about the nation's balance of payments. The fear was that in order to alleviate the trade deficit (an excess of imports relative to exports), interest rates would be raised, and that the higher interest rates would dampen the effect of the tax cut within the U.S. economy. President Johnson was also concerned about the federal budget deficit, which could also result in higher interest rates. He cut spending—primarily in defense—in order to reduce the deficit. The budget request for the War on Poverty was modest because of the size of the deficit. Few people believed that the tax cut would reduce poverty rates measurably.

The effects on business occurred over a longer period, through the accelerated corporate tax payment schedule. Prior to the bill's passage, corporations estimated their taxes in September and paid half of that amount at year end. Corporations with tax liabilities in excess of $100,000 would have to pay earlier and eventually would pay in quarterly installments. The most immediate positive impact on business was increased inventory investment, as firms prepared for increased consumer spending. The other major direct benefit for business was the change in the investment credit. The anticipated benefit from that change was a $160 million reduction in corporate taxes in 1964 and $195 million in 1965.

While the tax bill was making its way through Congress, the economy was well into a recovery. In 1963, steel production rose 11 percent over 1962. During the fourth quarter of 1963, 2.2 million new cars were produced, setting a record. Construction increased. Retail trade, business investment, and consumer spending all rose throughout 1963, before the tax cut was passed.

The tax cut was hailed as a monument to the ideas of economist John Maynard Keynes and as a significant shift in economic policy. President Franklin D. Roosevelt had used fiscal policy favored by Keynes to pull the country out of the Depression, but he favored increased spending as a tool rather than tax policy. The belief in a balanced budget was commonly held, in opposition to Keynesian economics. The significance of the tax cut was in the use of tax rather than spending policy and the use of planned budget deficits. The Kennedy-Johnson tax cut was more closely aligned to Keynes's theory than was the New Deal.

By June, 1964, the economy had been growing for forty months, in the longest period of economic growth since World War II. Prices remained stable. The Federal Reserve Index of Industrial Production was up 25 percent from the base period of 1957-1958. Production costs were stable. The Census Bureau's Index of Unit Labor Costs of Manufacturing showed that labor costs had actually fallen slightly from the same base period. According to the McGraw-Hill Capital Spending Survey, business planned a 14 percent increase in capacity over the next three years and expected a

19 percent increase in sales volume. Stock prices held steady, and consumer spending grew, as did the level of consumer debt.

In October, 1964, a major strike at General Motors idled 265,000 workers. The strike caused a reduction in auto production in the last quarter of 1964 and reduced projections for 1965. There was fear of a steel strike, and manufacturers began stockpiling steel in anticipation. A contract settlement at Chrysler exceeded the administration's wage guidelines and fueled fears of inflation. Raw material prices rose. By August, there was a 7 percent drop in construction contracts and an increase in home mortgage foreclosures. There was growing concern about business failures and the increase in consumer debt.

By 1965, the Gross National Product had increased 25.3 percent since 1961. Industrial production was up 27 percent. Personal income was 21.5 percent higher than in 1961, and corporate profits had risen 64 percent in the four-year period. The unemployment rate was still above 5 percent, and there remained concern over structural unemployment and poverty. Credit remained available because the Federal Reserve System increased the money supply as interest rates increased.

The impact of the tax cut was felt both before and after the legislation was passed. The congressional debate increased consumer and business expectations. Passage of the legislation then secured a recovery that was already well under way. The importance of the tax cut has more to do with the essential change in government policy that occurred. For the first time, tax policy was used deliberately to manipulate the economy. The government's role as economic manipulator was firmly accepted. The Keynesian concept of planned deficits took root. The ideal of a balanced budget remained, but the business community, voters, and Congress became willing to accept budget deficits as part of the economic picture.

Bibliography

Bernstein, Irving. "Keynesian Turn: The Tax Cut." In *Promises Kept*. New York: Oxford University Press, 1991. A history of the Kennedy Administration, with detailed description of the political process involved in the tax cut legislation. Good discussion of the relationship between the administration and business at the time.

Evans, Rowland, and Robert Novak. "Taming the Congress." In *Lyndon B. Johnson: The Exercise of Power*. New York: New American Library, 1966. An interesting narrative description of how President Johnson maneuvered the tax bill through Congress. Shows Johnson's struggle to come to terms with the new economics represented by the tax cut proposal.

Hughes, Jonathan R. T. *American Economy History.* 5th ed. Reading, Mass.: Addison-Wesley, 1998.

Solow, Robert M., and James Tobin. "The Kennedy Economic Reports." In *Two Revolutions in Economic Policy*, edited by James Tobin and Murray Weidenbaum. Cambridge, Mass.: MIT Press, 1988. Compares economic policy changes that occurred during the Kennedy Administration and during the Reagan Administration. A highly readable explanation of economic issues of the time and reasons for the tax cut proposal. The text also includes the presidents' economic reports for readers who want detailed statistics and data.

Sorensen, Theodore C. "The Fight Against Recession." In *Kennedy.* New York: Harper and Row, 1965. An insider's view of the thinking and discussions within the Kennedy Administration that led to the tax cut proposal. The chapter provides detail regarding the economic problems of the time and why the tax cut proposal was considered to be the best option.

"Tax Cut: Triumph of an Idea." *Business Week*, April 11, 1964, 180-182. Excellent synopsis of economic thought. Contains anecdotes about Keynes's thinking and shows the policy shift represented by the tax cut and its importance in the evaluation of economic theory. The style is informative and clear. A good background source for readers without training in economics.

Alene Staley

Cross-References

The General Agreement on Tariffs and Trade Is Signed (1947); Firms Begin Replacing Skilled Laborers with Automatic Tools (1960's); Reagan Promotes Supply-Side Economics (1981).

THE CIVIL RIGHTS ACT PROHIBITS DISCRIMINATION IN EMPLOYMENT

CATEGORY OF EVENT: Labor
TIME: July 2, 1964
LOCALE: Washington, D.C.

Under Title VII of the Civil Rights Act, victims of employment discrimination were legally entitled to a process for resolving grievances

Principal personages:
ROBERT F. KENNEDY (1925-1968), the U.S. attorney general, 1961-1964
LYNDON B. JOHNSON (1908-1973), the president of the United States, 1963-1969
MARTIN LUTHER KING, JR. (1929-1968), a civil rights leader and 1964 Nobel Peace Prize winner influential in drafting the bill
HUBERT H. HUMPHREY (1911-1978), the Senate floor manager of the bill
EMANUEL CELLER (1888-1981), the chairman of the House Judiciary Committee when the bill was proposed
WILLIAM MCCULLOCH (b. 1901), the senior Republican on the Judiciary Committee, instrumental in influencing undecided Republicans to vote in favor of the bill
PETER RODINO (1909-   ), the Democratic representative who proposed an amendment to establish the Equal Employment Opportunity Commission
EVERETT DIRKSEN (1896-1969), a conservative Republican senator who reversed his opposition to the bill and cast a pivotal vote to end the Senate filibuster against it

Summary of Event

Title VII of the Civil Rights Act of 1964 prohibits discrimination in employment. It is one of the eleven major provisions of the act, which prohibits discrimination in all sectors of society. The significance of the act in general is that it was more comprehensive and contained more power for enforcement than any previous civil rights legislation. Title VII in particular is significant because it drastically changed employment practices in efforts to provide equal opportunity and provided for legal means of resolving the grievances of people who had suffered from employment discrimination in the past and might face it in the future.

Prior to 1964, major legislation prohibiting discrimination in employment practices consisted of President Franklin D. Roosevelt's 1941 executive order creating the Fair Employment Practices Committee (FEPC) to prevent job discrimination in war industries, President Harry S Truman's order to desegregate the armed forces in 1948, and the Equal Pay Act of 1963, which prohibited sex discrimination, especially with respect to wages. In the opinion of civil rights advocates, none of these laws was comprehensive enough.

The period between the mid-1950's and the mid-1970's was one of widespread social unrest in the United States. The Civil Rights Act of 1964 came about in part as a response to a series of demonstrations against racial discrimination that began in the mid-1950's. Impatient with what they perceived to be slow progress in eliminating racial discrimination, African Americans and civil rights advocates of all races began to hold increasing numbers of protest demonstrations. Under the leadership of Baptist minister Martin Luther King Jr., and others, thousands of civil rights activists held a series of marches, sit-ins, and boycotts, mostly in the South. Although the civil rights demonstrations were generally nonviolent, opponents responded with arrests, attack dogs, and firearms. Because violent scenes, sometimes involving killing, were broadcast nightly on television, it was not long before the issue became national rather than merely regional. Regardless of where they stood on racial issues, most Americans were appalled at the treatment of demonstrators and the scenes of brutality they witnessed. Many feared a serious breakdown of social order and began to demand government action to put an end to the violence.

U.S. Attorney General Robert F. Kennedy perceived a potential threat and declared that there was an immediate need for stronger and broader legislation to put an end to the racism and inequality at the root of the unrest. He urged his brother, President John F. Kennedy, not to delay in drafting and sending a civil rights bill to the House of Representatives. In June, 1963, the president sent an eight-provision bill to the House. It was far more detailed and powerful than any previous civil rights bill, but amendments by a bipartisan group of civil rights advocates in the House and Senate made it even stronger.

In both houses, however, conservative Republicans and southern Democrats proved to be powerful adversaries of the bill. In the Senate, a thirteen-week filibuster, the longest in history, nearly killed the bill. When Senator Everett Dirksen, a powerful conservative Republican, reversed his opposition to the bill and cast a pivotal vote for cloture, the debate ended. On July 2, 1964, one year and thirteen days after the bill first entered the House, it was signed into law by President Lyndon B. Johnson.

Like the other provisions of the law, Title VII in its final form is far more comprehensive than first proposed. It prohibits discrimination on the basis of race, color, religion, sex, and national origin in the hiring and classification of employees as well as in the granting of labor union membership. It is administered by the Equal Employment Opportunity Commission (EEOC), an agency with legal enforcement powers. The EEOC investigates charges of discriminatory practices, establishes procedures for resolving grievances through mediation, or failing mediation, refers cases to local or state authorities for resolution. If voluntary compliance is not secured sixty days after these procedures, the aggrieved parties may file suit in federal court. Jury trial can be requested by either plaintiff or defendant. The EEOC can also request the court to permit the U.S. attorney general to intervene

President Lyndon Johnson signs the Civil Rights Act of 1964 as government and civil rights leaders look up. (Library of Congress)

in suits and can urge the attorney general to file suit whenever discriminatory employment practices are observed to exist.

In cases in which local and state laws regarding discrimination are more strict than federal law and more inclusive of the groups deemed entitled to protection from discriminatory practices, the EEOC can advise the plaintiff to file charges locally before filing with the federal agency. Generally, plaintiffs are able to have allegations investigated on both the state and federal levels.

Impact of Event

The long and contentious debate involved in passing the Civil Rights Act of 1964 is reflected in the difficulties in interpreting, applying, and enforcing the law. The most important impact of Title VII is that it made employment practices more equitable than they were prior to 1964 but also more complex and more subject to government regulation. Charges of discrimination and decisions regarding charges can involve lengthy and expensive disputes, and differing interpretations of the law have sparked controversy.

Under Title VII, substantiated charges of discrimination are backed by government agencies and the courts. Plaintiffs can receive compensatory damages for proven violations of Title VII, and when charges of past discrimination are proved, the damage settlement can be retroactive. In 1973, for example, American Telephone & Telegraph (AT&T), faced with a class action suit, paid $15 million in back wages to fifteen thousand women and minority-group men and an additional $23 million in raises to thirty-six thousand employees. The payments came as part of a settlement in which AT&T did not admit to having discriminated. This case was one of the most widely publicized, but there were many other cases against both large and small companies. Some went as far as the Supreme Court.

Employment practices did not change rapidly enough to satisfy some protected groups and their advocates. EEOC investigations often concluded that female employees and employees of various racial and ethnic backgrounds were not being promoted or given raises on a parity with white male employees. In cases in which companies had few or no minorities on the payroll even though minority workers were available, the EEOC declared that discrimination existed. Companies were advised to take proactive measures by establishing goals and objectives to rectify past or current discrimination. These proactive measures, known as affirmative action, consisted of aggressive programs of recruitment of minorities, fair employment testing methods, and training programs to ensure appropriate placement of employees and equal opportunity for advancement. Lack of nondiscriminatory and consistent training could result in charges of discriminatory failure to promote.

When employment testing came under the scrutiny of the EEOC, employers were required to prove that their tests were nondiscriminatory. Tests used to rank or evaluate applicants had to involve skills or abilities directly related to jobs. The EEOC believed that tests were often biased as to the sex, culture, or race of applicants and therefore could not be used as accurate assessments of skills or ability to perform jobs. Tests had to be validated as fitting job specifications and accurately assessing the skills of people of varying racial, cultural, and educational backgrounds. If the tests could not be validated as meeting these requirements, they were to be discarded. EEOC guidelines on testing were upheld by two Supreme Court decisions during the early the mid-1970's, *Griggs v. Duke Power Company* (1971) and *Albemarle Paper Company v. Moody* (1975).

Whether out of fear of reprisals or out of a sincere desire to provide a fair and balanced workforce, companies generally made good-faith efforts to comply with EEOC rules. It is important to note what is meant by "good-faith" efforts. They are accepted by the EEOC in lieu of desired results only when they can be proven to be the best that a company can do at a reasonable cost and in the light of any extenuating circumstances. Good intentions alone are not always a sufficient defense against charges of discrimination. If, for example, a company has a stated nondiscriminatory policy but has no workable affirmative action program to support it, charges of discrimination might hold up. The good-faith defense was rejected in *Griggs v. Duke Power Company*. On the other hand, good faith was accepted by a New York district court in *Rios v. Enterprise Association Steamfitters Local 638* in 1975. Affirmative action programs worked in many companies, and more female and minority workers were entering the workforce. Although their salaries were still lower than those of white men and although positions in upper levels of management were still out of reach for most of them, salaries slowly approached parity, and women and minorities advanced into positions of rank and responsibility.

Many civil rights advocates still considered the progress of affirmative action to be too slow, however, and the EEOC issued stricter guidelines. It decided that the percentages of minority workers in companies should reflect the composition of the surrounding community. When the EEOC concluded that the percentage of minority workers at a company did not reflect the numbers available for work, it concluded in most cases that discriminatory practices existed. Companies often were required to hire specified numbers of minority workers by specific dates.

Opponents of this type of quota program charged that it constituted a preferential practice. They argued that recruiting and hiring for the purpose of attaining a mandated number or percentage of members of a protected group would result in a workforce composed of people employed by virtue of their sex or ethnicity rather than their skills. They argued further this was both an invitation to possible poor job performance and an insult to the group or individual the program was designed to protect, because it implied inferiority and suggested that their employment resulted only from the EEOC mandate.

Opponents charged that such programs were in direct violation of Title VII, which states that nothing in the title should be interpreted as requiring an employer to grant preferential treatment to employees of any race, color, religion, sex, or national origin. Nevertheless, in 1986 the Supreme Court upheld affirmative action hiring quotas as a remedy for past discrimination.

Such disputes illustrate the complexities of complying with, interpreting, and applying EEOC guidelines. Regardless of the controversies, however, the Civil Rights Act of 1964 has come closer to putting into practice the theory of equal opportunity embodied in the Fourteenth Amendment than had any prior civil rights legislation. The long-term impact of Title VII will be a continuous challenge to business to operate efficiently while at the same time providing fair treatment to workers, in compliance with the law and in the spirit of the Constitution.

Bibliography

Farley, Jennie. *Affirmative Action and the Woman Worker*. New York: AMACOM, a division of American Management Association, 1979. A guideline for personnel management. Discusses affirmative action in recruitment, selection, and training, analyzing what works and what does not.

Glazer, Nathan. "From Equal Opportunity to Statistical Parity." In *Affirmative Discrimination: Ethnic Inequality and Public Policy*. New York: Basic Books, 1975. Although conceding that there have been benefits from affirmative action, Glazer argues that quota systems can harm the very groups and individuals they were designed to protect. Tracing the history of progressively stricter government mandates in employment, he discusses what he views to be inherent weaknesses in the language and interpretation of legislated equal employment opportunity. A complex and interesting argument.

Peres, Richard. *Dealing with Employment Discrimination*. New York: McGraw-Hill, 1978. A clearly written, objective discussion of civil rights legislation and how it can be applied to the best advantage of both employer and employee. The book defines unlawful discrimination and explains how complaints can be prevented or resolved. An extensive appendix contains reprints of Title VII and other pertinent equal employment opportunity legislation.

Sowell, Thomas. *Preferential Policies: An International Perspective*. New York: William Morrow, 1990. Comparing American affirmative action with similar policies in other countries, the author discusses the results and implications of these policies on society in general. For readers interested in a broad discussion of the impacts of nondiscriminatory policies.

Whalen, Charles, and Barbara Whalen. *The Longest Debate: A Legislative History of the 1964 Civil Rights Act*. Washington, D.C.: Seven Locks Press, 1985. Written in a lively style and meticulously documented, this book follows the progress of the act from its historical background to its enactment into law. Provides interesting insights into the legislative process.

Wofford, Harris. "Popular Protest and Public Power: Civil Rights." In *Of Kennedys and Kings: Making Sense of the Sixties*. New York: Farrar Straus Giroux, 1980. Narrates the events and discusses the personalities crucial to the passage of the 1964 Civil Rights Act.

Christina Ashton

Cross-References

Congress Passes the Equal Pay Act (1963); The Supreme Court Orders the End of Discrimination in Hiring (1971); The Pregnancy Discrimination Act Extends Employment Rights (1978); The Supreme Court Rules on Affirmative Action Programs (1979); *Firefighters v. Stotts* Upholds Seniority Systems (1984); The Supreme Court Upholds Quotas as a Remedy for Discrimination (1986).

AMERICAN AND MEXICAN COMPANIES FORM *MAQUILADORAS*

CATEGORY OF EVENT: International business and commerce
TIME: 1965
LOCALE: Mexico and the United States

In the mid-1960's, the Mexican and American governments encouraged formation of a series of factories along their border to provide economic boosts to cities on both sides

Principal personages:
LUÍS ECHEVERRÍA, (1922-   ), the president of Mexico, 1970-1976
RICHARD M. NIXON (1913-1994), the president of the United States, 1969-1974
GUSTAVO DÍAZ ORDAZ (1911-1979), the president of Mexico, 1964-1970
OCTAVIANO CAMPOS SALAS, the Mexican minister of industry and commerce in 1965

Summary of Event
In 1965, Mexico's minister of industry and commerce, Octaviano Campos Salas, proposed the establishment of a tariff-free zone along the United States-Mexico border. President Gustavo Díaz Ordaz wholeheartedly supported the idea. That marked the beginning of the *maquiladoras* program, officially known as the Border Industrialization Program, which may be considered the forerunner of NAFTA, the North American Free Trade Agreement, which Canada, Mexico, and the United States signed in 1992.

From the Mexican standpoint, the *maquiladoras*, or factories, were designed to benefit the entire country. Although they were located primarily in border areas, the intent was to open free trade zones in parts of Mexico that needed economic stimulation. The government envisioned that the spread of benefits from the areas would have a positive effect on the country as a whole. In fact, it hoped that the program would lead to the establishment of a de facto Mexican-United States free trade area all along the border. The *maquiladoras* did provide an economic boost to cities on both sides of the border, but they brought problems as well.

The *maquiladoras* were seen as labor-intensive businesses that would create sorely needed jobs in Mexico and keep American industries competitive in a global economy by lowering labor costs. They began as joint ventures between a variety of Mexican and American companies. A few Mexican companies established operations, and several plants formed around Mexican labor cooperatives. The bulk of the *maquiladoras*, however, were subsidiaries of American companies.

The Mexican government developed its program to allow manufacturers to use low-cost labor to assemble final products for re-export. The procedure was simple: Mexican manufacturers would import components and raw resources from the United States duty free. They would transform these materials into finished products and ship them back to the United States. Often, the shipping consisted of short trips across the border, since many of the American companies built component manufacturing "twin" plants on their side of the dividing line between the two countries. The only duty paid was on the added value (principally the cost of labor) of the goods.

There were other benefits as well. For example, American companies could, through thirty-year trusts created by Mexican credit institutions, gain control over their factories and office facilities through leases, or, in some cases, outright ownership. Without the trusts, they could have no control, since Mexican law prohibited foreign companies from owning any land in areas within sixty miles of the American border or thirty miles of the coast.

As the program grew, the Mexican government relaxed some of its limitations on American companies. For example, it eased its ban on American companies selling any of the finished goods in Mexico. Once that happened, the companies were allowed to sell up to 20 percent of their production within Mexico. Such benefits, combined with cheap labor, were magnets for American companies looking to cut production costs. The government also removed its restriction prohibiting United States companies from buying components in Mexico. This worked to the Mexicans' advantage, as by 1987, American companies had purchased nearly $300 million worth of local parts. The revisions strengthened a growing program and led to even more jobs in the border cities on both sides.

El Paso, Texas, for example, benefited tremendously. As the number of "twin plants" grew, so did El Paso's dependence on *maquiladoras*. Within twenty years of the program's inception, about 20 percent of jobs in the city were connected to *maquiladoras*. Mexicans near the border often spent their wages in American cities. In 1982, Mexicans bought an estimated 80 percent of the goods sold in Laredo, Texas, and spent about $200 million in San Diego, California. These figures indicate that both countries profited extensively from the *maquiladoras* program, which was nothing more than an extension of similar programs between Mexico and the United States.

The phenomenon of Mexicans working for American companies was not new. During the nineteenth century, Mexican peasants moved into border communities seeking employment. Many entered the United States looking for jobs with the expanding railroads, and business operators in northern Mexico tried to enter American markets. Subsequently, cattle ranching grew and became more modernized in the American Southwest and northern Mexico.

World War II increased cooperation between the United States and Mexico. The two governments negotiated the bracero program in 1942. American President Franklin D. Roosevelt and his Mexican counterpart, Manuel Avila Camacho, agreed to allow Mexicans to serve as agricultural workers in the American West. The United States needed these braceros to replace farm workers serving in its armed forces. Later, the Mexican workers spread into the American railroad industry. By July, 1945, there were an estimated fifty-eight thousand Mexicans working in the agricultural industry and another sixty-two thousand working for the railroads. There were also thousands of illegal immigrants working in various American industries.

In addition to the agricultural and railroad workers, thousands of other Mexican laborers rushed north to work in new defense plants all along the border, from El Paso to San Diego. Consequently, Mexican border cities such as Tijuana and Ciudad Juarez started growing considerably. This presented problems for the Mexican government, in that it all but created two Mexicos. The area along the United States border became known as Mexamerica.

For a long while after the war, the Mexican government concentrated on building up Mexamerica. Specifically, the government increased its investment in agriculture throughout Mexico, 75 percent of the funds going for irrigation projects. Most of the money was invested in the northern part of the country. The project turned a desert wasteland into a fertile, productive agricultural region. Many large modern farms emerged, similar to those on the American side of the border. The Mexican farmers grew crops including garbanzos, winter vegetables (especially tomatoes), cotton, citrus crops, grapes, and strawberries, most of which were destined for markets in the United States. Railroads expanded to connect the Mexican and American farming regions. The effect was an imaginary, but all too real, dividing line between northern and southern Mexico.

In 1964, the American government ended the bracero program. President Lyndon B. Johnson, however, did not want to abandon Mexico. Both governments acted independently to offset the loss of jobs in Mexico. The United States government encouraged American businesses to invest in Mexico and re-export to the United States. It pointed out to American companies that under U.S. tariff codes, they could export items "offshore" for processing or assembly, paying duty only on the value added when they sent the goods back to the United States. This idea appealed to many American manufacturers.

A year later, the Mexican government modified its foreign investment laws to allow American firms to establish plants in Mexico. The primary goal was to provide jobs in northern Mexico for returning braceros and others. Just how well it succeeded is evidenced by the fact that in the early stages of the program, 89 percent of the *maquiladoras* were located along the Mexico-United States border. The government also hoped to create a foundation for an industrial base. It succeeded in both aims, even though success did not always come easily. In 1969, President Richard M. Nixon virtually closed the U.S.-Mexico border during a controversy over drugs. Then, in August, 1971, he unexpectedly imposed a 10 percent duty on imports that severely affected Mexico, which sold more than 70 percent of its exports to the United States. Mexican President Luís Echeverría, a staunch supporter of the *maquiladoras* program, continued to push for better relations between the two countries. His diplomacy prevailed, and the program grew.

Impact of Event

The *maquiladoras* program attracted the hoped-for investment and foreign exchange earnings. Significantly, the *maquiladoras* became Mexico's second-largest source of foreign earnings, behind oil and ahead of tourism and migrant workers. In the first twenty years of their existence, the number of *maquiladoras* grew to almost one thousand. By 1987, American firms had invested approximately $2 billion in their "offshore" operations in Mexico. Those figures satisfied the Mexican government's foreign investment goals. There was similar success in the employment picture.

The *maquiladoras* program created jobs. Ironically, at its outset, young, single women filled as many as 78 percent of them. These were women who, for the most part, were born and reared in the borderlands. Without the *maquiladoras*, they probably would have been unemployed. This created a disruption in Mexico's social structure. Traditionally, Mexican women stayed home, and men worked outside the home. Many of the men who might have worked in the *maquiladoras*, however, had remained in the United States as the bracero program wound down. Those who returned did not want to work for the low wages offered in the border plants. Women therefore became the primary source of workers for the *maquiladoras*. The government had to find a way to change this situation. Gradually, through a series of incentives, the percentage of male workers increased. By 1985, it was up to 23 percent. A year later, the figure reached 32.9 percent.

There was also a turnover problem in the border cities. As the popularity of the *maquiladoras* program soared, so did the number of people moving from rural areas of Mexico to find work in the border towns. Many of them worked only a short while before moving into the United States for better-paying jobs. The Mexican government sought ways to keep its citizens at home. American companies helped by investing in training and motivation programs and by assisting higher education in the Mexican border states. Within a few years, Chihuahua had five technological schools, the most in the nation; Tamaulipas had four. These moves helped curb the outflow of workers to the United States. The Mexican government had other problems to deal with, though, such as the environment.

In the mid-1970's, approximately 450 *maquiladoras* plants employed about 70,000 workers. By 1987, the *maquiladoras* employed 310,000 Mexicans, and experts began predicting that the number would reach 1 million by 1995 and that U.S. imports of their products would reach $25 billion annually. The successes of the program, however, came at a price.

The *maquiladoras* attracted opposition both in Mexico and in the United States. Organized labor in the United States complained that the program took jobs away from Americans. Some Mexicans criticized the program because it exploited the nation's workers and did little to improve technology, train workers for better jobs, or increase wages. It is important to note that 83.1 percent of the *maquiladoras* jobs were considered technical. Worse, the critics said, the *maquiladoras* were strangling the Mexican border cities.

The Mexican government argued that the program provided Mexicans with a chance to escape the poverty so prevalent in the interior of the country. The buildings in which they worked contained amenities such as air conditioning and lighting that improved employment conditions and made the employees' lives easier. Regardless of the arguments pro and con, people flocked to the border cities to seek work, inadvertently creating problems.

The large number of workers moving into Tijuana, Ciudad Juarez, and other large border cities overtaxed the communities' facilities. They put a strain on electrical power, telephone lines, public transportation, housing, and border bridges. Crime increased, and health problems and water restriction caused difficulties for administrators. There was also concern over the mental state of workers who put in long hours doing repetitive tasks for low wages. Finally, there was an increase in the pollution generated by the growing number of plants.

The Mexican government took steps to alleviate as many of the problems as it could. One step was to establish industrial parks to concentrate the businesses as much as possible and to meet their infrastructure needs. The parks were located near ports, with easy access to labor and raw materials. They provided administrative services for individual companies, including payroll administration and plant maintenance. The administrators even handled customs requirements and provided feasibility studies for American companies interested in establishing plants in Mexico.

Another step was to spread out the *maquiladoras*. The Mexican government encouraged companies to relocate their plants or to build new ones in locations away from the most common bases of operations. *Maquiladoras* tended to concentrate in three cities in the early stages of the program, Tijuana, Mexicali, and Ciudad Juarez. As late as 1983, more than half of the plants were still concentrated in these three cities.

The Mexican government continued to adapt the *maquiladoras* program, which admittedly got off to a slow start. In 1966, for example, the dutiable value of *maquiladoras* shipments to the United States was only $3 million. Ten years later, it rose to $536 million. By 1979, it exceeded the $1 billion barrier. Significantly, in 1976, *maquiladoras* exports equaled more than half of Mexican exports to the United States of manufactured goods, excluding chemicals and some food, oil, and fiber products. About two-thirds of the exports consisted of items such as electronic and television parts, telephone switchboards, bicycles, textiles, and transportation and communication equipment. Over the years, the variety of goods produced by the *maquiladoras* increased.

In retrospect, the program has been beneficial to both countries in most respects. The program suffered through normal growing pains in the 1960's and grew erratically. In 1975, in Mexico, for example, the *maquiladoras* industry employed 67,000 workers. The following year, the government devalued the peso, which stimulated the program. By 1981, six hundred plants in Mexico provided 132,000 jobs. The government again devalued the national currency. Subsequently, by mid-1987, more than a thousand plants employed more than 279,000 people and generated $1.5 billion in earnings. One estimate suggested that *maquiladoras* could employ as many as three million workers by the year 2000. Such numbers justified the two governments' vision in implementing the program in the 1960's.

The United States also benefited from the program. American companies were able to match labor-intensive, high-technology industries with reasonably priced skilled and unskilled laborers, maintaining their competitive edge in the process. The United States government did face problems from critics regarding the loss of jobs to Mexicans and the one-sided benefits the Mexicans were seen to be gaining from the lack of tariffs on re-exported products. Those were the same arguments the U.S. government faced in 1965, at the onset of the program.

Trial and error resulted in a much larger program than the Mexican government planned on at the program's inception. Even though the original design dictated that all products assembled were to be re-exported to the United States, the government expanded the program to include some European and Japanese companies. These companies also have established operations on the border.

Bibliography

McBride, Robert H., ed. *Mexico and the United States*. Englewood Cliffs, N.J.: Prentice-Hall, 1981. This collection of essays includes a particularly informative essay by Laura R. Randall, titled "Mexican Development and Its Effects upon United States Trade," that presents meaningful statistics regarding the *maquiladoras* program.

Pastor, Robert A., and Jorge G. Castaneda. *Limits to Friendship: The United States and Mexico*. New York: Alfred A. Knopf, 1988. A uniquely formatted book in which the two authors present contrasting views in a series of essays devoted to a variety of topics affecting U.S.-Mexican relationships.

Raat, W. Dirk. *Mexico and the United States: Ambivalent Vistas*. Athens: University of Georgia Press, 1992. An easy-to-read book focusing on the manner in which the United States and Mexico have affected each other's history, including the impact *maquiladoras* have had on the border regions.

Riding, Alan. *Distant Neighbors: A Portrait of the Mexicans*. New York: Alfred A. Knopf, 1985. A concise overview describing Mexico's political and governmental structures and economic and social conditions from 1970 to 1985.

Roett, Riordan, ed. *Mexico and the United States*. Boulder, Colo.: Westview Press, 1988. A readable collection of essays that focuses on the economic agenda and key bilateral issues affecting U.S.-Mexican relationships.

Schmitt, Karl M. *Mexico and the United States, 1821-1973: Conflict and Coexistence*. New York: John Wiley & Sons, 1974. A highly readable treatise on the often stormy relationship between the two countries, with an excellent summary of the inception of the *maquiladoras* program.

Vazquez, Josefina Zoraida, and Lorenzo Meyer. *The United States and Mexico*. Chicago: University of Chicago Press, 1985. A concise history of U.S.-Mexican relations presented in two parts. Vazquez writes the history between 1821 and 1898, and Meyer picks up the story there. Includes discussions of ties among the United States, Mexico, and other Central and South American countries.

Arthur G. Sharp

Cross-References

The United States Begins the Bracero Program (1942); The Agency for International Development Is Established (1961); The United States Suffers Its First Trade Deficit Since 1888 (1971); The Immigration Reform and Control Act Is Signed into Law (1986); Mexico Renegotiates Debt to U.S. Banks (1989); The North American Free Trade Agreement Goes into Effect (1994).

JOHNSON SIGNS THE MEDICARE AND MEDICAID AMENDMENTS

CATEGORY OF EVENT: Government and business
TIME: July 30, 1965
LOCALE: Independence, Missouri

The passage of the Medicare and Medicaid amendments to the Social Security Act further opened medical care to the elderly and the indigent

Principal personages:
CLINTON P. ANDERSON (1895-1975), the Democratic senator from New Mexico who cosponsored the Medicare bill
ROBERT KERR (1896-1963), the Democratic senator from Oklahoma who sponsored efforts to cover costs of medical care for the "medically needy"
CECIL R. KING (1898-1974), the Democratic congressman from California who cosponsored the Medicare Bill
WILBUR MILLS (1909-1992), the chairman of the House Ways and Means Committee

Summary of Event

The notion of governmental funding for the medical needs of United States citizens was not new in the 1960's. The road to Medicare and Medicaid began during the Depression, when President Franklin D. Roosevelt's New Deal Administration set up programs to help those unable to provide for themselves. The Great Society administration of Lyndon B. Johnson finally saw passage of governmental medical insurance for the elderly and poor.

Private medical insurance had been available to consumers since the 1930's, when the nonprofit Blue Cross and Blue Shield programs began. During World War II, the War Stabilization Board exempted "fringe benefits," including health care and insurance, from its ban on wage increases. This gave employers an opportunity to place more value on their employees' work without violating the ban on pay increases and resulted in a dramatic increase in the number of Americans covered by medical insurance. Coverage, however, was largely limited to those in an employer or union plan and left the retired elderly and unemployed without coverage.

Postwar medical advances made health care more expensive. Advances in technology made for medical miracles but came at a cost. In 1945, President Harry S Truman recognized the financial burden of medical care on the elderly and called for the American Medical Association (AMA) and other groups to look into funding alternatives.

The 1950's brought more attention to the medical needs of the poor and elderly, as health care costs more than doubled during the decade. A program sponsored by Senator Robert Kerr (D-Oklahoma) and Congressman Wilbur Mills (D-Arkansas) that set up federal-state sharing of medical expenses for the "medically needy" helped lessen the cost burden. The program set up a vendor payments system whereby state agencies made direct payments to physicians and other medical providers. Aime Forand (R-Rhode Island) proposed a plan in 1959 that would provide hospitalization coverage for Social Security recipients and be funded through an additional Social Security tax.

By 1960, more than 17.5 million Americans had reached the age of sixty-five, and the proportion of elderly Americans was growing. Improved technologies had resulted in better medical care, which in turn meant longer lives. Studies showed that 15 percent of the average elderly person's income was spent on medical care, and concerns arose that this income (in most cases fixed) could not keep in step with rising medical costs. That same year, Health, Education, and Welfare Secretary Arthur Flemming proposed plans for medical insurance, using the term "medicare" for the first time. A year later, congressmen Cecil King and Clinton Anderson introduced an official proposal for a medicare plan. This program was similar to the Forand legislation but added an annual deductible and coverage of retirees from the railroads.

Opposition to this proposal came from an unexpected source, the AMA. The organization lobbied heavily against governmental involvement in the medical industry, fearing a loss of control over patient care. Doctors' groups publicly stated their intention not to treat patients under the program and spread fears within the American public of socialized medicine. The

AMA's alternative solution was a program called "Eldercare," introduced in the House of Representatives by some Republican members. This state-administered private health insurance plan would be funded by a premium based on the purchaser's income, with federal subsidies for the needy. The plan soon died, after Republican Party leadership did not lend support.

Committee hearings reached gridlock on the issue. The King-Anderson proposal was tabled so that Congress could concentrate on tax and civil rights legislation during 1963 and 1964. The 1964 election reopened the door for health insurance. President Lyndon Johnson called for immediate attention to the issue of medical care for the elderly and the poor. In addition, the election put Democratic majorities into both the Senate and the House of Representatives. The AMA realized that some type of insurance plan was coming, and in 1965, James Appel, the president of the AMA, called for a compromise and encouraged doctors to participate in shaping new regulations governing health care.

The Eighty-ninth Congress passed the Medicare and Medicaid bills in 1965 as amendments to the Social Security Act. Signed by President Johnson at the Harry S Truman Library in Independence, Missouri, on July 30, 1965, the new programs went into effect on July 1, 1966. The first Medicare cards were given to former president Harry S Truman and his wife.

Administered by the Department of Health, Education, and Welfare (HEW) and the Social Security Administration, Title XVIII of the Social Security Act (Health Insurance for the Aged), or Medicare, was divided into two programs. Part A, hospitalization, was an automatic program for those aged sixty-five and over and eligible for Social Security or railroad retirement benefits. People under the age of sixty-five could receive Medicare if they had been receiving Social Security for more two years as a result of a disability. The program was funded through a percentage of the Social Security taxes paid by all workers. It provided for sixty days of hospital care with a $40 deductible to be paid by the patient and an additional thirty days of coverage at a cost to the patient of $10 per day. Other provisions included one hundred days of nursing home care for treatment of certain medical conditions, with a $5 charge for each day after the first twenty, and up to one hundred home health-care visits after a hospitalization. The program did not cover long-term nursing home costs. Payments to medical providers were based on "usual, customary, and reasonable" charges.

The second program, Part B, had been an add-on amendment to the King-Anderson proposal in 1965. It offered medical benefits based on a voluntary enrollment; more than 90 percent of those eligible enrolled the program. Enrollees in the program had a monthly premium deducted from their Social Security payments ($3 per month in early years) which was then matched by the federal government from the general treasury. Once an annual $50 deductible was met, the plan paid for 80 percent of physicians' fees and supplies and an additional one hundred home nursing visits beyond those covered under Part A.

A second amendment, Title XIX, Grants to States for Medical Assistance Programs, set up Medicaid. Medicaid was a cooperative program with responsibility shared by state and federal governments. Consolidating the Kerr-Mills programs to include the poor regardless of age, Medicaid increased annual federal grants to the states and called for additional medical care and screening for children in impoverished families. The program required states to cover all persons receiving cash assistance, although criteria for assistance and funding levels were to be determined on a state-by-state basis. Generally, those receiving Aid to Families with Dependent Children (AFDC) or public assistance were eligible. Medicaid also set limits on the amounts to be paid for various services. In 1966, California became the first state to establish a program, called Medi-Cal. New York followed in the same year. By 1968, forty-eight states had started Medicaid programs.

Impact of Event

Both critics and proponents of the medical care programs hoped for better health care for elderly and poor Americans as a result of the passage of Medicare and Medicaid. Whether that goal was achieved depends on one's perspective. The almost 19.5 million elderly people who enrolled in the program during 1968 alone received more care, but that care came at an additional cost. Costs for prescription drugs and medical appliances such as walkers and braces, in addition to deductibles, kept medical costs at 15 percent or more of an elderly person's income. Medicaid recipients, especially children, received basic health care, but millions of small children still went without immunizations. Despite these problems, Medicare and Medicaid helped to encourage patients to play more active roles in their own health care. Patients began to question doctors about their options concerning treatment and providers. Patients and their families became a powerful consumer base as the medical industry became more of a business, with hospitals advertising to compete for patients in the early 1980's.

The Medicare and Medicaid programs underwent several revisions and amendments. Early changes brought about an extension in hospitalization from 90 to 120 days (1967) and gave certain patients with chronic kidney disease Medicare coverage (1972). Early Medicaid changes involved restrictions on funding and placed payments on a scale based on the Consumer Price Index (1970).

As costs increased, the federal government sought to control payments. In 1972, limits were placed on "reasonable costs," but it was not until the 1980's that major changes were made in the Medicare program. Beginning in 1983, Congress implemented the concept of Diagnosis Related Groups. This revision sought to level discrepancies between geographical areas by setting flat-fee payments for certain medical conditions instead of paying a percentage of fees and costs. Six years later, in 1989, Congress further limited funds paid by Medicare when it decreased payments to specialists by 11 percent while increasing payments to primary care physicians by 20 percent, effective in 1992. In addition, a Resource-Based Relative Value Scale was implemented in an attempt to balance unequal charges. The same year, a cap was placed on Medicare patient charges. For 1992, doctors could charge 20 percent more than Medicare covered; for 1993, the figure was 15 percent.

Despite numerous revisions and amendments, the Medicare and Medicaid programs retained several loopholes and gaps that raised costs either to the government or to consumers. Medicare did not cover long-term nursing home care or prescription drugs unless they were given in a hospital. The Medicaid program covered long-term care but only once a patient was eligible for the program. This meant that elderly persons virtually were forced to deplete their life savings to qualify for Medicaid-covered nursing home care. Several books and lecture series appeared to help elderly persons and their families learn to "hide" assets in order to keep them from going toward medical costs. Another alternative was the growing popularity of home health agencies, which Medicare did cover. These agencies provided home nurse visits for those still able to care for themselves at a basic level.

To help combat the shortcomings of Medicare, private insurance companies developed supplemental policies. These "Medigap" plans helped with costs of prescription drugs as well as deductibles and charges above what was covered by Medicare. For example, a doctor visit might cost $40, even though Medicare set the prevailing charge for the area at $35. Once the deductible was met, Medicare would then pay 80 percent of the prevailing charge, or $28. If the doctor did not accept assignment (Medicare payment accepted as payment in full), the patient would then be responsible for the remaining $12. Supplemental policies often paid 80 percent of the remaining balance.

Congressional investigations into Medicare problems resulted in the Medicare Catastrophic Coverage Act of 1988, which attempted to close the gap between actual and covered costs through expanding benefits. The program increased coverage of hospital benefits, added coverage for prescription drugs, and put a limit on out-of-pocket expenses. The plan was designed to be financed by an increased premium and a surtax on the incomes of wealthier Social Security recipients. Complaints flooded into Washington that the elderly, whom the act meant to help, were actually hurt by increased costs. Public opposition became so strong that the act was repealed in 1989.

Medicaid was not without its own problems. To be eligible, a person had to be receiving cash assistance. In most states, these programs left out men and women without children. Most recipients of aid under Medicaid were children, and a high proportion of expenditures went for nursing home care for the elderly. Medicaid also placed a tremendous burden on states' budgets, with a 583 percent increase in spending in the first ten years of the program.

The state programs sought to decrease this burden through spending limits on a variety of medical areas, including drugs and physicians' fees. New payment limits often fell so far below the prevailing charges in an area that some doctors refused to participate in the program, resulting in a reduction of primary care physicians. Those who did participate under the Medicaid and Medicare programs often found themselves forced to increase charges to other patients to make up for the low payments from those covered by Medicare and Medicaid, creating a cycle of increased costs.

The rising costs of medical care fueled a constant debate over funding. States found themselves overburdened by the costs of Medicaid programs, and both Medicaid and Medicare placed ever-increasing strains on federal funds. Five years into the programs, expenditures on Medicare had increased by 300 percent and those on Medicaid by 400 percent. By 1975, annual U.S. medical costs had reached $133 billion; by 1984, a billion dollars a day were spent on health care. By 1993, medical care costs were more than $700 billion a year and represented more than 12 percent of federal spending.

Administrative costs were often blamed for the rising costs, but a study conducted during the 1980's estimated administrative costs for Medicare and Medicaid at 3 to 5 percent of total costs, while private insurance plans had administrative costs ranging from 14 to 24 percent of the total bill. One administrative area that did promote problems was billing, in particular overcharging by hospitals and doctors. Numerous doctors and hospitals faced fraud charges for padding the bills of patients in order to make up the difference between program payments and actual costs or to make up for those patients who could not pay.

The spread of acquired immune deficiency syndrome (AIDS) also resulted in funding problems, as the high costs of treating patients fell heavily on the Medicaid program. How these already overburdened programs could face the growing medical epidemic was unclear. Alternative ways of funding Medicaid were needed to help keep the program alive.

Funding the Medicare and Medicaid programs had been a struggle since their passage. The initial plans for funding proved unable to keep up with growing costs. More Americans were reaching the eligibility age for Medicare, and economic problems resulted in dramatic increases in the number of people receiving state assistance and Medicaid. Even so, many Americans were left with no medical coverage. The programs had opened medical coverage to more Americans and transformed the medical profession, but to remain effective they needed to keep pace with rising medical costs by finding new sources of funding.

Bibliography

Budish, Armond D. *Avoiding the Medicaid Trap: How to Beat the Catastrophic Costs of Nursing Home Care*. Rev. ed. New York: Henry Holt, 1989. Suggests numerous solutions to the problem of protecting the assets and life savings of elderly persons. Contains charts covering the guidelines and provisions for each state.

Enthoven, Alain C. *Health Plan: The Only Practical Solution to the Soaring Cost of Medical Care*. Reading, Mass.: Addison-Wesley, 1980. Discusses the medical coverage options available to the American public, including private and publicly funded plans. Focuses on costs to the programs and consumers. Contains an author-developed Consumer Choice Health Plan to give consumers more control over health coverage.

Feingold, Eugene, ed. *Medicare: Policy and Politics*. San Francisco: Chandler, 1966. A detailed look at the history and passage of Medicare. Covers changes made as a result of congressional debates and reprints several testimonies and excerpts from speeches by members of Congress and the AMA.

Grannemann, Thomas W., and Mark V. Pauly. *Controlling Medicaid Costs: Federalism, Competition, and Choice*. Washington, D.C.: American Enterprise Institute for Public Policy Research, 1983. Discusses means to control the growing costs and inadequacies of the Medicaid programs. Outlines suggestions to provide more medical care at lower cost.

Witkin, Erwin. *The Impact of Medicare*. Springfield, Ill.: Charles C Thomas, 1971. Discusses the relationships between the Medicare program and hospitals, doctors, consumers, and insurance companies. Provides an early look at the program while recognizing its pitfalls. Appendices include the text of the law and a 1969 handbook.

Jennifer Davis

Cross-References

The Social Security Act Provides Benefits for Workers (1935); The First Homeowner's Insurance Policies Are Offered (1950); Health Consciousness Creates Huge New Markets (1970's); Nixon Signs the Occupational Safety and Health Act (1970); The Employee Retirement Income Security Act of 1974 Is Passed (1974).

CONGRESS LIMITS THE USE OF BILLBOARDS

CATEGORY OF EVENT: Advertising
TIME: August, 1965
LOCALE: Washington, D.C.

The 1965 Highway Beautification Act banned billboards within 660 feet of interstate or primary highways except in industrial or commercial areas

Principal personages:
LYNDON B. JOHNSON (1908-1973), the president of the United States, 1963-1969
LADY BIRD JOHNSON (1912-   ), the first lady of the United States, 1963-1969
PHILLIP TOCKER (1910-   ), the chairman of the Outdoor Advertising Association of America when the law was passed
LAURANCE SPELMAN ROCKEFELLER (1910-   ), an assistant to Lady Bird Johnson and a supporter of natural beauty
MRS. CYRIL FOX, the chair of the Pennsylvania Roadside Council
JOHN THOMAS CONNOR (1914-   ), the secretary of commerce

Summary of Event

In August of 1965, the Highway Beautification Act was passed into law, largely as a result of the persistence of President Lyndon B. Johnson, Lady Bird Johnson, and Laurance Spelman Rockefeller. Phillip Tocker, chairman of the Outdoor Advertising Association of America (OAAA), supported the bill as long as commercial and industrial zones were exempt and if people who were no longer allowed to rent land for billboards were compensated. The act stated that all signs within 660 feet of interstate and primary highways were banned, except for official direction signs and on-premise advertising. Commercial and industrial areas were exempt. States that did not enforce removal of all offending signs by 1970 could lose up to 20 percent of their federal highway funds.

Before the Highway Beautification Act of 1965 was passed, there was only one federal law specifically concerning billboards. It was passed in 1958 and stated that a bonus would be given to any state that controlled billboards within 660 feet of the federal interstate highway system. Only seven states qualified for bonuses: Kentucky, New York, Maine, New Hampshire, Ohio, Wisconsin, and Virginia.

The billboard industry had grown so rapidly that in most cities there were more billboards than it was possible for a driver, or perhaps even a passenger, to read. The movement against billboards started in citizens' roadside councils and garden clubs throughout the United States. These groups disliked billboards for two reasons. First, they thought billboards were ugly and blocked out landscape. Second, there were numerous reports linking increased numbers of accidents to prevalence of billboards. Some studies showed that there were three times as many accidents in areas with billboards as compared to similar areas without billboards. Billboard opponents reasoned that drivers were distracted by the advertisements. A growing interest in removing billboards initiated the Highway Beautification Act.

In May of 1965, President Johnson held a conference at the White House to discuss the bill. Mrs. Cyril Fox, chair of the Pennsylvania Roadside Council and a representative of various roadside councils and garden clubs, attended this meeting. The bill that she and most beautification activists wanted to pass prohibited billboards within one thousand feet of interstate and primary highways, with no exempt areas. Her version of the bill also addressed other areas, including junkyards, landscaped areas, and scenic roads. New junkyards would be prohibited within one thousand feet of interstate and primary highways, and existing junkyards would either be removed or be screened by a fence of shrubbery within five years. States were to use 3 percent of their federal highway aid for landscaping and beautifying roadsides. States also would have to use one-third of their federal highway aid for secondary roads and access roads to recreational and scenic areas.

Phillip Tocker was invited to this May conference. His suggestions outraged the beautification activists. He would support the bill only if the distance restriction were changed to 660 feet, commercial and industrial areas were exempt, and the federal government would compensate for losses. Mrs. Cyril Fox, the roadside councils, and the garden clubs were displeased not only with Tocker but also with Laurance Rockefeller and his staff. The roadside councils and the garden clubs believed that since they had been fighting for years against billboards, they should have a more powerful position, the one that Rockefeller and his staff were fulfilling. At the end of the conference, Tocker's version of the bill was read to President Johnson. Fox, the roadside councils, and the garden clubs were disillusioned. After that conference, they no longer supported the bill, which they thought did not solve the problem. This lack of support made it difficult to pass the bill.

President Johnson's advisers were convinced that the bill had no chance of passing unless it exempted commercial and industrial areas, largely because of the influence of the OAAA. The OAAA was a strong organization with six hundred companies throughout the nation as members. They accounted for nearly 90 percent of all standardized outdoor advertising.

Even after the compromises made at the White House conference in May the bill was held up in Congress. Some supporters thought that it would be best to wait until 1966 and try to get a stronger bill passed. In August, President Johnson sent out an urgent message that he wanted the bill passed that year.

The bill that eventually passed had even more compromises than the one read to President Johnson in May. The Treasury Department was to compensate billboard owners and farmers who had rented out their land for billboards if their business was affected by the new law. The federal government would pay three-fourths the cost of the bill, with states paying the remaining one-fourth. Junkyards were exempt from screening or removal in commercial and industrial areas. The bill also authorized the use of federal funds for landscaping roadsides and for building scenic and recreational areas. These funds could be used for landscaping in right-of-way areas, work that states were supposed to be doing. The areas of commercial and industrial exemptions would be determined by the states, with the approval of the secretary of commerce. Secretary of Commerce John Connor assured Congress that a state's decision would rarely be overturned.

Although the bill that was passed was not nearly as strong as the original proposal, its passage proved difficult. Even though 83 percent of existing billboards were located in exempt areas and more could be added in those areas, the loss of even 15 percent of a $200 million a year industry caused opposition to the bill.

Impact of Event

The OAAA thought that it had preserved the heart of its business through the compromises in the bill. Only 15 percent of its business would be cut, and the cuts would not take their full effect for five years. Losses would be compensated by the government. In addition, advertisers could put up larger signs beyond the restricted 660 feet, thus reaching essentially the same audience, and they could put up more signs on exempt roads.

Even with these opportunities, billboard use steadily declined after 1965. There are several reasons for the decline in billboard advertising. First, billboard advertising was not as effective as most other advertising media, particularly television advertising. Second, many cities were inundated with billboards. Many people became immune to them and stopped reading them. Some cities also enforced sign laws that were more strict than the federal law. Finally, beautification activists encouraged boycotts on products and services advertised on billboards. This did not make an enormous difference, but it had some effect.

The lure of billboard advertising was that the advertiser paid one fee and then had an advertisement in place for an extended period of time, usually months. With most other advertising media, the advertising lasted for only a short time. Many advertisers discovered, however, other media produced more sales per dollar spent on advertising. Billboards did not have much text, since drivers and passengers were not able to read much in the limited time that a billboard was in view. This was a major reason for the lack of success from billboard advertising. All other advertising media, except newspaper advertisements, reported increases in 1966 and continued expansion through the 1970's.

Before 1965, there were many types of users of billboard advertising. Products advertised included cigarettes, cars, hotels and motels, candy, soda, alcohol, restaurants, airlines, dance clubs, drug stores, laundry and dishwashing detergents, toothpaste, and events. Both local and national advertisers used the medium, as a single billboard could target a specific geographical market. Advertisers worked on the premise that because so many people passed by their advertisements, they must be effective in creating sales. Many companies gradually learned that this was not true. The fact that someone drove past a ten-foot bottle of Palmolive dish detergent every day did not necessarily make that person more likely to switch to that brand. Audiences became immune to ads, ignoring them as part of the background, and the limited advertising features possible on billboards made them ineffective for many products.

Certain types of products lent themselves better to billboard advertising than did others. For example, products or services aimed at travelers were prime candidates for successful billboard advertising. Many automobile travelers left aspects of their trips unplanned and thus were susceptible to suggestions offered by billboards. Billboard advertising was particularly effective for restaurants (especially fast food), hotels and motels, gas stations, and, to a lesser degree, entertainment services.

Ads for the products were generally effective since potential customers had a need, could interpret the offer quickly, and knew where to receive the offer. Since the advertisements supplied the required information, they were successful. Some other types of companies also did well. For example, advertisements for specific events did well. Without a billboard, many people would not have been able to anticipate an event, and visitors would not know about it.

Many companies, especially ones that sold supermarket products, discovered that billboard advertising was not very effective. There were many reasons that billboards were not effective for these types of products. Most viewers of billboards did not have an urgent need for toothpaste, for example, and billboards could not give any reasons to choose one brand over another.

Procter and Gamble, a large producer of household products, was the number one advertiser on television in 1966. Television advertising was more expensive than billboards, but the company created more sales through television than through billboards. When Procter and Gamble compared sales produced in relation to cost, television advertising was less expensive.

As another example, after being required to dismantle a Camel cigarette billboard in Times Square, the Reynolds Tobacco Company focused more of its advertising efforts on television. After 1970, however, when cigarette commercials were banned from radio and television, its efforts focused on billboards again.

Local laws against sign use also hurt the billboard industry. In the 1970's, Denver passed laws further restricting billboards and signs. The chief supporter of these tougher laws was Gerald Dixon, head of television at Columbia Broadcasting System (CBS). His advocacy hinted that declines in billboard use caused increases in television advertising.

The Highway Beautification Act did not have a major direct effect on the decline of billboards. The first removal of a billboard as a result of the law did not occur until April 27, 1971. The main reason that offending billboards were not removed sooner was that the law stated that the owner of the billboard must be compensated. Because the federal government did not authorize a significant amount of funds until 1970, the states could not afford to compensate billboard owners. Many offending billboards existed long after the law passed. Some states even inquired if they could remove offending billboards and then compensate owners later, when federal funds came through. The answer was no, since the law clearly stated that there must be compensation for every billboard removed.

The Highway Beautification Act of 1965 was only one of several reasons for the decline in billboard usage. Although billboards did not decline as much as roadside council and garden club members would have liked, the billboard industry certainly declined, while television and radio advertising continually increased. Advertisers found that broadcast media often proved to be worth their higher cost per message.

Bibliography

"Beauty and the Billboards." *The New Republic* 154 (April 23, 1966): 8-9. Discusses the Outdoor Advertising Association of America and use of billboards by its members. Describes details of the law and funding for removal of billboards.

Drew, Elizabeth Brenner. "Lady Bird's Beauty Bill." *The Atlantic Monthly* 216 (December, 1965): 68-72. Gives the details of the White House conference on the bill. Discusses the compromises made to get the bill passed and describes advertisers' options under the bill.

Gotfryd, Bernard. "Signs of the Times." *Newsweek* 65 (March 8, 1965): 89-90. Describes the law concerning billboards before the Highway Beautification Act was passed. Discusses the billboard industry in general.

Gould, Lewis. *Lady Bird Johnson and the Environment*. Lawrence: University Press of Kansas, 1988. This book accurately and in minute detail describes the Highway Beautification Act of 1965 and other programs of beautification on which Lady Bird Johnson worked. It also stresses the importance and rising power of first ladies.

Pell, Robert. "Escalating Ugliness." *America* 122 (June 12, 1965): 848-849. Discusses President Johnson's initial desire for the beautification act and the White House conference on the bill.

"The Sign Busters." *Newsweek* 77 (June 7, 1971): 116-117. Discusses how the law has not had a large effect overall but how more stringent laws in some cities have been more effective in controlling billboard usage.

Dan Kennedy

Cross-References

Advertisers Adopt a Truth in Advertising Code (1913); The Federal Trade Commission Is Organized (1914); The U.S. Government Bans Cigarette Ads on Broadcast Media (1970).

CONGRESS PASSES THE MOTOR VEHICLE AIR POLLUTION CONTROL ACT

CATEGORIES OF EVENT: Transportation; government and business
TIME: October 20, 1965
LOCALE: Washington, D.C.

The Motor Vehicle Air Pollution Control Act authorized federal government standards to control emissions from cars, beginning with the 1968 model year

Principal personages:
A. J. HAAGEN-SMIT (1900-1977), a professor of biochemistry and chief consultant on smog to the Los Angeles County Air Pollution Board in the 1950's and 1960's
KENNETH HAHN (1920-1997), a Southern California politician
EDMUND MUSKIE (1914-1996), a U.S. senator from Maine, 1959-1980; chairman of the Senate Subcommittee on Air and Water Pollution in the late 1960's
RALPH NADER (1934-   ), a leading consumer and environmental activist

Summary of Event

Air pollution existed as a byproduct of industrialization as early as the nineteenth century, in London. The term "smog" was coined to describe the combination of coal smoke and fog that periodically blanketed London. Somewhat inaccurately, the term began to be used in the United States in the late 1940's and early 1950's to describe a new kind of air pollution in the Los Angeles basin, a brownish, hazy, and eye-irritating atmospheric phenomenon resulting in large part from photochemical reactions to vehicular emissions. For a long time, smog was considered to be a peculiarity

465

of Southern California, with its legendary dependence on the private automobile and a topography and weather patterns conducive to atmospheric
pollution.

A. J. Haagen-Smit, a professor of biochemistry at the California Institute
of Technology, was a member of the scientific committee of the Los
Angeles Chamber of Commerce. Increasing numbers of complaints came
to the chamber from local farmers who protested the increasing and unusual
damage to their crops. His initial findings indicated that the area's smog was
not caused by the kinds of gasses emitted by industrial operations. His
continued investigations in the early 1950's began to point to motor vehicles
as the primary source of Los Angeles' pollution. He found that automobiles
emit pollutants in the following three ways: exhaust through the tailpipe
includes carbon monoxide, nitrogen oxides, particulates, and hydrocarbons; evaporation from both the carburetor and gas tank contributes hydrocarbons; and "blowby" of hydrocarbons and particulates from the pistons
to the crankcase puts these pollutants into the air.

As air quality continued to worsen, the Southern California region set up
the Air Pollution Control District, which had the power to declare "smog
alerts" that were supposed to immediately result in decreased burning,
restrictions in emissions from factory or refinery smokestacks, and decreased physical activity on the part of schoolchildren. All "nonessential"
motor vehicle traffic was supposed to cease, but this regulation proved
almost impossible to enforce on the increasingly clogged Los Angeles
freeways.

In correspondence with the chairman of the Los Angeles County Board of
Supervisors as late as 1953, key automobile industry spokespersons seemed
unwilling to concede the close connection between motor vehicle emissions
and photochemical air pollution. It became increasingly difficult, however, to
refute the growing evidence of this connection. The automobile companies
began to concede that motor vehicles were a major factor in producing smog
in Los Angeles but questioned whether that type of pollution could exist
elsewhere in the country. Research in various locations, funded by the federal
government beginning in 1955, provided good evidence that photochemical air
pollution was not confined to Los Angeles. The surgeon general was directed
to conduct studies of the physical damage caused by smog, but no other action
occurred immediately at the federal level.

Meanwhile, the problem became a major public policy issue in California. Not satisfied with the slow response from Washington, the increasingly
powerful Southern California Air Pollution Control District pushed the
California legislature to create a Motor Vehicle Pollution Control Board in
1960. It had the power to certify smog control technology and require its

installation in new vehicles. The major automobile manufacturers by then had developed a positive crankcase ventilation device, which was to recycle blowby air back into the cylinder. California required this device to be installed in cars beginning in the 1961 model year. Increasing evidence from studies undertaken in California indicated that a significant reduction of air pollution, particularly hydrocarbon emissions, would depend on widespread adoption and usage of exhaust emission devices. Under continuing pressure from California, the largest single-state market for new cars, manufacturers promised to have exhaust devices ready by the 1967 model year.

Recognition of air pollution caused by automobiles spread nationwide. In 1962, Congress approved the first of a series of laws that, over the next eight years, moved the federal government into a leadership position in antipollution efforts. This legislation directed the Department of Health, Education, and Welfare (HEW) to develop air quality criteria and to begin planning for investigative and abatement functions like those already in effect for water pollution. Guidelines developed by HEW remained advisory; state and local governments could choose whether to follow them. The 1962 act also directed HEW to encourage the automobile industry to develop devices to help control emissions of pollutants.

HEW's 1964 report *Steps Toward Clean Air* suggested that the growing air pollution problem would not be solved until there were national standards for vehicular emissions. This report attracted the attention of politicians such as Senator Abraham Ribicoff of Connecticut and Senator Edmund Muskie of Maine, who was named chairman of the new Senate Subcommittee on Air and Water Pollution. Appropriately, that subcommittee's first public hearing was held in Los Angeles, in January of 1964. Governor Edmund G. "Pat" Brown of California testified that the continued enormous growth in the numbers of motor vehicles on his state's roads meant that the problem could not be brought under control until the federal government used the interstate commerce clause to regulate emissions in newly manufactured cars. On the basis of these hearings, the subcommittee's report concluded that automobile exhaust was "the most important and critical source of air pollution and it is, beyond question, increasing in seriousness."

Also in 1964, HEW issued a report documenting that automotive emissions posed a serious threat to physical health. Although automobile manufacturers claimed that they were working as fast as possible to upgrade abatement technology, they recognized the political reality that federal legislation was inevitable. They offered to drop their strong opposition to mandated exhaust standards in return for a two-year lead time and uniform nationwide (rather than diverse state) standards for exhaust manifold devices.

The result of this heightened public awareness and political pressure was the passage on October 20, 1965, of the federal Motor Vehicle Air Pollution Control Act. Section 202 required the secretary of HEW to set emission standards, which would require that new vehicles achieve prescribed performance standards. Manufacturers could choose the most attractive technical means of reaching the standards, which were set by HEW in 1966 to be applicable nationwide in the 1968 model year. These regulations dealt primarily with carbon monoxide and hydrocarbons, under standards similar to the ones earlier mandated by California. Section 203 specified the ways in which manufacturers could apply for a certificate of compliance based on their prototype (rather than production line) vehicles.

Impact of Event

The automobile industry was concerned about this vast new area of government regulation. Business critics such as Ralph Nader, however, complained that the legislation was too loose and would lead to lax enforcement of standards. As a result of these criticisms, Congress in 1967 passed even tougher federal standards under the Air Quality Act. This piece of legislation mandated that federal emission standards for new vehicles were binding in all states except California. This cleared up a controversy as to whether the 1965 legislation permitted more stringent standards for individual states. California was now explicitly permitted to adopt, under certain circumstances, more stringent standards to meet its special needs.

After 1967, vehicular pollution control policy, even in California, became more influenced by the federal government. This was especially true after the Clear Air Act Amendments of 1970 set up uniform air quality standards for the nation and also mandated controls to eliminate gasoline evaporation. This piece of legislation would soon be enforced by the powerful new Environmental Protection Agency (EPA), which set standards directed at controlling nitrogen oxides, carbon monoxide, lead, and particulate matter as well as hydrocarbons. This policy ultimately impelled the use of such control devices as catalytic converters and electronic carburetors on vehicles to control all these pollutants.

Such new governmental controls affected other major industries as well. As one example, the Clean Air Act caused the EPA to encourage catalytic converter technology to control motor vehicle exhaust emissions. These converters required usage of unleaded gasoline, which requires much more intensive processing by refiners than does leaded gasoline.

Although the Clear Air Act of 1970 had originally "required" America's air to be clean by 1975, this soon proved impossible. The act was amended several times in later years. In addition, as automobile manufacturers pointed out, there never was an explicit and scientifically agreed upon standard as to what constitutes "clean air." Nevertheless, much evidence indicates that progress was made in cleaning up the nation's air in the 1970's and 1980's. In spite of millions of additional residents and cars in the Los Angeles basin, for example, there were fewer "smog alerts" in the early 1990's than in the 1970's.

The 1977 amendments to the Clean Air Act made it more difficult to achieve new fuel conservation standards, as cleaner technology was not as fuel efficient. The largest American automobile producer, General Motors, estimated in a public interest report issued in the late 1970's that the new emissions control equipment would add more than $200 to the cost of each vehicle. Furthermore, at the same time new vehicular safety features such as mandatory seatbelts added hundreds of dollars more to the price tag. Because of these high costs and, particularly in the early years, negative effects on automobile performance, emissions regulation was always controversial with the public as well as with manufacturers.

In retrospect, questions should be raised about the price paid for emissions reduction on a set of rather stringent deadlines. As a study released by the Brookings Institution in 1986 concluded, Congress acted precipitately in constructing a program with tight deadlines and extremely ambitious goals. Congress had little information or theory on the effects of automobile pollution on human health. Blaming a combination of stringent standards and tight deadlines for jerry-built technologies, especially for the 1974 model year, the report cited higher costs and automobiles that suffered from less reliability and fuel efficiency as results of regulation.

These negative effects of greater government controls occurred at a time of increasing competition from foreign automobile producers. Because of antitrust laws, American manufacturers were not allowed to cooperate in developing new technology for emissions control. In contrast, Japanese manufacturers were able to share research and development costs for an excellent emission control system, saving money for each company and making each more competitive in the American market.

The enactment of federal regulations on automobile emissions during the 1960's and 1970's was a manifestation of the government's perceived mandate to regulate that followed the Great Society era. Before 1965, the American automobile industry was subject to relatively little regulation of either its product or its manufacturing processes. Safety regulations, energy efficiency standards, and pollution regulations markedly changed this within a few years following 1965.

Bibliography

Crandall, Robert W., Howard K. Gruenspecht, Theodore E. Keeler, and Lester B. Lave. *Regulating the Automobile*. Washington, D.C.: Brookings Institution, 1986. This study provides analysis of the economic impact of three major types of federal regulation of the automobile. In particular, it points out the conflicting goals of each of the three programs (fuel economy, safety, and emission standards), which operated independently of one another.

Kennedy, Harold W., and Martin E. Weekes. "Control of Automobile Emissions: California Experience and the Federal Legislation." *Law and Contemporary Problems* 33 (Spring, 1968): 297-314. Details the growth of political pressure in the 1950's from Southern California constituents on Congress to adopt federal legislation regarding motor vehicle pollution control.

Lees, Lester. *Smog: A Report to the People*. Pasadena: California Institute of Technology, 1972. A landmark multidisciplinary study concerning air pollution in Southern California. Provides outstanding historical data on growth of the smog problem and development of alternative strategies to comply with the Clean Air Act in Southern California.

Rae, John B. *The American Automobile Industry*. Boston: Twayne, 1984. An outstanding interpretive history. Chapter 11, "The Government and the Automobile Industry," illuminates the critical combination of air pollution, automobile safety, and fuel efficiency regulation and how these had major effects on the financial and operating aspects of the automobile business.

White, Lawrence J. *The Automobile Industry Since 1945*. Cambridge, Mass.: Harvard University Press, 1971. A scholarly study focusing on the economic aspects of the industry and how these were affected by both antipollution and safety legislation in the 1960's. Discusses possible future technological breakthroughs but expresses doubt (which the passage of time has supported) that automobiles powered by the internal combustion engine will soon have major competition for transportation of individuals.

Anthony Branch

Cross-References

Nader's *Unsafe at Any Speed* Launches a Consumer Movement (1965); Congress Passes the Motor Vehicle Air Pollution Control Act (1965); The Banning of DDT Signals New Environmental Awareness (1969); The Environmental Protection Agency Is Created (1970); The United States Plans to Cut Dependence on Foreign Oil (1974); Bush Signs the Clean Air Act of 1990 (1990).

NADER'S *UNSAFE AT ANY SPEED* LAUNCHES A CONSUMER MOVEMENT

CATEGORY OF EVENT: Consumer affairs
TIME: November 29, 1965
LOCALE: New York, New York

Ralph Nader's publication Unsafe at Any Speed *led to the passage of federal automotive safety regulations and began the U.S. consumer rights movement*

Principal personages:
RALPH NADER (1934-   ), an attorney and consumer advocate, author
   of *Unsafe at Any Speed*
LYNDON B. JOHNSON (1908-1973), the U.S. president who signed the
   1966 National Traffic and Motor Vehicle Safety and Highway Safety
   acts
WILLIAM HADDON, JR. (1926-1985), a physician and first administrator
   of the National Traffic Safety Agency
WARREN GRANT MAGNUSON (1905-1989), the Senate Commerce Committee chairman who conducted congressional automobile safety
   hearings

Summary of Event

Ralph Nader's 1965 publication *Unsafe at Any Speed: The Designed-in Dangers of the American Automobile* posited a connection between the number of automobiles manufactured with mechanical or design defects between the years 1955 and 1965 and an increased number of vehicular accidents. This publication led to a greater public awareness of deficiencies in the manufacturing safety and design regulations of the United States automotive industry. The information provided by Nader was supplemented by testimony given during congressional automobile safety hearings which were promoted by Nader's revelations. Data gathering and debate led to drafting of the National Traffic and Motor Vehicle Safety Act and the Highway Safety Act, signed into law by President Lyndon B. Johnson in 1966. These acts federally regulated the design of motor vehicles and marked the beginning of the United States consumer movement.

Nader's publication was based upon his research on the manufacturing of automobiles and how U.S. automakers resisted numerous governmental attempts to require improved safety standards. A 1959 Department of Commerce report predicted that by 1975 automobile accidents would cause fifty-one thousand deaths annually. Nader found that this automobile fatality number would be reached by 1965, with the increase in fatalities resulting from several defects that existed in the mechanical designs of automobiles. In response to these predictions, automobile manufacturers attributed the increased number of automobile deaths to driver negligence rather than mechanical failure.

The 1960-1963 Chevrolet Corvair models manufactured by General Motors (GM) received significant attention from Nader. The car's rear engine design resulted in several wheel suspension problems that caused many drivers to lose control of their automobiles. More than one hundred lawsuits against GM were initiated, prompting GM to redesign its 1964 and 1965 Corvair models to eliminate this defect.

A 1965 study conducted by Consumers Union, the organization that tests products for the publication *Consumer Reports*, found that since 1955, when new automobile sales in the United States totaled approximately eight million, there had been a decrease in the quality standards of automobiles manufactured. Of the thirty-two automobiles randomly tested by Consumers Union, all were found to have defects within the first five thousand miles of test driving. In another study, in 1963, the American Optometric Foundation tested fifty-six automobiles and found that not one could provide a suitable visual environment for daytime driving. In 1965, a public television program entitled *Death on the Highway* connected specific design hazards with several brand-named automobiles, bringing national attention to the growing concern with automobile safety.

Even with increased public awareness, the U.S. automobile manufacturers would not improve their safety standards. For example, in 1959, the New York State Joint Legislative Committee on Motor Vehicle and Traffic Safety had recommended that seat belts be sold as standard factory-installed equipment. In 1960, the automobile manufacturers' lobbyists used their influence to defeat a bill that required seat belts on all new automobiles sold in New York. New York, like many other states, was unable to require rigid automobile safety standards because of the lobbying power of the automobile manufacturers.

Undaunted by the automotive industry's resistance to more stringent safety standards for the manufacturing of automobiles, Nader continued his consumer movement. In his testimony before Senator Warren Grant Magnuson's automobile safety committee, Nader recommended that all automobiles should have seat belts, collapsible steering wheels, and passive passenger restraints. He also urged that automobile windows should be made of tempered glass, as in Europe, rather than the laminated glass in use in the United States. Laminated glass consists of a plastic glass core with glass bonded to it, while tempered glass is solid glass treated by heat. In an accident, laminated glass will not prevent a passenger from being ejected through the window and then being pulled back, with extensive facial lacerations a likely result. The stronger tempered glass would reduce the chances of a passenger being thrown through a window.

Through his magazine articles, the book *Unsafe at Any Speed*, and testimony before Congress, Nader argued that the automobile industry had permitted stylistic concerns to take precedence over safe design and proper construction. He further believed that not only automakers were blameworthy; the general state of American industry favored profit over improved technology, even at the expense of the consumer. Nader contended that food and drug violations, defective automobiles, professional malpractice incidents, and other business crimes were more detrimental to the safety and health of society than were violent street crimes. Nader's publications and publicized testimony before Congress began a consumer movement and eventually influenced Congress to pass laws to protect the safety of consumers.

Impact of Event

In 1966, the National Traffic and Motor Vehicle Safety Act and the Highway Safety Act were signed into law, largely because of the influence of Nader's book *Unsafe at Any Speed*, which built public and congressional support for stronger automobile safety legislation. These acts listed twenty-six safety standards for 1968 automobile models that were to be implemented by January 31, 1967. These standards included provision of equipment as recommended in Nader's book: collapsible steering columns, safety glass and glazing materials, air pollution control devices, anchors for both lap and shoulder belts, and recessed instrument panels. In addition, the National Traffic Safety Agency was formed to ensure that automobile manufacturers complied with these acts. The first administrator in charge

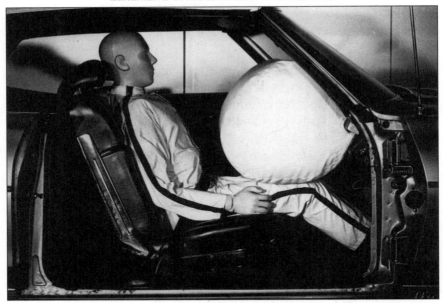

A crash-test dummy is used in early testing of automobile air bags. (National Highway Safety Administration)

of the National Traffic Safety Agency was William Haddon, Jr.

The important aspect of this legislation was the power given to the federal government to regulate American automobile manufacturers. This legislation marked the first time that the government departed from its "hands-off" approach. It also represented some of the first proconsumer legislation to be passed by the government.

In 1967, the National Traffic Safety Agency became the National Highway Safety Bureau (NHSB), part of the newly formed Department of Transportation. Haddon was named as the first director of the NHSB. Within the first two years of the NHSB's existence, twenty-nine motor vehicle safety standards were issued, and ninety-five more were proposed. The automotive industry had made seat belts standard equipment, but the NHSB required shoulder harnesses to be installed on all new automobiles manufactured on January 1, 1968, or after.

In 1969, automobile air bags received national attention as a result of public hearings before Senator Magnuson's Commerce Committee. Nader by that time had recruited several attorneys from Harvard Law School into his consumer movement. With funding from Consumers Union and from Nader's own sources, lobbyists urged legislators to support a requirement that all new automobiles manufactured be equipped with air bags. General Motors had quietly tested air bags in the early 1950's, but technical difficulties and lack of adequate proof that the air bags reduced passenger injuries during an accident led GM to discontinue this program.

In November, 1970, after an executive reorganization, the NHSB became the National Highway Traffic Safety Administration (NHTSA). It interpreted the safety laws differently than had its predecessor, the NHSB. According to the NHTSA, air bags were not the only equipment that complied with the passive resistance safety standards set forth earlier by Magnuson's committee hearings. Alternatives included fixed cushions within the vehicle interior, self-fastening seat belt systems, and crash-deployed blankets. It was not until 1989 that federal legislation required automakers to provide passive restraints on all new automobiles.

Automobile safety served as a starting point both for Nader as a consumer advocate and for the consumer movement in general. Throughout the late 1960's and early 1970's, Nader exposed the unsafe environment that existed for consumers and society. Nader demonstrated that packaged foods in supermarkets sometimes contained carcinogenic (cancer-producing) ingredients to preserve their visual appeal to consumers. In addition, he castigated the meatpacking industry for transforming diseased and decayed meat into supposedly safe items. In his research, Nader found that poor sanitation facilities led to the inclusion of insect remains and rodent fragments in the frankfurters sold in the supermarkets. He contended that the chemical colorings that cosmetically improved the appearance of meat could also impair the health of the consumer. As a result, Congress passed the Wholesome Meat Act (1967) and the Wholesome Poultry Act (1968).

Nader's research extended to the workplace, based on his premise that workers were part of his consumer advocacy movement. Nader publicized occupational hazards that ranged from numerous cases of brown lung disease in cotton mill workers to cancer-producing X-ray radiation doses to which medical technicians were exposed. In 1967, Congress passed the Radiation Control for Health and Safety Act as a result of Nader's consumer safety public campaigns.

Nader believed that three principal forces were necessary to strengthen the consumer movement: pressure on federal, state, and local legislators; workers "blowing the whistle" on illicit practices of their companies; and development of a citizen-initiated political action organization to be a "watchdog" for corporate abuse. Nader testified and lobbied for numerous reforms. As a result of his pressure, consumer laws were passed relating to natural gas and pipeline safety, occupational health and safety, and coal mine health and safety. Although Nader could not infiltrate corporations, Nader's movement encouraged employees to speak out against their corporations. With his own funding, Nader created Public Interest Research

Groups (PIRG) in the 1970's on college campuses. He urged students to set up PIRG organizations to research issues and lobby for consumer causes. By 1975, more than 145 PIRGs were on campuses throughout twenty states, thus completing Nader's dream to mobilize a nation of consumer advocates.

Nader's investigations on automotive safety tied into the belief that highway laws could reduce the number of vehicular accidents. One such law involved requiring seat belts. In 1978, Tennessee became the first state to require seat belt restraints for young children. By 1985, all fifty states had enacted child restraint laws. Another debate focused on the issue of lowering speed limits, both as a means of promoting safety and as a way of conserving gasoline.

Nader's efforts and the consumer movement in general won widespread approval but led to some questions. Manufacturers continued to raise the argument that free markets provided the safety measures that consumers demanded. If consumers truly wanted increased safety, the argument ran, some entrepreneur would be willing to offer it on the market for a profit. Legislation requiring additional safety measures therefore forced consumers to purchase more safety than they were willing to pay for and more than they thought worth the cost. As consumers became more aware of safety issues, sellers were forced to confront lawsuits charging products with being unsafe. A dilemma remained of how many accidents were worth paying to prevent.

Bibliography

Burda, Joan M. *An Overview of Federal Consumer Law*. Chicago: American Bar Association, 1998. Practical guide prepared by the American Bar Association.

Graham, John D. *Auto Safety: Assessing America's Performance*. Dover, Mass.: Auburn House, 1989. Explains the thirty-year struggle to resolve the controversy over the use of occupant restraint systems in motor vehicles. Depicts the effect of the 1966 safety acts on the automobile industry and the consumer.

_____, ed. *Preventing Automobile Injury: New Findings from Evaluation Research*. Dover, Mass.: Auburn House, 1988. A representation of then-current research on motor vehicle-related injuries and recommendations to prevent automobile injuries. The findings are based upon the collaborative efforts of several medical and educational institutions. Consists of major papers and comments by those who made presentations at or participated in the New England Injury Prevention Research Center Conference in December, 1987.

Holsworth, Robert D. *Public Interest Liberalism and the Crisis of Affluence: Reflections on Nader, Environmentalism, and the Politics of a Sustainable Society.* Cambridge, Mass.: Schenkman, 1980. A discussion of the beginning of the consumer movement and Ralph Nader's contributions to it. Although the book discusses the consumer consciousness of the 1960's, it also depicts the apathy of consumers in the 1970's. This book is intended more for academicians than for the general reading public.

McCarry, Charles. *Citizen Nader.* New York: Saturday Review Press, 1972. Discusses Nader's consumer movement and his enemies. Focuses on the negative aspects of Ralph Nader as a consumer advocate, private citizen, and writer. This book's merit is that the reader can view Nader from an oppositional stand. Good psychological portrait of Nader.

Nader, Ralph. *Unsafe at Any Speed: The Designed-in Dangers of the American Automobile.* New York: Grossman, 1965. An attack on the U.S. automobile manufacturing industry. Its central argument is that automobile manufacturers sold vehicles that they knew were unsafe in the name of profit.

Sanford, David. *Me and Ralph: Is Nader Unsafe for America?* Washington, D.C.: New Republic, 1976. Book about Nader by a personal associate. The focus is on the events that surrounded Nader and Sanford's interpretation of Nader's reaction to these events. Some of the stories are trivial and biased, but they give interesting perspectives on Nader.

U.S. Congress. House. Committee on Government Operations. Government Activities and Transportation Subcommittee. *The Administration's Proposals to Help the U.S. Auto Industry.* 97th Congress, 1st session. Washington, D.C.: Government Printing Office, 1981. Hearings before a subcommittee held on May 13 and 14, 1981. Contains transcripts, statements, and letters.

Martin J. Lecker

Cross-References

Congress Passes the Pure Food and Drug Act (1906); Congress Passes the Motor Vehicle Air Pollution Control Act (1965); Congress Passes the Consumer Credit Protection Act (1968); The United States Bans Cyclamates from Consumer Markets (1969); Congress Passes the Fair Credit Reporting Act (1970); Nixon Signs the Consumer Product Safety Act (1972).

ATLANTIC RICHFIELD DISCOVERS OIL AT PRUDHOE BAY, ALASKA

CATEGORY OF EVENT: New products
TIME: December 26, 1967
LOCALE: Prudhoe Bay, Alaska

The search for new oil fields produced a major find at Prudhoe Bay, Alaska, setting off a lengthy battle with environmentalists over the development of this resource

Principal personages:
ROBERT O. ANDERSON (1917-　　　), the head of Atlantic Richfield and one of the great oil wildcatters
TED STEVENS (1923-　　　), the state of Alaska's primary spokesman in the Senate
MO UDALL (1922-1998), the most vocal critic of the Alaskan oil pipeline in the United States House of Representatives

Summary of Event

The Naval Petroleum Reserve was created on the North Slope of Alaska in 1923, nearly a half century before the first oil was to flow from wells in America's northernmost state to consumers in the lower forty-eight states. During the 1920's and again in the 1930's, the challenge of Alaska's uncharted resources combined with projected shortages in the United States and world petroleum markets to encourage exploratory drilling in Alaska. On both occasions, however, the exploratory wells came up dry. The exploratory ventures were seen more as a hedge against the future than the first step in massive commercial development of Alaska's oil wealth. The cost of drilling in Alaska appeared prohibitive, and the technology for

478

transporting significant quantities of any oil discovered there did not yet exist. During the late 1940's and early 1950's, oil was discovered in Kuwait and in new, rich oil fields elsewhere in the Middle East. Oil could be produced much more cheaply in those fields than in the United States. Transportation costs had fallen as well. Interest in Alaska's unproven reserves therefore fell even lower. Given the conditions of the 1950's, when American leaders still talked in Congress about America's strategic petroleum reserves in Saudi Arabia and when the danger of market gluts and depressed prices resulting from the new fields in the Middle East had become the principal problems confronting producers, concern with the danger of shortfalls in supply faded fast. Most of the remaining interest in further exploratory drilling in Alaska disappeared as well.

The world oil market changed dramatically during the late 1950's and early 1960's. The major Western oil companies that had controlled the world petroleum market for nearly a half century began to lose their hold on the market. The existing profit-sharing system with host governments, which a decade before had replaced the concession system, no longer satisfied the governments of the states in which oil was produced, especially in an era of falling oil prices and concomitant falling governmental revenue. In 1960, Standard Oil of New Jersey's unilateral attempt to reduce the posted price of oil spurred governments of five oil-producing states, representing three-fourths of the oil then being exported, to unite in an openly declared effort to wrest control over price and production from the major oil companies. Out of their frustration was born the Organization of Petroleum Exporting Countries (OPEC). OPEC would not achieve major international status until the Arab oil embargo of 1973, but its creation served as an early warning that the United States would be better served by having its strategic petroleum reserves nearer to home, as in the Naval Petroleum Reserve in Alaska.

Also contributing to reawakening interest in Alaska were increases in the posted price of oil during the 1960's. The expanding Western economies increased their demand for oil and, at the urging of the producer state governments, the Western petroleum corporations regularly increased the posted price of oil on the international markets. The cost of producing oil in Alaska no longer seemed quite as commercially prohibitive as it once had.

During the mid-1960's, the increasing price of oil and decreased confidence in maintaining a supply of cheap oil from abroad combined to lure an expanding number of American firms into exploratory ventures abroad (for example, Occidental in Libya) and at home (chiefly along the Outer Continental Shelf). Consistent with this atmosphere, the California-based

Richfield Company, together with its Humble subsidiary, launched a joint exploratory project with the Atlantic Refining Company on the North Slope of Alaska's Prudhoe Bay. Under the leadership of Robert O. Anderson, one of America's last great oil wildcatters, the Atlantic Richfield Company (later ARCO) obtained the majority of the government leases then being granted for exploratory and developmental activity in Alaska. Even after its initial well proved to be dry in 1966, Atlantic Richfield pressed on with its exploratory efforts.

The exploratory well Atlantic Richfield began drilling in 1967 might well have been the last such well tried in Alaska for some time, if not forever, had it too come up dry. On December 26, 1967, however, the well christened Prudhoe Bay State Number 1 produced oil. Approximately six months later, a second well confirmed the presence of a vast commercial-scale pool of oil beneath Prudhoe Bay's frozen banks. In time, the pool would be estimated to contain ten billion barrels, making it the largest oil field ever discovered in North America. With the potential to produce two million barrels of oil a day, the field was estimated to have a higher production capacity than all but two other fields in the world.

Impact of Event

Had the oil field been developed rapidly, the history of the petroleum industry during the next quarter century could have been written differently. The United States would have had far less need for imported oil in the early 1970's, and the Arab oil embargo in 1973 would have been far less effective. Additional years might even have been required for OPEC to obtain control over the price and production of oil in its member countries. As it was, the significance of finding oil in Alaska was initially blunted by the technological problem of transporting the oil eight hundred miles to port facilities for shipment south and by equally vexing political problems making it difficult for oil producers in Alaska to get the oil to American consumers in the lower forty-eight states.

Technologically, moving the oil from wellhead to gas tank meant overcoming the obstacles to producing the oil in volume in the subzero temperatures of Alaska's North Slope and transporting it by pipeline through the frozen tundra either to the port of Valdez for shipment by tankers to California or across Alaska and then Canada to consumers in the United States. These obstacles appeared surmountable to Atlantic Richfield, which supported the Valdez route and initially expected to ship oil from that port within three years. No sooner had the second well confirmed the presence of large reserves than the heavy equipment for constructing a pipeline began to arrive in Alaska.

The political obstacles to exploiting the oil field proved to be less negotiable. Many environmentalists doubted that the petroleum industry had the knowledge to build a safe eight-hundred-mile pipeline across Alaska's frozen landscape without doing significant ecological damage. If a pipeline did have to be built, most environmentalists advocated as less risky the longer route across Canada. They made it clear that they would do everything in their power to prevent the construction of the Valdez pipeline.

The Santa Barbara oil spill in 1969 and the National Environmental Protection Act (NEPA) passed in its wake came at approximately the same time that the oil companies were requesting a federal right of way to build the Valdez pipeline. The NEPA required the United States Department of the Interior to prepare a justifying environmental impact statement before granting permission to begin activity on any project likely to have a substantial impact on the environment. On March 20, 1970, the Department of the Interior sought to comply with the letter of the law by issuing an eight-page statement of impact that downplayed potential damage to the environment. Within a week, the Wilderness Society, the Friends of the Earth, and the Environmental Defense Fund jointly sued the Department of the Interior for violating the National Environmental Protection Act and the 1920 Mineral Leasing Act. Three weeks later, on April 13, 1970, a court injunction halted construction on the pipeline until a definitive court ruling on compliance with the NEPA could be obtained.

Work on the pipeline remained suspended for nearly four years. Two of those years were spent in judicial wrangling. On March 20, 1972, the Department of the Interior produced an expanded nine-volume environmental impact statement to justify its approval of the pipeline's construction, but the injunction remained in effect until August 15, 1972, when the case was appealed to the Supreme Court. The equipment sent to Alaska to build the pipeline was still idle in October, 1972, when the Arab-Israeli war triggered the Arab oil embargo against Western countries assisting Israel. That embargo made the Organization of Petroleum Exporting Countries a cartel effectively in control of the price and production of oil in the petroleum exporting world and produced an almost overnight quadrupling in the price of imported oil from slightly less than $3 a barrel to nearly $12 a barrel.

Also almost overnight, the atmosphere in Congress changed on the matter of constructing the trans-Alaskan pipeline. A measure to approve the Interior Department's last environmental impact statement, relieve the Department of the Interior of further obligations under the NEPA, and approve the construction of a pipeline from Prudhoe Bay to Valdez was passed on November 16, 1973, less than a month following the announcement of the

Arab oil embargo. By April, 1974, the monumental $10 billion task of constructing an environmentally friendly pipeline was at last under way.

The pipeline was completed in 1977. Within a year it was carrying a million barrels of oil per day from the North Slope to port facilities in Valdez. By the early 1980's, the amount being transported had doubled, stemming America's appetite for imported oil. The development came too late to prevent a second oil crisis in 1979 from driving the price of imported oil to almost $38 per barrel but not too late to contribute to a general decline in Western demand for OPEC oil in the mid-1980's. The availability of Alaskan oil exerted such pressure on the cohesiveness of the OPEC organization that it lost substantial control over the production rates of member states and was powerless to prevent the posted price for a barrel of oil from slipping briefly below $10 before stabilizing in the late 1980's at approximately $20. Political issues played a large part in the decline of OPEC's power, but the availability of Alaskan oil surely contributed to that decline.

Bibliography

Berry, Mary Clay. *The Alaska Pipeline: The Politics of Oil and Native Land Claims.* Bloomington: Indiana University Press, 1975. An insightful account of the impact of the Alaska pipeline on the development of the "two Alaskas"—the one of natives and the one of oil.

Chasan, Daniel Jack. *Klondike '70: The Alaska Oil Boom.* New York: Praeger, 1971. A good account of the impact of oil on Alaska in the form of a very readable narrative covering the first days of the oil rush that followed Atlantic Richfield's discovery of oil.

Coates, Peter A. *The Trans-Alaska Pipeline Controversy: Technology, Conservation, and the Frontier.* Bethlehem, Pa.: Lehigh University Press, 1991. A good study of the confrontation between environmentalists and the energy developers seeking to build the trans-Alaskan pipeline, examined in the context of a century of confrontation between environmentalists and developers over Alaskan resources.

Davidson, Art. *In the Wake of the Exxon Valdez.* San Francisco, Calif.: Sierra Club Books, 1990. An in-depth, often technical analysis of the spill of approximately ten million gallons of petroleum in Prince William Sound.

Dixon, Mim. *What Happened to Fairbanks? The Effects of the Trans-Alaska Oil Pipeline on the Community of Fairbanks, Alaska.* Boulder, Colo.: Westview Press, 1979. Two years of fieldwork produced a volume of considerable insight and a few surprises pertaining to the unintended effects of the pipeline's construction on life in Fairbanks.

Jorgensen, Joseph G. *Oil Age Eskimos.* Berkeley: University of California

Press, 1990. A solid interpretation of the effect of energy development and monetary compensation for oil rights on one of the poorest groups of Native Americans.

Joseph R. Rudolph, Jr.

Cross-References

Discovery of Oil at Spindletop Transforms the Oil Industry (1901); The Teapot Dome Scandal Prompts Reforms in the Oil Industry (1924); Arab Oil Producers Curtail Oil Shipments to Industrial States (1973); The United States Plans to Cut Dependence on Foreign Oil (1974); The Alaskan Oil Pipeline Opens (1977).

CONGRESS PASSES THE CONSUMER CREDIT PROTECTION ACT

CATEGORIES OF EVENT: Consumer affairs and finance
TIME: May 29, 1968
LOCALE: Washington, D.C.

The Consumer Credit Protection Act required creditors to provide clear and adequate information about the cost of borrowing and enacted protection regarding wage garnishment and loan sharking

Principal personages:
PAUL DOUGLAS (1892-1976), a Democratic senator from Illinois who introduced truth-in-lending legislation in the Senate
WILLIAM PROXMIRE (1915-), a Democratic senator from Wisconsin who supported passage of the bill in the Senate
LEONOR SULLIVAN (1903-1988), a Democratic member of the House of Representatives from Missouri who authored and gained passage of the House version of the bill
A. WILLIS ROBERTSON (1887-1971), a Democratic senator from Virginia
RICHARD H. POFF (1923-), a Republican member of the House of Representatives from Virginia who offered the loan-sharking amendment to the bill as part of an anticrime program

Summary of Event

The Consumer Credit Protection Act was signed into law by President Lyndon B. Johnson on May 29, 1968. The law had the longest legislative history of any consumer bill. It was introduced each year in the Senate beginning in 1960 but failed to receive committee approval for eight years. Despite the long struggle to get it passed, the final legislation was stronger than the original version.

Consumer protection began early in the history of the United States, primarily as governmental regulation of economic activities. The Interstate Commerce Act of 1887 was the first federal legislation that regulated an industry. It resulted in the creation of the first regulatory commission, which produced rules that were models for later legislation designed to ensure consumer protection. Legislation in the early twentieth century focused on the safety, purity, and advertising claims of foods, drugs, and cosmetics. The Federal Trade Commission was set up in 1914 to maintain free and fair competition and to protect consumers against unfair or misleading business practices.

After World War II, Americans were eager to buy new products. Because they had come to trust producers and believed themselves to be protected by government oversight, they had little concern about the quality or safety of products. Goods were produced as quickly as possible to satisfy demand. Advertising gained a new level of sophistication by playing to the psychological needs of individuals. In 1957, these tactics were exposed in a book called *The Hidden Persuaders* by Vance Packard, and the buying public became indignant. The consumer movement began to take shape.

The idea of truth in lending originated with Senator Paul Douglas, who believed that lenders deceived borrowers about the true annual rate of interest. The practice of charging interest on the original amount of the loan, rather than on the declining balance as an installment loan was paid off, resulted in a true annual rate that was sometimes as high as twice the stated rate. Consumers, who generally were not knowledgeable in financial matters and were unaware of the methods of interest calculation, were paying a high cost for credit. They were unable to compare the costs of borrowing from various lenders because there was no requirement of standard, accurate, and understandable disclosures of the actual cost of borrowing.

In 1960, Douglas introduced a truth-in-lending bill in the Senate. In addition to requiring disclosure of the dollar amounts of the loan, the down payment, charges not related to the financing, and the total financing charges, the bill also required finance costs to be disclosed as an annual interest rate, based on the unpaid balance of the loan. Retailers, banks, and loan companies objected to the annual percentage rate (APR) disclosure requirement. First, it was argued that consumers were accustomed to the monthly rates currently reported and would find the change confusing. Second, many sellers believed that the reporting of a much higher "true" annual rate of interest would result in reduced consumer purchases. Some argued that this would seriously hurt the economy. Other objections included the contention that the law would not do any good, since the cost of merchandise could simply be increased to hide the cost of credit, and that regulations in this area were the responsibility of the states, not of the federal government. In addition, it was feared that it would be costly and difficult to train retail personnel in the new credit procedures necessary to comply with the requirements.

Consumer protection supporters and activists were primarily liberal Democrats, and consumer protection bills were initially seen as part of a liberal agenda. Voting in committees was mostly partisan. This slowed consumer legislation in Congress. Business organizations also lobbied against most consumer legislation. Interference from the federal government was considered to be unnecessary and an infringement on their rights.

In 1960, John F. Kennedy campaigned for election as president as an advocate of consumer protection. Once elected, he proposed a "Consumer Bill of Rights," to include the right to safety (protection against dangerous products), the right to be informed (protection against fraud and misinformation), the right to choose (adequate competition), and the right to be heard (government responsiveness to consumer issues). Kennedy asked Congress to enact new food and drug regulations, strengthen antitrust laws, and pass truth-in-lending legislation.

In the version of the bill proposed in 1964, revolving credit arrangements, such as retail store credit accounts, were exempted from the annual percentage rate disclosure. The bill gained more acceptance, but it died because of strong opposition by the chair of the Committee on Banking and Currency, Senator A. Willis Robertson. In the 1966 election, senators Douglas and Robertson lost their bids for reelection so were no longer on that committee in 1967 when Senator William Proxmire reintroduced the bill. Senator Proxmire was more willing than Senator Douglas had been to bargain and compromise. The bill was debated in the Financial Institutions Subcommittee of the Committee on Banking and Currency. The bill cleared the subcommittee and the committee, then was passed by the Senate by a 92-0 vote.

Congress' attitude toward consumer bills was changing dramatically as a tide of consumer activism grew in the United States. The National Traffic and Motor Vehicle Safety Act of 1966 had proved to be a popular bill. Media coverage played an important role in the passage of that bill and helped gain attention for other pending consumer legislation.

Leonor Sullivan, an eight-term Democratic congresswoman on the Consumer Affairs Subcommittee of the House Committee on Banking and Currency, authored the House version of the truth-in-lending bill. After battling unsuccessfully to strengthen the bill in the committee, she fought vigorously on the House floor, where several amendments were added, making the bill stronger than the Senate version. The APR disclosure exemption for revolving credit was dropped. Restrictions were included on wage garnishment, whereby an individual's earnings are withheld from his or her paycheck for repayment of debt. Loan sharking was made a federal offense, with severe penalties when interest rates were charged in excess of the usury levels in each state. The bill also established a Consumer Finance Commission to study the consumer finance industry. Publicity and strong public support for the bill resulted in the stronger House version clearing the conference committee.

The main section of the bill is Title I, the Truth-in-Lending Act, which requires, before credit is extended, disclosure of the APR and all finance charges, as dollar amounts, along with other loan terms and conditions. Advertisements that included certain financing terms required further elaboration. Specifically, any advertisement that included the down payment, the amount of each payment, the number of payments, the period of repayment, the dollar amount of any finance charge, or a statement that there was no charge for credit also had to disclose the cash price or the amount of the loan; the amount of down payment or a statement that none was required; the number, amount, and frequency of payments; the annual percentage rate; and the deferred payment price or the total dollar amount of the payments. Additionally, the bill provided for the right of the consumer to cancel a consumer credit agreement within three days if a second mortgage was taken on the consumer's residence. The Federal Reserve Board was required to draft regulations that implemented the law. Regulation Z was issued on February 10, 1969. Regulations were to be enforced by nine different federal agencies, including the Federal Trade Commission, the Federal Reserve Board, the National Credit Union Administration, the Comptroller of the Currency, the Federal Deposit Insurance Corporation, the Federal Home Loan Bank Board, the Interstate Commerce Commission, the Civil Aeronautics Board, and the Agriculture Department.

Impact of Event

In 1960, when Senator Douglas first introduced truth-in-lending legislation, there was little support for consumer issues in Congress. The powerful business community and the credit industry were opposed to the bill. Politics, partisanship, and special interests stalled the bill for many years. The refusal of Senator Douglas to publicly question the ethics of members of Congress with special interests or to question banks' opposition to the bill helped enable the fight to go on for years without much publicity. Growing consumer support for protective legislation was in part the result of the consumer protection activities of Ralph Nader. Nader's investigation of shortcomings in automobile safety resulted in General Motors (GM) having him followed and investigated. The public was outraged at GM's attempts to discredit Nader. Media coverage further fueled consumer demands for protection from unscrupulous business practices. The Ninetieth Congress, which finally passed the Consumer Credit Protection Act, was described by President Johnson in his 1968 State of the Union message as "the Consumer Congress."

The Consumer Credit Protection Act was intended to protect unsophisticated consumers from the hidden costs of borrowing or buying on credit. The concern of business that customers would buy fewer goods and borrow smaller amounts when they became aware of the true annual cost of borrowing apparently was unfounded, although it is impossible to say what consumer behavior would have been in the absence of the law. Continued use of credit in the early 1980's, with its high inflation and high interest rates, seemed to indicate that consumers were willing to use credit at almost any cost. When inflation was high, consumers learned that delaying their purchases resulted in a higher cost of goods, leading them to purchase immediately even at high interest rates. They continued to use credit even when the APR rose above 20 percent. Interest rates generally dropped in the later 1980's, but credit card interest rates remained high. Consumers, however, continued to increase their credit card debt.

The original truth-in-lending bill of Senator Douglas was intended to introduce competition to the area of consumer credit. Douglas had hoped that with comparable APR information, consumers would be able to shop for the best rates. One of the results of the legislation appeared to be that some businesses ceased to advertise their credit terms and rates. Whether this was a result of the truth-in-lending act or the tight supply of money soon after the law was enacted is difficult to ascertain. The main purpose of the bill would not have been realized if creditors gave little or no information in attempts to avoid violating the law.

Businesses were concerned about the cost of implementing the regulations. Costs arose from training employees, redesigning credit agreement forms to comply with required standards, educating customers about the information being provided to them, and calculation of complex APRs. In general, businesses found that these costs were not as high as had been anticipated. The government provided rate tables to figure APRs, and training and education did not require much time for most businesses.

In 1971, the act was expanded to include a restriction on credit card issuers that they could not send unsolicited credit cards to consumers. A fifty-dollar limit was put on a credit cardholder's liability if there was unauthorized use of the card (for example, in case of a lost or stolen card). If the issuer was notified before any unauthorized use occurred, the cardholder was not liable for any charges. The Truth-in-Lending Simplification and Reform Act of 1982 was passed with a revised Regulation Z that corrected several weaknesses and ambiguities in the original law.

Further legislation covered other areas of concern. The Fair Credit Reporting Act (1971) dealt with credit reporting agencies, their practices, and consumers' rights regarding information in their credit files. The Fair Credit Billing Act (1974) dealt with billing errors and procedures to handle them. The Equal Credit Opportunity Act (1975 and 1977) prohibited discrimination in the granting of credit and provided for prompt responses to consumers regarding the acceptance or rejection of their credit applications. This act especially benefited women, who had previously had difficulties obtaining credit. The law required that credit decisions be made on the basis of qualifications regarding financial status rather than characteristics such as sex, marital status, race, age, religion, or national origin. The Fair Debt Collection Practices Act (1978) protected consumers from deceptive and abusive debt collectors and established procedures for debt collection. The Electronic Funds Transfer Act (1978) established the rights and responsibilities of users of electronic funds transfers.

Consumer outcries and the pressure put on Congress to act in the interest of its constituents, the consumers, led to this flood of legislation that followed the Consumer Credit Protection Act of 1968. It brought much more regulation to business than was previously envisioned. The cost of the regulation and the resulting benefit to consumers are difficult to measure. The impact clearly has been an increase in consumer rights and a better-informed buying public.

Bibliography

Blackburn, John D., Elliot I. Klayman, and Martin H. Malin. *The Legal Environment of Business*. 3d ed. Homewood, Ill.: Irwin, 1988. In a chapter on debtor-creditor relations, this college textbook for business students describes the laws that apply to consumer protection. It includes cases to illustrate the application of the law and the opinion of the courts on those cases.

Burda, Joan M. *An Overview of Federal Consumer Law*. Chicago: American Bar Association, 1998. Practical guide prepared by the American Bar Association.

Eiler, Andrew. *The Consumer Protection Manual*. New York: Facts on File, 1984. Describes the laws that protect consumers and gives specific advice to consumers so that they can demand the rights they have under those laws. Gives detailed information about the legal system. This is a how-to book with sample letters to help consumers put their complaints into writing to achieve results.

Faber, Doris. *Enough! The Revolt of the American Consumer.* New York: Farrar, Straus and Giroux, 1972. This well-written book gives a fascinating history of the consumer movement. Much of the book is based on interviews. Suggests additional readings that would provide the interested reader with a detailed background.

Nadel, Mark V. *The Politics of Consumer Protection.* Indianapolis: Bobbs-Merrill, 1971. Part of a policy analysis series that describes and analyzes public policies generated by national, state, and local governments. It examines consumer politics, participants in policy decisions, and the role of the press and consumer activists in influencing policy decisions.

"The Truth About Credit Is Coming." *Consumer Reports* (August, 1968): 428-431. A report from Consumers Union, a consumer protection organization that tests and reports on consumer products and consumer issues. This article informs consumers about the law and how it will affect them. The article gives opinions as well as facts.

Rajiv Kalra

Cross-References

Congress Passes the Pure Food and Drug Act (1906); The Federal Trade Commission Is Organized (1914); Congress Passes the Fair Credit Reporting Act (1970); Congress Prohibits Discrimination in the Granting of Credit (1975).

THE UNITED STATES BANS CYCLAMATES FROM CONSUMER MARKETS

CATEGORY OF EVENT: Consumer affairs
TIME: October 18, 1969
LOCALE: Washington, D.C.

Evidence that consumption of cyclamates may be harmful to humans' health led to their removal from the United States marketplace

Principal personages:
HERBERT LEY (1923-   ), the commissioner of the United States Food and Drug Administration, 1968-1969
ROBERT FINCH (1925-1995), the secretary of Health, Education, and Welfare, 1969-1970
MARVIN S. LEGATOR (1926-   ), an FDA scientist who studied the effect of cyclohexylamine injections on rats
UMBERTO SAFFIOTTI (1928-   ), a doctor affiliated with the National Cancer Institute who was instrumental in forwarding the results of cyclamate research to the Department of Health, Education, and Welfare

Summary of Event

On October 18, 1969, Secretary of Health, Education, and Welfare Robert Finch announced that food products containing cyclamates would be banned from the U.S. markets effective February 1, 1970. This decision was made after several scientific studies revealed that certain amounts of cyclamates were harmful to chicken embryos and rats.

Prior to the development of artificial sweeteners, only natural sugars, in forms such as sugarcane, corn syrup, maple sugar, and honey, were used in food products. These sugars are high in calories and are unhealthy for a small proportion of people afflicted with medical conditions such as diabetes. Artificial sweeteners have much lower caloric contents than natural sugars and can be used by consumers who cannot safely ingest sugar. Only a small percentage of the United States population must abstain from sugar, but many consumers choose to purchase foods and beverages produced with low-calorie sugar substitutes as part of weight-control programs.

A growth in consumption of artificial sweeteners would coincide with a reduction in the market for sugar. This shift threatened sugar producers, who supported testing and research on the artificial substances to determine if they might have adverse physiological effects on consumers.

Because some consumers need to restrict or discontinue consumption of sugar for medical reasons and other consumers wish to reduce caloric intake, a substantial market for artificial sweeteners had developed in the United States by the mid-1960's. Ideally, a sugar substitute should taste identical to sugar, perform as sugar does in food preparation, and not adversely affect the health of those consuming it. Chemists have attempted to create such a product, but time and research have shown that many artificial sweeteners have limited merits.

In the two decades prior to 1969, cyclamates had been the primary substitute for sugar in diet-type food products. A cyclamate is an artificial (chemically produced) salt of sodium or calcium. Cyclamates have a sweet taste similar to that of sugar and contribute virtually no calories to foods and beverages in which they are used. By the late 1960's, the consumption of diet soft drinks, diet fruit jams and jellies, and table sugar substitutes had become widespread. Using cyclamates as sweeteners, soft drinks were made calorie free, and canned fruits and jams were produced with significantly reduced caloric contents.

Diet soft drink producers consumed more than half the cyclamates produced in the United States and, according to *Business Week*, collectively manufactured products worth $420 million at retail prices in 1969. Of all soft drinks sold in 1969, 15 percent were diet drinks. These drinks thus had substantial effects on the financial performance of manufacturers.

Producers of artificial sweeteners pursued development of their products because they believed there was a potentially large market of diet-conscious people who would willingly pay for the sweetening agents. The possibility for large profits was a motivating factor for producers, as artificial sweeteners sold for more than four times as much as granulated sugar. Furthermore, it was expected that consumers would eagerly purchase low-calorie prepared canned foods and beverages. A government advisory panel for the Food and Drug Administration (FDA) estimated in 1968 that 75 percent of the U.S. population consumed artificial sweeteners and that 70 percent of these sweeteners were used in soft drinks. At that time, about half a dozen companies were marketing brands of artificial sweeteners for table use, most of which contained cyclamates. Brand names of the sweetening products included Sugarcane 99, Crystal Sweet, Sweet'n Low, Sweetness & Light, Zero-Cal, and Sugarine. Diet soft drinks were sold under brand names such as Diet Pepsi, Fresca, Like, Tab, and Diet-Rite.

As new food and pharmaceutical products are developed, the FDA must approve their distribution in the United States. Once products have been approved for distribution, researchers may continue to test them to better observe the physiological effects the products have on humans. Such research is often initiated when a group or organization suggests that there may be a potential hazard as a result of consumption. In 1958, an amendment to the Food and Drug Administration Act known as the Delaney Amendment was passed. It requires that food additives that are shown to cause cancer in either animals or humans be removed from the consumer market.

Research concerning the effects of consumption of cyclamates occurred throughout the time they were marketed in the United States. Several preliminary research panels concurred that consumption of cyclamates was safe. In December, 1968, a government advisory panel, in a report to the FDA, concluded that no research warranted a reduction from the current recommended consumption limit of 5 grams (the equivalent of more than three quarts of artificially sweetened beverages) of cyclamates per day. The FDA responded with a more guarded recommendation to the public that research was ongoing and that, pending results, consumers should consume no more than 50 milligrams per day. The panel reported that according to soft drink labeling information, a 12-ounce can contained between 0.3 and 0.6 grams of cyclamates. Even one soft drink would exceed the lower recommended limit. In April, 1969, changes in labeling of products containing cyclamates were recommended by the FDA to allow consumers to more easily stay within the safe consumption levels. At that time, concern about safe intake levels was primarily in response to the knowledge that consuming more than 5 grams of cyclamates per day has a laxative effect on humans and to the results of laboratory experiments that had shown liver changes in animals that consumed cyclamates.

Early in October, 1969, researchers hired by Abbott Laboratories, which manufactured more than half of all cyclamates sold in the United States, found possibly malignant tumors in rats that were fed high doses of cyclamates. This information was passed along to the Department of Health, Education, and Welfare (HEW) through reports from the National Cancer Institute and

Abbott Laboratories. As a result of the reports and as advised by the National Academy of Sciences, Robert Finch announced on October 18 that cyclamates would be removed from U.S. markets.

Impact of Event

The immediate reaction to the ban by manufacturers of cyclamates and of foods and beverages containing cyclamates was surprise. Earlier in 1969, new products containing cyclamates had been introduced to the consumer market. Other products were continuing to be developed, and HEW statements had recently ruled cyclamates to be safe for consumption.

Consumers responded with mixed reactions to the cyclamate ban. Some were concerned for their health and immediately wanted products without the controversial cyclamates. Others were concerned that they might not have low-calorie alternatives to their favorite products. As a result, many stores reported unusually heavy sales of cyclamate-containing products in the week immediately following the ban. Apparently, consumers stocked up on the items that they expected to be removed from supermarket shelves. The Royal Crown Cola company, producer of Diet-Rite, the leading diet soft drink in 1969, surveyed consumers to determine their reactions to the cyclamate issue. The results of the survey indicated that consumers were not concerned about their consumption of cyclamates even though they were aware of the controversy.

Many retail stores chose to remove cyclamate-containing products before the February 1 deadline. Other stores left cyclamate products on the shelves but discontinued orders of new products. Most stores endured a slowdown in sales of diet products following the announcement of the ban.

Producers of diet-plan beverages that were formulated and marketed as substitutes for traditional meals found an exemption from the ban by repackaging their products and distributing them through drugstores as prescription items. This move enabled them to avoid huge losses on their inventories.

Diet soft drink manufacturers dealt with the transition to cyclamate-free products remarkably well. Fortunately for the manufacturers, the ban was announced in October, a traditionally slow sales and advertising period. Soft drinks are not produced very long in advance of distribution, so manufacturers were not hampered by large inventories that might become worthless.

Fruit canners did not fare as well as soft drink producers, as they had just completed a seasonal pack when the ban was announced. Further, canners and jam producers generally had proportionately more diet products in their product mix than did soft drink producers. Manufacturers of diet-type canned fruits and vegetables successfully secured an extension in the phase-out time for cyclamates. They effectively extended the deadline to September 1, 1970. This extension enabled them to deplete most of the inventory that had been canned prior to the ban announcement.

With the impending deadline for the ban of cyclamates quickly approaching, manufacturers of foods and beverages were eager to discover a cyclamate replacement that would save the market for their products. Soft drink manufacturers overwhelmingly switched from cyclamates to saccharin. Saccharin did not replicate the taste of sugar as well as did cyclamates. Saccharin also had the unfortunate drawback of a bitter aftertaste. A small amount of sugar could be added to a drink to squelch the bitter aftertaste, but this added approximately forty calories to the product. Manufacturers were concerned about the marketability of this substitute, afraid that consumers would not consider the reduction of a few calories to be enough of a benefit to purchase the diet drink and that consumers concerned about the effect of sugar on teeth would not be satisfied with the addition of sugar.

Following the October announcement of the cyclamates ban, advertising was heavy among diet product producers, both those that used cyclamates and those that did not. Many products that were marketed as diet or sugar-free and never did use cyclamates increased their advertising for two reasons. First, they now had an advantage over the cyclamate-containing products. Second, their producers wanted to be certain that consumers knew that cyclamates were not used in the products.

Although it is difficult to measure the effectiveness of advertising, it is clear that consumers responded favorably to new diet products that replaced those containing cyclamates. Saccharin had been produced since 1901. It became the sweetener of choice for diet products for more than two decades, until health risks similar to those earlier discovered for cyclamates were associated with it. Nutra Sweet emerged as the replacement of saccharin in the 1980's. Because of the potential volume of sales and profits generated from diet foods and beverages, research targeting the physiological effects of currently consumed artificial sweetener and the development of new artificial sweeteners continues.

Bibliography

Burda, Joan M. *An Overview of Federal Consumer Law.* Chicago: American Bar Association, 1998. Practical guide prepared by the American Bar Association.

Cohen, Stanley E. "Cyclamates Incident May Raise Some Questions for Government Marketers." *Advertising Age* 40 (October 27, 1969): 107. Discusses controversial issues and the impact of the cyclamate ban on producers and policymakers.

"Cyclamates: How Sweet It Isn't. . ." *Chemical Week* 105 (October 29, 1969): 30-31. Discusses the economic impact of the cyclamate ban on producers of cyclamates.

"Diet Industry Has a Hungry Look." *Business Week* (October 25, 1969): 41-42. Discusses the impact of the cyclamate ban on producers of diet soft drinks and other diet foods.

Donlon, Thomas B., and Kathryn Sederberg. "Food, Drink People React Swiftly to Cyclamate Ban: Ads May Increase." *Advertising Age* 40 (October 27, 1969): 1. Discusses the impact on advertising resulting from the cyclamate ban. Specific companies' strategies for new advertising are shared.

Semling, H. V., Jr. "FDA Establishing Cyclamate Policy, Economic Woes Being Heard." *Food Processing* 31 (April, 1970): 71-72. Highlights the new policy on cyclamates used for pharmaceutical products and the phase-out schedule for cyclamates in food products. The economic impact of the ban is discussed.

Virginia Ann Paulins

Cross-References

Congress Passes the Pure Food and Drug Act (1906); Congress Sets Standards for Chemical Additives in Food (1958); Health Consciousness Creates Huge New Markets (1970's).

THE BANNING OF DDT SIGNALS NEW ENVIRONMENTAL AWARENESS

CATEGORY OF EVENT: Consumer affairs
TIME: November 20, 1969
LOCALE: Washington, D.C.

By banning the use of DDT, the United States took a first step in addressing environmental concerns relating to many products

Principal personages:
RACHEL CARSON (1907-1964), a marine biologist, the author of *Silent Spring*
PAUL HERMANN MÜLLER (1899-1965), the inventor of DDT
WILLIAM LONGGOOD (1917-   ), a Pulitzer Prize-winning journalist, author of *The Poisons in Your Food*

Summary of Event
In the spring of 1972, amid considerable controversy, the Environmental Protection Agency (EPA) banned dichloro-diphenyl-trichloroethane (DDT) for use as a pesticide in the United States. This followed a ban on use in residential areas issued by the federal government on November 20, 1969. The DDT ban had a far-reaching impact on humanity, the environment, and business. Widespread use of other toxic or dangerous pesticides, however, continued in the United States and elsewhere.

DDT, which consists of chlorinated hydrocarbons or organochlorides, was acquired by the United States from Switzerland in 1942. It was discovered by Paul Hermann Müller, who won a Nobel Prize for the

497

discovery. Prior to the discovery of DDT, there were hundreds of different pesticides in use. Many of these pesticides were effective on only one or a few pests. Some of the more infamous pesticides included Paris green, which contained arsenic but was extremely effective on potato bugs; lead arsenate, used to eliminate gypsy moth caterpillars; and calcium arsenate, used against cotton pests in the South. One problem associated with early pesticides was that they were often as dangerous to plants as they were to insects.

DDT was an important discovery because insecticides that had been in use were scarce because of World War II. In addition, DDT was effective against a variety of insects, including lice and mosquitoes. It was discovered after the war that DDT also was effective against a number of agricultural pests that plagued American farm production and Americans in general.

By 1960, DDT was a household word. Its use was so widespread that almost every person in the United States either had used the product or had heard of its use. It was partially because DDT was so well known that it was singled out for study by scientists who noticed irregularities in the environment.

At this time, during the peak of DDT use, two books were written about pesticides and their impact on the environment. One of the books, *Silent Spring* (1962), written by marine biologist Rachel Carson, extensively outlined the effects of DDT on humans and on the environment. According to Carson, humans can become poisoned by DDT in a number of ways: by breathing the oily fumes that occur when it is sprayed, by ingesting food that has been sprayed with DDT, and by absorbing it through the skin. Because DDT is fat soluble, it is stored in organs rich in fatty substances such as the liver, the kidneys, and the adrenal and thyroid glands. DDT had been linked to cancer and blood disorders.

DDT did not disseminate in the environment. Accumulations of DDT remained in the soil and continued to contaminate plants and insects. Birds or other animals that ate insects or animals contaminated by DDT died or passed the contamination on to other animals through the food chain. There were questions as to whether DDT poisoning could be passed from a mother to her child through mother's milk and about a variety of illnesses that could result from DDT poisoning.

Another significant book written during this time was *The Poisons in Your Food* (1960) by journalist William Longgood. It was an important work because it was the first major journalistic attack against pesticides. It caused the general public to become aware of the dangers of pesticides, outlining a number of toxic pesticides that had been used to restrict insects and promote agricultural growth. The book indicated that many poisons remained in food and were therefore consumed by human beings.

Both these books stirred public interest in environmental concerns. That public concern led to the establishment in 1970 of the Environmental Protection Agency (EPA), whose purpose was to protect and improve the environment. The EPA was responsible for controlling pollution through standard setting, enforcement, and research in the areas of solid waste, toxic substances, radiation, and noise. One of the first acts of the EPA was to amend the Federal Insecticide, Fungicide, and Rodenticide Act of 1947 to restrict the use of DDT.

The federal government had banned use of DDT in residential areas on November 20, 1969, and called for a virtual halt to its use by 1971. Other countries took similar action. The EPA issued a cancellation order on the use of DDT in January, 1971. The Department of Agriculture appealed the order. In October of 1971, the EPA held hearings to determine the nature of the hazards of DDT use or misuse and the nature of benefits of the use of DDT. The EPA tried to determine if harms to humans associated with DDT occurred because it was misused or necessarily resulted even with proper use. The harms of using DDT then had to be weighed against the benefits of its use. One of the benefits of its use was increased food production, particularly important for countries that were dense in population. Land had to be very productive to feed the people of such countries. The use of DDT also had eliminated hoards of mosquitoes, which had caused epidemic outbreaks of malaria, and it had eliminated lice infestations, which were responsible for numerous typhus epidemics. The EPA determined, however, that the harmful effects of DDT outweighed the benefits. If it remained in the environment for a long enough time, it could endanger a large number of people. DDT therefore was banned for use and production in the United States. European countries later followed suit.

Impact of Event

The banning of DDT in the United States and in Europe, along with hearings on pesticides and their use, alerted the public to the importance of environmental and ecological issues. The American public became involved by joining groups such as Greenpeace, the Sierra Club, the Audubon Society, the National Wildlife Federation, and the Wilderness Society. Membership in these groups soon numbered in the millions. These groups lobbied Congress to pass additional laws to protect the environment. Lobbying efforts soon resulted in legislation concerning clean air, water pollution, noise control, drinking water, and toxic substances. These acts identified pollutants and set standards for their release into the environment.

Standards were meant to identify the levels at which certain pollutants would be dangerous to people or the environment and to restrict emissions to those levels or below. The standards focused on factories and sewage plants at first. Later, standards would be expanded to include all polluters.

Compliance with the standards was expensive. The EPA forced many companies to develop new processes or products in order to conform to standards. For example, auto companies were forced to alter their auto emissions systems to include a part called a catalytic converter. Auto companies also were forced to design more fuel-efficient vehicles, since gasoline had been identified as a pollutant as well as a natural resource. These changes added an estimated $800 to the cost of each American car. Other companies were required to find alternative places to dump their refuse or to do research and development on alternate uses for refuse. Even biodegradable refuse and, under some conditions, clean but warm water were deemed harmful to the environment. Areas previously used as dump sites were discovered to contain toxic substances, and companies found to have used the sites were forced to pay to have these sites cleaned.

During 1988, corporations paid an estimated $86 billion for pollution control, an amount equal to 2 percent of the Gross National Product. The Comprehensive Environmental Response, Compensation, and Liability Act was passed in 1980 in part to help firms pay the high costs of cleaning up old dump sites. Under this act, firms unable to pay to clean sites received assistance from the government, which had funds from petroleum and chemical production taxes set aside for this purpose. Business costs escalated in other ways, as firms were sued because of harm done to the environment. Hooker Chemical Company faced one such suit. When dangerous chemicals seeped from its barrels into the groundwater, people in a small community near Niagara Falls, New York, since called Love Canal, experienced increased rates of cancer, birth defects, and other illnesses. The costs of settling the resulting suit was in the billions of dollars.

Costs continued to rise as other harmful or possibly harmful practices were identified. For American business, making a profit became complicated by concerns over environmental issues and possible future liabilities. Companies producing pesticides, for example, had to be concerned about the health and welfare of the populations of areas in which the pesticides were produced and used. The Food and Drug Administration (FDA) and the Environmental Protection Agency shared the responsibility for protecting the public from harmful substances in food. Manufacturers of pesticides and chemicals had to perform tests and prove the safety of their products as well as showing that residues did not accumulate beyond allowed levels. The FDA and EPA relied largely on tests conducted by the manufacturers themselves when registering pesticides. Consequently, some harmful pesticides, including Dieldrin, Diazinon, Malathion, and Lindane, remained in use. Pesticides by nature are harmful to at least some forms of life and may cause cancer, birth defects, or nerve damage in humans. Some chemicals have not been tested for possible harmful effects. During the Ronald Reagan Administration, testing all but halted. Concern mounted about pesticides such as alar in apples, heptachlor in dairy products, and ethylene dibromide (EDB) in muffin and cake mixes. The release of toxic fumes from a chemical plant in Bhopal, India, in 1984 served as an example of the potential deadliness of pesticides. Thousands of people were killed in their sleep by toxic pesticide fumes, and hundreds of thousands more were injured.

The banning of DDT led to banning of other harmful substances in the United States and elsewhere. For countries with weaker economies or that are densely populated, the choice to restrict pesticides carried different costs and benefits. The risks of using harmful pesticides had to be balanced against the possibility of starvation or epidemic, and some countries could not afford the chemicals that could be used instead of those proved to be harmful. Pesticides will continue to be produced and used as long as insects continue to develop immunities to the chemicals being used. The challenges for business are to continue to balance pesticide use with other forms of pest control and to develop new safe and effective products. That concern with safety will also hold for wider environmental problems such as air and water pollution.

Bibliography

Beatty, Rita Gray. *The DDT Myth*. New York: John Day, 1973. Defends the use of DDT and refutes the findings of previous studies. Recounts studies of successful use. Includes tables comparing DDT to other sources of pollution and identifies some natural toxins found in the environment. Contains a selected list of references and an index.

Carson, Rachel. *Silent Spring*. Boston: Houghton Mifflin, 1962. An in-depth report on the results of early studies on the use of DDT and other dangerous chemicals. Outlines the dangers to the environment and to humans. Contains an index and an excellent list of principal sources.

Duggleby, John. *Pesticides*. New York: Macmillan, 1990. This forty-five-page hardcover book discusses what pesticides do, how to measure danger, and alternatives to pesticide use. Juvenile reading. Contains a section with addresses to write for further reading, a glossary of terms, and an index.

Greer, Douglas E. "Environmental Protection." In *Business, Government, and Society.* New York: Macmillan, 1993. This chapter in a textbook reviews the topic of environmental policies by asking relevant questions. Contains an appendix on clean air and a section of notes which contains lists for additional reading. Written for undergraduate students.

Gunn, D. L., and J. G. R. Stevens. *Pesticides and Human Welfare.* Oxford, England; Oxford University Press, 1976. Presents a balanced opinion on the use of pesticides. Discusses the problems, strategies for use, and the legal environment up to 1975. Detailed appendix outlining terminology, reading lists at the end of each chapter.

Mott, Lawrie, and Karen Snyder. *Pesticide Alert: A Guide to Pesticides in Fruits and Vegetables.* San Francisco: Sierra Club Books, 1987. This softcover manual discusses pesticide residues and federal regulation of pesticides. Lists several fruits and vegetables and pesticide uses for each. Intended for the adult reader, this manual contains notes, a section on sources of additional information, and further reading. Also contains a glossary, a bibliography, and an index.

Taylor, Ron. *Facts on Pesticides and Fertilizers in Farming.* New York: Franklin Watts, 1990. Discusses pesticides and their uses in thirty-two pages. Contains four-color illustrations and color photos. An excellent and very brief introduction to ecology for the juvenile reader. Contains a glossary, an index, and a list of relevant addresses to write for additional information.

Wharton, James. *Before Silent Spring.* Princeton, N.J.: Princeton University Press, 1974. Discusses recognition of insect problems and regulations in force prior to 1962. Also includes a history of pesticides and public health. Contains bibliographic notes by chapter and an index. Meant as a source of information for the adult reader.

Elizabeth Gaydou

Cross-References
Congress Passes the Pure Food and Drug Act (1906); Congress Passes the Motor Vehicle Air Pollution Control Act (1965); Health Consciousness Creates Huge New Markets (1970's); The Environmental Protection Agency Is Created (1970); The Three Mile Island Accident Prompts Reforms in Nuclear Power (1979).

HEALTH CONSCIOUSNESS CREATES HUGE NEW MARKETS

CATEGORY OF EVENT: Marketing
TIME: The 1970's
LOCALE: The United States

Growing awareness of the importance of a healthy diet and exercise opened new markets among American consumers

Principal personages:
ADELLE DAVIS (1904-1974), a biochemist and author of four books on nutrition
BENJAMIN GAYELORD HAUSER (1895-1984), a nutritionist and chiropractor
CARLTON FREDERICKS (1910-1987), a psychiatrist and biochemist
LINUS PAULING (1901-1994), a biochemist and proponent of Vitamin C as a preventive medicine
RACHEL CARSON (1907-1964), a marine biologist
RALPH NADER (1934-   ), a consumer advocate who wrote about the dangers of chemicals in food

Summary of Event

In the 1970's, several health issues generated concern about nutrition and exercise. The pesticide DDT and cyclamates, an artificial sweetener, were banned in the United States in 1969. Other pesticides and food additives soon came under scrutiny. Doctors and researchers made news by linking cholesterol and heart attacks; findings showed that exercise could reduce cholesterol while strengthening the heart. People began to take up jogging; joggers then began buying clothing and shoes for their exercise.

Manufacturers of athletic shoes touted specialized shoes for that form of exercise.

The World Food Congress, sponsored by the United Nations Food and Agriculture Organization (FAO) at The Hague in June, 1970, brought together nations concerned with a host of problems including agricultura productivity and the purity of the environment. Addeke H. Boerma, director-general of the FAO, stated that it would be futile to discuss hunger and malnutrition in isolation from other related problems such as overpopulation. He believed that radical steps had to be taken to cure the entire problem as a whole; if such steps were not taken, the problems could result in outbreaks of violence. At this same conference, delegates expressed concern regarding new plant varieties that were the backbone of the green revolution and the large amounts of fertilizer, pesticides, herbicides, and irrigation required to grow these new plants. Chemical use would prove to be problematic in a monsoon country such as India, where such herbicides, fertilizers, and pesticides would be washed into the River Ganges and the Bay of Bengal, causing pollution of unpredictable magnitude. There was also fear for the oceans of the world, not only from pollutants that were meant to increase yields of food plants but also from future oil spills that could reduce another valuable food source, marine life.

Meanwhile, these same concerns were being addressed by scientists in the United States and elsewhere. Numerous books were published on the subject of pesticides and herbicides as well as on the effect of food additives on the human body. Health-conscious biochemists such as Adelle Davis and Benjamin Gayelord Hauser wrote books about the benefits of pure food. James Trager stated in an article that three groups of people buy what had become known as health foods: people who have a desire for good food, people concerned about environmental decay brought on by persistent use of pesticides and herbicides, and people who believe that what they eat affects their health and well-being. Trager stated that in 1971 there were fifteen hundred to two thousand health food stores in the United States, adding a billion dollars a year to the economy. Davis stated that health food stores appealed to both the "establishment" and the "young, hip" generation. With a master's degree in biochemistry from the University of Southern California, she had sold nearly two million copies of her books on the subject of pure food by 1970.

With the rise in popularity of health food stores and growing awareness of the environment, farmers and ranchers took up organic farming, producing food without artificial fertilizers, pesticides, or herbicides. California growers in particular reflected the increase in interest in organic food. That state appeared to lead the U.S. movement toward health consciousness.

Farmers there were among the first in the country to adopt organic methods on a large scale, and consumers swarmed to health food stores and embraced healthy food products. Furthermore, the California climate was conducive to year-round outdoor exercise.

In 1970, organic food was found mostly in health food stores, small country stores, and through co-ops, groups of people that got together to order large amounts to take advantage of quantity discounts. The leaders of this movement were found mostly on the two coasts and in the Midwest in 1970. As of 1992, the amount of revenue generated by the sale of organic foods in the marketplace had grown to an estimated $1.4 billion dollars.

In 1976, psychiatrist and biochemist Carlton Fredericks published a book, *Psycho-Nutrition*, in which he showed how diets planned on an individual basis could heal people with a wide variety of ailments ranging from simple allergies to chemical imbalances and schizophrenia. His appearances on television talk shows provided publicity for that book and his later publications. The buying public appeared to be willing to accept broad claims of the benefits of a proper diet.

While the World Food Congress addressed problems raised by the new plant strains that began the green revolution, researchers continued to test new plant strains. They also rediscovered plant varieties that had fallen out of use. Examples include amaranth, and ancient Aztec grain with a buckwheat flavor; spelt, an ancient grain that first had its resurgence in Europe and then gained popularity in the United States; quinoa, a complete protein grain known as the Chilean mother grain, grown high in the Andes; and kamut, a grain brought to the United States from Egypt. Health food producers soon marketed these rediscovered grains in pasta form and in cereals.

Health consciousness affected markets in addition to that for food. People became increasingly aware of the importance of exercise. Markets for athletic shoes, equipment, and clothing grew tremendously. As exercise gained in social status, equipment became a status symbol. Sweatsuits came out in glamorous lines and were worn by people who rarely exercised but wanted to give the appearance that they did. General-purpose gym shoes were replaced by shoes designed for specific forms of exercise. Jogging shoes proved to be particularly popular, even for people who never went jogging. Exercise equipment that found new markets ranged from rowing machines and stationary bicycles to large, multiuse home gyms. Sales of bicycles boomed. Later, mountain bikes would become popular, in part as a result of the increasing desire to escape urban life and get in touch with nature, at least temporarily.

Athletic equipment and footwear took sophisticated turns in regard to comfort and utility. Wooden tennis rackets were replaced by ones made of metal and other materials, for example. Sophistication naturally came at a price, and innovators with new ideas reaped substantial profits.

Consumers in many cases needed to be educated about healthy practices. Cookbooks and exercise books proliferated, as did periodicals. *Vegetarian Times*, for example, promoted the benefits of a diet without meat. Magazines also developed around the many newly popular participant sports.

One way in which consumers have sought to improve their diets has been finding ways to buy fresh food products closer to their sources of production. (PhotoDisc)

Impact of Event

From health food stores to organic gardening and farming to the growth of interest in exercise, the entire health movement has proliferated since the 1970's. Many of the new products and trends introduced in that decade became entrenched parts of the marketplace.

Doctors recommend exercise to keep circulatory systems in good shape, and people discovered that they felt better as a result of exercise. The result was often an overall increase in fitness consciousness, with greater attention also paid to diet. Many people attracted to health consciousness in the 1970's remained steady consumers of health-related products. By 1990, many of those early converts had passed their health consciousness on to their children, a new generation of consumers.

Health consciousness extended into the field of health care itself. Consumers of medical care gradually became aware of alternatives to traditional Western medicine as it became more expensive and as the alternatives proved to be effective. *The New England Journal of Medicine* reported that by 1990, one-third of all Americans were using some form of alternative health treatment. These alternatives included relaxation techniques, spiritual healing, biofeedback, acupuncture, and herbal medicine. These alternative treatments accounted for $10.3 billion in expenditures in 1990, with insurance covering $2.4 billion of that total. Traditional physicians began to take notice of this trend and studied these alternatives. In 1992, the National Institutes of Health in Bethesda, Maryland, established an office for the study of unconventional medicine.

Surveys on the sales of sporting goods show steady increases in sales. From 1980 to 1991, for example, the market for sporting goods as a whole grew from $16.7 billion to $45.1 billion. Sales of athletic clothing grew from $3.1 billion to $11.9 billion over the same period of time. Footwear sales, including shoes for jogging and running, tennis, aerobics, basketball, golf, and other sports, grew from $1.7 billion to $6.8 billion. Equipment sales nearly doubled, from $6.5 billion to $12.5 billion. Sales of bicycles and related supplies more than doubled, from $1.2 billion to $2.5 billion.

Part of the increase in sales came from the increased sophistication of products. The large number of buyers made it feasible to develop new products, such as basketball shoes with air pumps. Buyers proved eager to try out each innovation, and prices of products skyrocketed. Sophisticated products became so popular that simpler products were crowded out of the market. Single-speed bicycles, for example, are almost impossible to find for adult riders.

Athletes became conscious of the link between exercise and diet, partly as a result of the many books and articles published on the subject. Endurance athletes load up on carbohydrates before they begin strenuous activity and consume drinks containing electrolytes while they exercise. Backpackers carry food, often in the form of dried fruits and nuts, while on the trails.

Organic foods increased in sales, but their market share remained small. In 1992, organic foods accounted for $1.4 billion in sales out of the approximately $200 billion for all farm products.

Health consciousness created huge new markets in the United States and elsewhere in the industrialized world. Other parts of the world, however, still struggled with basic problems of food distribution, overpopulation, and the difficulties created by herbicides, pesticides, and fertilizers. These were the very problems that had, in part, spurred the movement toward health consciousness.

Bibliography

Detje, F. W. "Reform, Revolution, and Food." *Science News* 98 (July 25, 1970): 86. Discusses concerns voiced by representatives attending the World Food Congress in 1970. These concerns included use of pesticides and herbicides and how Third World nations can avoid contamination when monsoon rains wash toxins into rivers.

Eisenberg, David M., et al. "Alternative Medicine in the United States: Prevalence, Costs, and Patterns of Use." *The New England Journal of Medicine*, January 28, 1993, 246. Gives statistics on use of alternative medicine. By 1990, one-third of all Americans were using some form of health treatment alternative such as relaxation techniques, spiritual healing, biofeedback, acupuncture, and herbal medicine. Americans spent $10.3 billion on these treatments; insurance covered $2.4 billion.

Goldman, M. C. "Sharp Rise in Organic Food Demand." *Organic Gardening and Farming* 17 (April, 1970): 66-70. Reports the rising interest in food produced without herbicides, pesticides, or fertilizers. Tells how farmers and ranchers successfully provided organic food.

Jacobson, Michael F. *The Complete Eater's Digest and Nutrition Scoreboard.* 1st ed., rev. and updated. Garden City, N.Y.: Anchor Press/Doubleday, 1985. A consumer's fact book of food additives and healthful eating. A good source for understanding what is listed on food labels and how it may affect the consumer.

Lansing, Elizabeth. "Image to Shed, More Food to Grow." *Life* 69 (December 11, 1970): 52. Discusses how the organic gardening movement is growing and why. Also tells how families and other groups are succeeding with this enterprise.

Trager, James. "Health Food: Why and Why Not." *Vogue* 157 (January 1, 1971): 122-123+. Casts a somewhat skeptical eye at much of the health food movement. Covers extremes in the health food movement.

Corinne Elliott

Cross-References

Congress Passes the Pure Food and Drug Act (1906); Congress Sets Standards for Chemical Additives in Food (1958); The United States Bans Cyclamates from Consumer Markets (1969); The Banning of DDT Signals New Environmental Awareness (1969); Bush Signs the Clean Air Act of 1990 (1990).

THE U.S. GOVERNMENT REFORMS CHILD PRODUCT SAFETY LAWS

CATEGORY OF EVENT: Consumer affairs
TIME: The 1970's
LOCALE: Washington, D.C.

Federal legislation prevented the marketing of potentially harmful children's products

Principal personages:
EDWARD M. SWARTZ (1934-   ), an attorney, and child toy safety advocate
RALPH NADER (1934-   ), an attorney and consumer advocate
TERRENCE SCANLON (1939-   ), the chair of the Consumer Product Safety Commission
JAMES FLORIO (1937-   ), the chairman of the House Reauthorization Subcommittee on Commerce, Consumer Protection, and Competitiveness
PEGGY CHARREN (1928-   ), the founder of Action for Children's Television

Summary of Event
During the 1970's, the federal government of the United States undertook a concerted effort to improve the safety of toys and other products used by children. This effort was presaged by passage of the Child Protection Act of 1966, which prohibited sale of any hazardous substance that might cause harm to children, if it failed to display a warning label on either the product or its package. The Food and Drug Administration (FDA) was responsible for enforcing this act, which amended the Hazardous Substances Labeling

509

Act of 1960. Prior to this act, signed into law on November 3, 1966, toy manufacturers were not held accountable for product safety or for reducing the risk of injuries sustained to children using their products.

On November 6, 1969, the Child Protection and Toy Safety Act was passed, extending the requirements of manufacturers by prohibiting any toxic, corrosive, or flammable toy or article that could cause personal injury or illness to children. In addition, if a product could cause an electrical, fire, or mechanical hazard to children, a label was to be displayed on the product or its package warning of its potential danger. The law gave the secretary of health, education, and welfare the authority to ban what the FDA classified as a hazardous substance.

The FDA was also responsible for carrying out the 1953 Flammable Fabrics Act, passed to ban highly inflammable nightgowns and children's clothing that would burst into flame when exposed to open flames. Unfortunately, the standards were not stringent. For example, if a six-inch sample of a material was held at a 45 degree angle from a flame for one second and did not catch fire, it passed the test. If the material burned at a rate of five inches or less in three and one-half seconds, it passed the test.

On October 27, 1972, the Consumer Product Safety Act established the Consumer Product Safety Commission (CPSC), which was empowered to develop safety standards for most consumer products other than food, drugs, and automobiles. The CPSC was charged with protecting the public against unreasonable risks of injury from consumer products, assisting consumers in evaluating the relative safety of competing product brands, reducing the conflicts between state and local regulations, and promoting research and investigation into the causes and prevention of product-related death, illness, and injury.

Prior to the establishment of the CPSC, the toy industry regulated itself. In 1968, the National Commission on Product Safety (NCPS) found in its final report to the United States Congress that self-regulation by trade associations such as the Toy Manufacturers of America (TMA) and organizations that give seals of approval, such as Good Housekeeping, were ineffective. The TMA did not force its members to comply with its standards, and organizations such as Good Housekeeping were more concerned that advertising claims were truthful than with testing and certifying products' safety to children.

One toy safety advocate who testified before the NCPS was Edward M. Swartz, an attorney who represented several clients in court to obtain compensation for injuries suffered by their children as a result of playing with hazardous toys. At the 1968 NCPS hearings, Swartz demonstrated how dangerous toys could be to their child users. Swartz became an advocate on

Among the important provisions of federal laws regulating the manufacture of children's clothing are requirements that materials be fire retardant. (PhotoDisc)

toy safety issues and wrote several books, including *Toys That Don't Care* (1971) and *Toys That Kill* (1986).

Swartz's research uncovered several unsafe products that were marketed in the 1970's having not been found to be dangerous by the CPSC. One product was the Wham-O Manufacturing Company's boomerang. Another unsafe product, marketed by PBI Incorporated, was a projectile toy that was advertised to the wholesale trade as a safe, flexible plastic toy, even though it had sharp edges and was potentially blinding. FAO Schwartz marketed a fiberglass bow and wooden arrow set. The wooden arrows had rubber tips, but they were removable. The toy was advertised as being harmless.

During the 1970's, the Ideal Toy Corporation made a "Kookie Kamera" that was marketed as nontoxic and not intended for internal consumption. The product caused several cases of nausea, which may have led to vomiting and even asphyxiation as a result of blockage of the trachea in small children. Another product, the Newman Company's "Loonie Straw," was designed to be reusable. The problem was that instructions called for the straw not to be washed in hot water. It was intended to be used to drink milk, making it probable that bacterial germs would be bred in the unsanitary straw.

From 1973 to 1977, the CPSC received more than one hundred death certificates related to the ingestion of small objects. Forty-five of these deaths were related to toys and nursery products. In 1976, it was estimated by a CPSC study that 46,500 children under the age of ten were treated in hospital emergency rooms for injuries related to small parts. Twenty-five of forty-five deaths involving children's products were of children less than three years old.

During 1978, the CPSC received more than 180 oral and written comments from businesses, trade associations, and consumer groups regarding the safety of consumer products. In response, on August 7, 1978, the Consumer Product Safety Act tightened up safety regulations and required every manufacturer, distributor, or retailer who obtained information that a product either was unsafe or did not comply with the CPSC regulations to immediately inform the CPSC.

Impact of Event

The effects of regulation on how toys were manufactured and marketed were mixed. In 1980, the CPSC banned the sale of toys with small parts intended for children under the age of three if the parts could accidentally be swallowed or become dangerously lodged in their throats. By 1989, however, the CPSC still had not clearly defined what constituted a small part and if small-part toys should be banned in general. Toymakers still claimed that accidents being researched were isolated incidents; the CPSC concurred in most cases.

On the other hand, many products were banned because of the CPSC's enforcement of the Child Protection Act and Child Protection and Toy Safety Act. In the 1970's, products called crackerballs were categorized as hazardous substances. Crackerballs consisted of small quantities of gunpowder and particles of sand or flint in papier-mâché coatings. When thrown against any hard surface, they would explode with a loud noise. Lawn dart sets were required to carry warning labels, and they could not be sold at toy stores. In 1977, the CPSC required bicycles to have capped brake wires, treads on the pedals to prevent foot slippage, and reflectors for night riding.

One area of concern for product safety advocates was that under product safety laws, toy manufacturers were permitted to market products with labels recommending the age group for which the toy would be most suitable. The labels did not indicate that the toy would be hazardous to any child younger than the recommended age. As a result, many adults believed that the recommended age group was based on intellectual capacity or dexterity, not on safety standards.

In 1977, Parker Brothers marketed a product called Rivitron, a plastic construction toy for children aged six to twelve. After an eight-year-old boy died from ingesting a small part of the toy, the CPSC found the death to be an isolated case. Parker Brothers added chemicals to the toy rivets, giving them a bad taste so that children would be deterred from putting the parts in their mouths.

In 1987, the CPSC under Commissioner Terrence Scanlon seized goods valued at almost $4 million during spot checks. Seizures represented 1.5 million units of toys. James Florio, chairman of the House Reauthorization Subcommittee on Commerce, Consumer Protection, and Competitiveness, criticized the CPSC for being relatively weak during the 1980's. Florio and his committee believed that confiscating $4 million worth of products from a $12 billion industry showed ineffectiveness as a safety commission.

Many critics of toy manufacturers believed that the public was unaware of the dangers that children faced when playing with toys that were not being stringently monitored by the CPSC. On the other hand, toy manufacturers believed that regulations were too stringent and the public too demanding. They argued that many injuries to children were not caused by the children and their toys but by the lack of parental supervision.

In 1968, Peggy Charren had founded Action for Children's Television (ACT). Charren was a critic of toy-based programs, which she believed were exploiting children and should have been scrutinized by the television industry and the Federal Communications Commission. In 1987, when Mattel announced a line of gun toys to be used in interaction with a television show, she unsuccessfully tried to stop the marketing of these products, claiming that simulating the shooting of a television figure would give children the wrong impression of real shooting. Charren's movement gave a new interpretation to product safety, expanding beyond physical features and taking into consideration the potential danger of marketing products that could lead to an unsafe situation or foster dangerous behavior.

Toy manufacturers were faced with other criticisms that may have led to decreased sales. In 1987, consumer advocate and attorney Ralph Nader found that television advertising manipulated child viewers to buy toy products that were not safe. For example, Nader found that plastic toy parts were more hazardous than were wood products, but that television advertising focused on plastic toys. Toy manufacturers responded that critics were more concerned with an antibusiness philosophy than with objections to the actual safety of toys.

Although the CPSC generally supported consumer advocates, in 1991 Toys "R" Us was permitted to sell wind-up dolls, even though children under three years of age could be injured by choking on some of the parts. Sale of the dolls was allowed because they were not intended for children of that age. Throughout the 1980's and 1990's, attorney Edward Swartz compiled lists of dangerous toys. Although many legal battles were won by the toy manufacturing industry, advocates such as Swartz, Nader, and Charren influenced the CPSC and the toy manufacturers to ensure that toys were safe. Toy manufacturers became more cognizant of their market and of the pressure that consumer advocates placed by lobbying legislators to strengthen product safety rules for children. Efforts that began in earnest in the 1970's thus continued to bear fruit into the 1990's, with effects sure to continue.

Bibliography

Dadd, Debra Lynn. *Non-Toxic and Natural: How to Avoid Dangerous Everyday Products and Buy or Make Safe Ones.* Los Angeles: Jeremy P. Tarcher, 1984. Designed to enable the selection of products that are nontoxic. Describes how to make safe products, choose brands that are safe, and pick products that will help protect the environment. A special section on toys describes the safest toys to purchase for young children.

Office of the General Counsel, ed. *Compilation of Statutes Administered by CPSC.* Washington, D.C.: U.S. Consumer Product Safety Commission, 1998. Unofficial compilation of laws relating to the Consumer Product Safety Act assembled for consumer use. Indexed.

Oppenheim, Joanne. *Buy Me! Buy Me!* New York: Pantheon Books, 1987. The first section describes the toy business as an industry and how it changed what children play with in the 1980's. The second section lists toys that are appropriate and safe for children of various age groups. The third section is a directory listing the names and addresses of organizations and toy suppliers, enabling the reader to obtain further information on purchasing toys for children.

Stern, Sydney Ladensohn, and Ted Schoenhaus. *Toyland: The High Stakes Game of the Toy Industry.* Chicago: Contemporary Books, 1990. A brief history of the toy industry, with a focus on the 1980's. Gives an objective and reasonably unbiased account of the toy industry's response to its customers from a safety perspective.

Swartz, Edward M. *Toys That Don't Care.* Boston: Gambit, 1971. Discusses the unsafe toys manufactured and purchased for children and what can be done to increase safety. Written by an attorney who is an advocate for safe toys. An excellent source, but written from a subjective viewpoint, that of a product liability and negligence trial attorney.

_____. *Toys That Kill.* New York: Vintage Books, 1986. A sequel to *Toys That Don't Care.* A history and list of unsafe toys manufactured in the 1970's and 1980's. An excellent source, but subjective.

Martin J. Lecker

Cross-References

Congress Sets Standards for Chemical Additives in Food (1958); The United States Bans Cyclamates from Consumer Markets (1969); Nixon Signs the Consumer Product Safety Act (1972).

AMTRAK TAKES OVER MOST U.S. INTERCITY TRAIN TRAFFIC

CATEGORIES OF EVENT: Transportation; government and business
TIME: 1970
LOCALE: Washington, D.C.

New modes of transportation threatened railroads with extinction and forced the federal government to take radical measures to save them, including passing the Rail Passenger Service Act

Principal personages:
RICHARD M. NIXON (1913-1994), the president of the United States, 1969-1974
JOHN A. VOLPE (1908-1994), the U.S. secretary of transportation under Nixon
ROGER LEWIS (1912-1987), the first president of the Amtrak corporation
RONALD REAGAN (1911-   ), the president of the United States, 1981-1989

Summary of Event
When the U.S. Congress created Amtrak in 1970, it took one in a series of steps increasing government involvement in railroad transportation. Railroads had an important role in the development of the United States. Trains carried passengers and supplies to the frontier and brought back food, lumber, and minerals to the population centers of the East. The federal government encouraged the growth of railroads by giving their builders enormous land grants, including not only rights-of-way but millions of acres on both sides of the tracks. This land increased tremendously in value because of the presence of the railroad tracks.

In the Midwest, railroads were responsible for the change from subsistence farming to the raising of single crops such as wheat and corn. In the West, ranchers were able to thrive because they had a means of shipping their cattle and sheep to major markets. California became a rich state in part because growers were able to ship fruits and vegetables to the eastern markets on rapid trains that had freight cars specially designed to prevent spoilage in transit. Cities such as New York and Chicago were able to grow to enormous proportions because trains brought in abundant food.

The so-called "railroad barons" received their land grants and exclusive operating territories on the condition that they provide efficient and equitable transportation for both passengers and freight. When rapid growth of railroads took place in the nineteenth century, no one could foresee the changes in transportation that would be wrought by the Industrial Revolution and later technological and social developments.

One of the earliest developments that threatened railroads was Henry Ford's adoption in 1913 of assembly lines for mass production of his famous Model T automobiles. This innovation allowed the price of cars to fall dramatically, changing automobiles from toys of the rich to a practical means of transportation for the entire population and marking the beginning of the end of the golden era of passenger travel on railroads.

Automobiles became an American passion. More women began driving as manufacturers competed by making their products more stylish and easier to handle. U.S. auto manufacturers began making annual style changes to encourage sales. Trade-ins of good used cars on new models made it possible for nearly every American to own some kind of car. Two-car families with two-car garages became a common part of the American scene.

The demand for automobiles brought a demand for paved highways. State governments responded by creating more highways, and the attractive highways increased the demand for automobiles. In the 1960's, under President Lyndon Johnson's administration, the government spent billions of dollars on a nationwide system of superhighways.

Along with automobiles came trucks and buses. Large long-haul diesel trucks encroached on the railroads' freight business, while buses encroached on the railroads' passenger business. Buses of the Greyhound line in particular became a common sight across the nation. Cars, trucks, and buses, not being confined to steel rails, could take people anywhere they wanted to go. As a result, the entire American landscape changed. New towns and cities sprang up that were not dependent on any linkage to railroad tracks.

At the end of World War II came the worst blow of all to the railroads' passenger business. The federal government was eager to encourage the growth of airlines for many reasons. For one thing, the business of manufacturing airplanes had long been an important asset to the American economy. The federal government helped to encourage air transportation by setting strict safety standards through the Civil Aeronautics Board.

There were plenty of pilots to fly these planes, because the government had trained thousands of men to be aviators during World War II. These experienced pilots provided safe, reliable service that helped to build the public image of air travel. Flying a passenger plane was easy for men who had flown bombing raids over Germany and Japan.

In spite of dramatic air crashes that sometimes killed hundreds of passengers, the public came to realize that, statistically speaking, air travel was the safest form available. The incredible savings in time made air travel hard to ignore. It took the fastest trains three full days to carry a load of passengers from Los Angeles to New York, while an airliner could make the same trip in a few hours. A business traveler could zoom from San Francisco to Los Angeles in one hour, while the same trip could easily take ten hours by car, covering four hundred miles of highways.

Trains were subject to long delays because of weather conditions, but airliners could avoid most adverse weather by flying above the clouds. Younger people, especially business travelers, abandoned train travel, and it became apparent that train clientele increasingly consisted of elderly people who were afraid of flying and had plenty of time on their hands.

Eventually, only one-third of 1 percent of Americans traveling between cities used trains. By the mid-1950's, 85 to 90 percent of the total passenger traffic in the United States went by automobile. The volume of traffic on interstate highways connecting America's cities illustrated that trains could no longer handle the endless stream of humanity hurtling along in private automobiles.

The basic problem was that railroads had become outmoded as a means of human transportation. Railroad companies, however, had obtained their rights-of-way from the government on the basis of a commitment to provide public transportation. Passenger traffic now not only caused the railroads to lose money but also interfered with the profitable transportation of freight. Freight trains had to be shunted off to sidings to stand idle while passenger trains that were half empty sped by. One possible solution was to build separate lines for passenger trains, but this was so obviously unprofitable that no railroad company considered such an investment.

President Richard M. Nixon supported the idea of government subsidization of passenger trains and was influential in the creation of Amtrak, the official nickname for the National Railroad Passenger Corporation, created by the Rail Passenger Service Act of 1970. Amtrak soon took over virtually all intercity passenger train service, although the semi-independent corporation was not involved in rail commuter service. Amtrak management eliminated many famous old passenger trains and cut down service to approximately 240 trains each day serving about 500 stations over 23,000 miles of tracks. Even with radical cost cutting, Amtrak continued to lose money, and there were periodic outcries to stop wasting taxpayers' money on an obsolete form of transportation and to let passenger trains pass into history, along with stagecoaches and riverboats.

Impact of Event

Many American railroad corporations were in desperate financial straits by 1970. The federal government was forced to subsidize them to prevent a complete collapse of rail transportation. Amtrak brought immediate relief. Freed from the duty of running passenger trains full of empty seats, the railroads were able to concentrate on hauling freight, the business that brought them profits.

The railroads were able to cash in on mushrooming international trade by providing "land bridges" across America. Japan, the largest exporting nation in the world, found that it was relatively inexpensive and fast to send cargo ships to ports in Seattle, San Francisco, and Los Angeles, where cargoes could be off-loaded onto flatcars and whizzed across the continent to ports such as New York, Baltimore, and Atlanta. The cargoes would then proceed to Europe, Africa, and the Middle East. The alternative was to send ships thousands of miles on circuitous routes around the Cape of Magellan or through the Panama Canal to reach their final destinations.

New methods of transporting freight were developed to adapt to changing conditions of international trade. The most innovative idea was containerization. Instead of being packaged in whatever form manufacturers chose, manufactured goods came to be customarily packed in huge, standard-size, all-metal containers that are weatherproof and tamper-proof. Freight no longer had to be slowly loaded into the holds of freighters in small parcels that had to be carefully placed but instead could be piled quickly. The containers were easy to tie down and easy to load and unload with winches. When they reached American ports, the containers could be quickly unloaded onto ordinary railroad flatcars. Huge "doublestack" freight trains requiring minimal crews became a familiar sight. Containerization was bitterly fought by labor organizations representing stevedores and other cargo ship employees. Unions obtained some concessions for their senior members but had to accept the loss of many jobs.

Amtrak did not provide much help for train travelers. Service continued to deteriorate under the new federally subsidized corporation. Many business leaders, government officials, economists, and journalists agreed that long-distance passenger trains were nothing but a form of amusement, like the trains at Disneyland. The only passenger trains that were needed were those providing commuter service over relatively short distances, and these did not need government support. The dominant modes of transportation between cities continued to be planes and automobiles.

With the coaches and Pullman cars getting older and shabbier, the wonderful dining cars of the past being replaced by canteen cars serving packaged food, and the rails themselves deteriorating so that passengers were sometimes badly shaken, the incentive to travel by train decreased. Older people who could remember the glory days of train travel were dying or traveling less frequently.

In the light of these developments, President Ronald Reagan, faced with huge budget problems, called for the breakup of Amtrak and the destruction of the remaining intercity passenger trains. Long-distance train travel managed to continue because of political pressure; some of the most famous surviving trains passed through states represented by influential United States senators. The future of Amtrak remained uncertain. It continued to operate passenger trains between major cities and acquired badly needed new equipment to provide greater speed and comfort.

It became obvious that trains were not an efficient means of transporting people in a vast country such as the United States. American travelers valued their time too greatly and became accustomed to the convenience and speed of travel by automobile and airline. Passenger trains continued to exist primarily because some people were afraid to fly, because some nostalgia buffs favored them for aesthetic reasons, and because some politicians continued to fight for them for their own political advantage.

Intercity passenger trains likely will remain part of the American scene, especially in areas of exceptional scenic beauty and areas of high population density, such as the Northeast Corridor between Boston and Washington, D.C. The passenger train, however, can never hope to recapture more than a fraction of its former glory.

Bibliography

Frailey, Fred W. *Zephyrs, Chiefs, and Other Orphans: The First Five Years of Amtrak*. Godfrey, Ill.: RPC Publications, 1977. A detailed study of the first five years of Amtrak's operations, attempting to determine which trains were attracting passenger business and which were operating at a loss, and why. Frailey, who is nostalgic about the golden years of train travel, is critical of management and government. Contains many facts and figures. Illustrated with photos of Amtrak trains.

Hilton, George W. *Amtrak: The National Railroad Passenger Corporation.* Washington, D.C.: American Enterprise Institute for Public Policy Research, 1980. Hilton, a professor of economics at the University of California, Los Angeles, describes the decline of passenger traffic and blames railroad management for deliberately discouraging passenger travel by downgrading the quality of service. Concludes that Amtrak serves no useful function but subsidizes people who enjoy traveling by train. Predicts that Amtrak will eventually pass out of existence.

Itzkoff, Donald M. *Off the Track: The Decline of the Intercity Passenger Train in the United States.* Westport, Conn.: Greenwood Press, 1985. Itzkoff concludes that the glamour of railroad travel has vanished forever. He is pessimistic about the future of Amtrak. Extensively footnoted and supplemented with an excellent bibliography. Contains photographs of interiors and exteriors of great passenger trains of the past.

Kidder, Tracy. "Trains in Trouble." *The Atlantic* 238 (August, 1976): 29-39. A survey of the American passenger trains operating under Amtrak. Explains the factors leading to the gradual deterioration of passenger service and discusses possible hope for rail travel revival because of increasing congestion on highways and freeways.

Lyon, Peter. *To Hell in a Day Coach: An Exasperated Look at American Railroads.* Philadelphia: J. B. Lippincott, 1968. An amusing and informative history of American railroads from their beginnings up until the time when it became obvious that the federal government was going to have to take drastic action to preserve passenger service. Lyon blames the railroads for sabotaging their passenger service in favor of the more lucrative freight business.

Orenstein, Jeffrey. *United States Railroad Policy: Uncle Sam at the Throttle.* Chicago: Nelson-Hall, 1990. An explanation and evaluation of U.S. public policy toward American railroads by a political scientist. Presents an overview of the history of American railroading. Discusses Amtrak in considerable detail and offers recommendations for improving government's subsidization and supervision of the nation's railroads.

Pindell, Terry. *Making Tracks: An American Rail Odyssey.* New York: Grove Weidenfeld, 1990. Pindell is a passenger train enthusiast and recounts the history of America's great passenger lines. He spent most of 1988 riding all twenty-one Amtrak routes, covering thirty thousand miles and visiting all but three states. He is a staunch advocate of preserving and improving passenger train service through Amtrak.

Bill Delaney

Cross-References

Ford Implements Assembly Line Production (1913); The Railway Labor Act Provides for Mediation of Labor Disputes (1926); The DC-3 Opens a New Era of Commercial Air Travel (1936); Truman Orders the Seizure of Railways (1946); Carter Signs the Airline Deregulation Act (1978).

THE U.S. GOVERNMENT BANS CIGARETTE ADS ON BROADCAST MEDIA

CATEGORY OF EVENT: Advertising
TIME: April 1, 1970
LOCALE: Washington, D.C.

As of January 1, 1971, cigarette advertising was banned from the American broadcast media

Principal personages:
LUTHER TERRY (1911-1985), the United States surgeon general in 1962; formed the Advisory Committee on Smoking and Health
FRANK E. MOSS (1911-   ), the chair of the Senate Commerce Committee hearings on the effects of smoking
JOSEPH CULLMAN III (1912-   ), the chair of Philip Morris and spokesperson for tobacco manufacturers at the Senate Consumer Subcommittee hearings
WALLACE BENNETT (1898-1993), the U.S. senator who introduced the bill that required health warning labels on cigarette packages beginning in 1965
JOHN F. BANZHAF III (1940-   ), the executive director of Action on Smoking and Health, an antismoking public interest group

Summary of Event
The Public Health Cigarette Smoking Act of 1969 banned cigarette advertising from American radio and television beginning January 1, 1971. It also allowed the Federal Trade Commission (FTC) to consider warnings in printed advertising after July 1, 1971. Warnings on cigarette packages were changed, and under the act, the FTC was required to give Congress

six months notice of any pending changes in rules concerning cigarettes. The legislation was signed by President Richard Nixon on April 1, 1970. After passage of the act, two voluntary agreements were reached between the FTC and cigarette manufacturers. The companies agreed to list tar and nicotine content in their advertising and also agreed to feature the health warning label in print advertising.

Pressure to curb cigarette advertising originated with a 1939 study that for the first time scientifically linked smoking with lung cancer. Between 1950 and 1954, fourteen major studies linked cigarette smoking with specific serious diseases. In response to these studies, cigarette manufacturers created the Tobacco Industry Research Committee, a lobby group to fund research on the use and health effects of tobacco. The group later changed its name to the Council for Tobacco Research—USA. In 1957, the Legal and Monetary Affairs Subcommittee of the House Government Operations Committee held six days of congressional hearings, with John A. Blatnik as the chair. As a result of these hearings, Senator Wallace Bennett introduced a bill that would require cigarette packs to carry warning labels, and Senator Richard Neuberger proposed removing tobacco from the list of crops that qualify for agricultural price supports. Five years later, in 1962, Surgeon General Luther Terry formed the Advisory Committee on Smoking and Health.

Two years later, on January 11, 1964, the surgeon general announced the results of that committee's findings. The press conference to announce the results was held on a Saturday in anticipation of the adverse effect the study might have on the stock prices of tobacco companies. The study established a link between cigarette smoking and diseases ranging from lung cancer to cardiovascular diseases and cirrhosis of the liver. Two weeks later, the Public Health Service announced its acceptance, in full, of the Advisory Committee's report. In subsequent weeks, several congressmen introduced legislation related to the controversy and called for hearings.

On March 16, 1964, three days of Federal Trade Commission hearings on cigarette labeling and advertising rules began. A proposed rule had been circulated in advance. One section required that a health warning appear in all advertising and on cigarette packages. Drafts of two warning statements were presented, each indicating that cigarette smoking can lead to death. Another section of the rule attempted to ban "words, pictures, symbols, sounds, devices or demonstrations . . . that would lead the public to believe cigarette smoking promotes good health or physical well-being."

The FTC was overruled by Congress on part of its proposal. Warnings were to be required only on packages, not in advertising, according to the Cigarette Labeling Act of 1965. The ban on radio and television advertising came later, by an act of Congress, not through the FTC or the Federal Communications Commission (FCC). The required inclusion of the health warning on all print advertisements also came later. This was the result of a voluntary agreement between the commission and cigarette manufacturers in 1972, when a congressional ban on commission action forcing this requirement was expiring.

The ruling requiring warning labels was to take effect on January 1, 1965. In the nine-month period between the commission's hearings and the first of January, the cigarette industry mobilized. Within one month of the hearings, the industry announced the creation of a voluntary code, intended to signify to Congress and the public that the industry was interested in regulating itself and that the FTC was an obstacle to self-regulation. Robert B. Meyner, a former governor of New Jersey, was hired to administer the code and given the authority to issue fines of up to $100,000 to violators. Essentially, the code prohibited advertising aimed at persons under twenty-one years of age and prohibited cigarette advertising from making positive health claims. The code limitations were difficult to interpret and enforce. These difficulties eventually led to an agreement that eventually banned cigarette advertising from the broadcast media.

The agreement was prompted by the pending expiration on July 1, 1969, of the Cigarette Labeling Act of 1965. The Federal Communications Commission unexpectedly announced in February, 1969, that if Congress allowed the 1965 act to expire, the FCC would propose a rule that would ban cigarette advertising from the airwaves.

At this point, several options were available. If Congress did not act and allowed the 1965 legislation to expire, this would permit the FCC to enact its proposed restrictions. Alternatively, Congress could have extended the 1965 ban or could have taken action on the health warning label, making it more or less stringent.

Antismoking forces hoped that Congress would not act, thereby allowing for the more encompassing regulations proposed by the FCC. Instead, the House Interstate and Foreign Commerce Committee held thirteen days of hearings two months before the ban was to expire. The arguments and many of the witnesses were the same as those heard in the 1965 hearings.

In testimony before the House Commerce Committee, Warren Braren, former manager of the New York office of the Code Authority, made it clear that the National Association of Broadcasters (NAB) deliberately misled Congress and the public into believing that voluntary industry self-regulation in reducing youth appeal was meaningful. He revealed that television networks and advertising agencies regularly overruled Code Authority staff members in interpretation of standards. The Code Authority operated entirely on voluntary submissions by advertising agencies. Some tobacco sponsors simply had not subscribed to the code, and those that did made their own judgments on whether their commercials needed to be reviewed.

The bill that passed the House of Representatives on June 18, 1969, however, appeared to represent a victory for the cigarette industry. It prohibited the states permanently, and the federal agencies for six more years, from enacting regulations on cigarette advertising, in exchange for a strengthened package warning label.

The bill as passed by the House, however, sparked a severe backlash in the Senate and at the state level as well as in the private sector. *The New York Times*, for example, announced that it would require a health warning in any cigarette advertisement appearing in that newspaper.

The Senate Commerce Committee, chaired by Frank E. Moss, held a one-day hearing, with only five witnesses appearing. Speaking for the tobacco manufacturers in July, 1969, Joseph Cullman III, chairman of Philip Morris, told the Senate Consumer Subcommittee that the industry was ready to end all advertising on television and radio on December 31, 1969, if the broadcasters would cooperate, and in any event would agree to cease advertising by September, 1970, when existing agreements expired. The announcement by Cullman caught many broadcasters by surprise. They had proposed to phase out cigarette ads over a three-year period beginning in January, 1970. Cigarette advertising accounted for $225 million a year in revenue to broadcasters, and they had hoped that a gradual reduction would help in the development of contingency plans to recover a portion of the lost revenue.

Meanwhile, the National Association of Broadcasters (NAB) Television and Radio Code Review Boards announced a plan on July 8, 1969, to stop advertising on radio and television beginning January 1, 1970. In addition, cigarette manufacturers were required to continue carrying warning labels on their packages. The agreement stipulated that member stations of the NAB would phase out cigarette commercials on the air beginning January 1, 1970. The Review Boards also said that they would prohibit cigarette commercials during or adjacent to any program that was primarily directed at youth and would further study ways to reduce the appeal of cigarettes to minors. The announcement amounted to a victory for critics of tobacco, most notably the FCC, which had threatened to ban all cigarette commercials from the airwaves.

The tobacco industry, in presenting its proposal, showed concern that broadcasters might sue for antitrust violations, on the grounds that the cigarette companies had acted in collusion. The industry included a request for antitrust protection in presenting its proposal.

The bill that emerged from Congress on March 19, 1970, called the Public Health Cigarette Smoking Act of 1969, banned cigarette advertising from radio and television beginning January 1, 1971. It also agreed to allow the FTC to consider warnings in printed advertising after July 1, 1971. Cigarette package warning labels were changed to: "Warning: The Surgeon General Has Determined that Cigarette Smoking Is Dangerous to Your Health."

Impact of Event

Attitudes within the tobacco industry regarding the ban were mixed. It is commonly assumed in the industry that advertising does not increase the size of the overall cigarette market. Instead, it affects the competitive position of the various brands. The primary effect of the advertising ban, therefore, would be to freeze the market shares currently held by each of the brands. Print ads could still affect market share but were not believed to be as powerful. The money saved by not producing and placing advertising in the broadcast media would be substantial. As an added bonus, the industry hoped that a cessation of cigarette advertising would yield a respite in the growing volume of antismoking advertising.

It was expected that the industry's decision to discontinue expensive television campaigns would be accompanied by stepped-up spending on print advertising, coupons, and contests. The chairman of American Brands predicted that "the battleground for cigarette sales advertising will probably switch to other media." Newspaper and magazine publishers, unlike broadcasters, are not federally licensed and are protected by the First Amendment's freedom-of-speech provision. There was no indication that publishers would voluntarily ban cigarette advertising, since it amounted to approximately $50 million in annual revenue. Furthermore, there was less pressure to ban print advertising of cigarettes, since these ads primarily reached an adult audience and were less intrusive than television ads.

Opinions varied on how cigarette sales would be affected by a ban on broadcast advertising. In Great Britain, where cigarette ads were banned from television in 1965, sales initially fell but then recovered to reach record levels. In the United States, per capita cigarette sales had begun declining in 1968. This decline had been attributed in part to a drop in the number of new, young smokers. This market segment had become increasingly concerned about the health threats of smoking. That concern resulted in part from antismoking advertisements that the television networks were required to run, free of charge, after passage of the 1967 Fairness Doctrine.

The tobacco industry's initial response to the broadcast advertising ban was to find alternative means to get its message to the public. Liggett &

Myers, Philip Morris, and R. J. Reynolds all signed contracts with automobile racing organizations as a way to keep their brands on television, announcing that the races would be named after popular brands, for example the "L&M Continental Championship," the "Marlboro Championship," and the "Winston 500." Some industry observers saw this as an attempt at a "rear door" reentry by cigarette makers into the television market. Advertisers also positioned displays strategically at racetracks so that they would be captured by television cameras covering the events.

Within one month of the imposed ban on broadcast media advertising, the number of pages of cigarette advertising in consumer magazines more than doubled as compared to the same period of the previous year. Although some increase was anticipated, its magnitude caught the magazine industry by surprise and created a controversy. This stemmed from the impression that the increase in cigarette advertising might convey in the light of the magazine industry's somewhat delicate position regarding health warnings. Congress had barred the Federal Trade Commission from requiring health hazard warnings in cigarette print ads before July 1, 1971, but not after.

Twenty months after the broadcast advertising ban went into effect, the FTC urged the government to buy broadcast time for antismoking advertising. Smoking had hit record high levels since the ads left the airwaves. In 1972, a total of 554 billion cigarettes were smoked, 3 percent more than in the preceding year. The tobacco industry apparently had survived the controversy that began with the 1964 surgeon general's report. Analysts correctly predicted that the industry would witness at least a decade of strong, steady growth. Some attributed this growth to the increase in the 25-to-44 age bracket, a group that accounted for a large proportion of cigarette consumption. Others argued that the ban had not yet had its full effect, since most young consumers had seen cigarette ads for most of their lives. John F. Banzhaf III, executive director of Action on Smoking and Health, an antismoking public interest group, stated that to date the greatest impact of the ruling was that antismoking messages were appearing far less frequently, since broadcasters no longer had to air them for free to balance cigarette ads. The effects of cigarette advertising were seen to be long term, while the antismoking ads seemed to have an effect for a shorter period.

In the 1970's, public and medical research interest turned to the effects of smoking on nonsmokers. In 1972, the surgeon general issued the first report suggesting that secondhand smoke was dangerous to nonsmokers. In 1975, Minnesota passed the first state law requiring businesses, restaurants, and other institutions to establish nonsmoking areas. The concern regarding secondhand smoke continued, with an increasing number of local governments and businesses restricting smoking in public areas.

The cigarette industry continued to target new generations of smokers. Through print and billboard advertising, sales promotions, public relations, and giveaways, the industry continued to aggressively promote its brands. In 1988, tobacco companies spent more than one billion dollars on advertising and more than two billion dollars on promotion. The restriction on broadcast advertising and the required warning labels on packages and advertisements appear to have had a limited impact in the face of advertising that promises smokers increased status, social acceptance, and glamour. The cigarette industry has defended itself against charges of irresponsibility by claiming that individuals are free to decide whether to smoke and that it simply is meeting an existing consumer demand. The industry is particularly defensive regarding charges that ads are targeted toward children. It argues that ads do not encourage people to start smoking, but rather to switch brands.

Bibliography
Doron, Gideon. *The Smoking Paradox: Public Regulation in the Cigarette Industry*. Cambridge, Mass.: Abt Books, 1979. Provides a succinct overview of the conflicting interests at the center of the debate regarding cigarette smoking.
Fritschler, A. Lee. *Smoking and Politics: Policymaking and the Federal Bureaucracy*. 3d ed. Englewood Cliffs, N.J.: Prentice-Hall, 1983. A comprehensive review of the debate and negotiations that surrounded the decision to ban cigarette advertising from television and radio. Provides an insightful summary of the political maneuvering that accompanied the decision.
Sobel, Robert. *They Satisfy: The Cigarette in American Life*. New York: Anchor Press, 1978. An extensive history of the tobacco industry and its changing economics, with a dispassionate account of the political struggle regarding cigarette advertising.
Tollison, Robert D., ed. *Smoking and Society: Toward a More Balanced Assessment*. Lexington, Mass.: Lexington Books, 1986. Presents an assessment of the debate regarding cigarettes from the standpoint of its impact on society. Does not directly review legal aspects, but provides a collection of articles that provide essential background information.
White, Larry C. *Merchants of Death: The American Tobacco Industry*. New York: Beech Tree Books, 1988. A somewhat biased presentation (as evidenced by its title) that provides a readable account of the techniques that tobacco companies have used to market their brands.

Elaine Sherman

Cross-References

Congress Passes the Pure Food and Drug Act (1906); Station KDKA Introduces Commercial Radio Broadcasting (1920); The A. C. Nielsen Company Pioneers in Marketing and Media Research (1923); Congress Establishes the Federal Communications Commission (1934); Cable Television Rises to Challenge Network Television (mid-1990's).

CONGRESS PASSES THE RICO ACT

CATEGORY OF EVENT: Business practices
TIME: October 15, 1970
LOCALE: Washington, D.C.

Congress passed the Racketeer Influenced and Corrupt Organizations Act to fight organized crime, but it was used most prominently to prosecute white-collar criminals

Principal personages:
G. ROBERT BLAKEY (1936-   ), an attorney who drafted the RICO Act
RUDOLPH GIULIANI(1944-   ), the prosecutor most famous for using RICO
CARL ICAHN (1936-   ), a prominent takeover artist who was one of the first to be threatened with RICO indictments
MICHAEL MILKEN (1946-   ), a powerful investment banker who was Giuliani's chief target
WILLIAM REHNQUIST (1924-   ), the Chief Justice of the United States who criticized prosecutors for using RICO in ways not intended by Congress

Summary of Event

In 1970, Congress wound up debates on what appeared to be a simple piece of legislation but actually, as the financial community would learn, was quite complex. Signed into law on October 15, it became known as the Racketeer Influenced and Corrupt Organizations (RICO) Act. The origin of the name was evocative, since its intended target was organized crime.

The measure's history stretched as far back as the Senate investigations of organized crime in 1950. These investigations demonstrated strikingly, through testimony by underworld figures, that legitimate businesses had

531

been infiltrated by criminal elements. Congress considered legislation to prevent this infiltration and a few weak statutes actually were passed, but the problem remained. In 1967, a presidential commission recommended a stiff new law to deal with the issue. Discussions that followed culminated in the 1970 debates.

G. Robert Blakey, who as a Senate committee counsel in 1969 drafted the bill that became the RICO Act, later claimed that the resulting law would make fair the fight between legitimate businesses and the twin Goliaths of organized crime and white-collar crime. Almost all the legislators debating the issue, however, indicated that the primary objective was to provide penalties for gangster elements. Senator Robert Dole (R-Kansas) said that it was impossible to put too much stress on the importance of the legislative attack on organized crime. White-collar crime received little attention.

Even so, the term "organized crime" did not appear in the final version of the law, partly in deference to the sensibilities of the Italian American community. Representative Mario Biaggi (D-New York) was vocal on this score, as were others. Some members of Congress doubted that a precise definition of organized crime was possible. Instead, the term employed was "racketeering activities," defined to include a pattern of racketeering activity or the collection of an unlawful debt as well as the establishment or operation of any illegal enterprise engaged in, or the activities of which affect, interstate or foreign commerce. Also included were "acts or threats of murder, kidnapping, gambling, arson, robbery, bribery, extortion, or dealing in narcotics or other dangerous drugs." In addition, counterfeiting, embezzlement from pension and welfare funds, extortionate credit transactions, obstruction of criminal investigations, and certain dealings with labor unions fell under the racketeering label. All of this was expected, since all of these activities were within the purview of criminal elements.

The acronym for the law, RICO, came into question. One account is that the name was inspired by the character played by Edward G. Robinson in the 1930 film *Little Caesar*, Rico Bendello. Apparently no connection was meant to be made to the Italian American community.

Mail fraud also came under the strictures of the new act, as did fraud in the sale of securities and the felonious manufacture, importation, receiving, concealment, buying, selling, or otherwise dealing in narcotic or other dangerous drugs, punishable under any law of the United States. The context makes it clear that the target of the law was individuals and groups collectively known as organized crime.

Activities falling under the rubric of white-collar crime were not intended to come under the RICO statute. One of the few moments of levity during the debates on the bill came from a congressman who voiced objection to the measure on the basis that whatever the original motives of lawmakers, the courts would be flooded with cases involving all kinds of things not intended to be covered. The law already was recognized to have the potential for overreaching by zealous prosecutors. For example, the congressman suggested, suppose several members of Congress played poker for money on a regular basis. Would this mean that they had been running an organized gambling business and could get twenty-year prison sentences? Could the federal government also confiscate the pot?

Subsection (a) of section 1962, which deals with prohibited activities, contains a laundry list of illegal activities. Securities activities are mentioned in this section. The act regulates the disposition of income that comes, directly or indirectly, from a pattern of racketeering activity or through collection of an unlawful debt in which a person has participated as a principal. That income, or the proceeds of such income, cannot be used to invest, directly or indirectly, in the acquisition of any interest in, or the operation of, any enterprise engaged in interstate or foreign commerce or any enterprise that affects interstate or foreign commerce. The purchase of securities with such income is not necessarily illegal. Securities purchases made in the open market for purposes of investment and without the intention of controlling or participating in the control of the issuer of the securities are not unlawful. Securities purchases would be lawful if the holdings (after the purchase) of the purchaser, the members of his or her immediate family, and any accomplices in any pattern of racketeering activity or the collection of an unlawful debt come to less than 1 percent of the outstanding securities of any single class; further, these holdings cannot confer, either in law or in fact, the power to elect one or more directors of the issuer of the securities.

The penalties for RICO violations were severe. Even if a business were run legitimately, it could be confiscated if it had been purchased with illegally obtained money, and in civil cases treble damages could be levied. Funds and assets could be seized even prior to any trial; suspected criminals thus could be punished before their guilt was assessed. The penalties were so severe that even as the law was passed, some attorneys doubted its constitutionality. RICO's defenders replied that such measures were needed to ferret out money obtained from "mob" activities.

The RICO Act provided for both civil and criminal prosecution when an enterprise engaged in two or more predicate acts within a ten-year period that involved interstate commerce. Under terms of the legislation, even two acts within this time period would constitute a pattern of racketeering activity.

There is debate as to whether legislators considered targets for the law other than "mob" activity and organized crime. Definitions included in the measure describe racketeering activity as including "any offense involving . . . fraud in the sale of securities, or the felonious manufacture, importation, receiving, concealment, buying, selling, or otherwise dealing in narcotic or other dangerous drugs, punishable under any law of the United States."

The context indicates that the legislators meant to address organized crime specifically, not the more common white-collar variety. The wording of the law, however, provided opportunities for energetic and imaginative prosecutors to bring cases outside the scope of organized crime. The initial cases under RICO did involve criminal activities undertaken by career criminals. That was the public's understanding of the purpose of the law. As late as 1980, a reporter wrote,

> RICO stands for the Racketeer Influenced and Corrupt Organizations statute, a federal law enacted in 1970 that gave the government a powerful new weapon in its fight against organized crime's takeover of legitimate businesses. . . . The idea, as the Justice Department put it in a training memo to its lawyers and agents, is "to hit organized crime in the pocketbook."

Impact of Event

Contained in the law were provisions for civil cases, which were used mostly against financial operators. It took time for this use of RICO to become widespread and gain acceptance. There was only one decision involving "civil RICO" in 1972, and only one other case before 1975. Only nine decisions were reported before the 1980's. It was then that matters changed. As New York federal judge Gerard Goettel noted, virtually any fraud case or even a commercial case with overtones of fraud might qualify as racketeering, since use of the mail and telephones brought illegal activity under the definition of racketeering.

One of the first uses of civil RICO in the securities industry came in 1982, when financier and takeover artist Carl Icahn was attempting to raid the Marshall Field organization, in his biggest attempted takeover up to that time. Attorneys for the large department store alleged violations of securities law in Icahn's strategy and also invoked RICO provisions, charging that Icahn had obtained some of the funds for the raid from a "pattern of racketeering." This pattern was evidenced by a consent order from the New Jersey Bureau of Securities, a New York Stock Exchange censure, four fines from the Chicago Board Options Exchange, and other minor charges. Nothing came of this, as Marshall Field entered into a merger with Batus, and the matter was dropped.

Of the approximately 270 trial court decisions before 1985, 3 percent were decided before 1980, 2 percent in 1980, 7 percent in 1981, 13 percent in 1982, 33 percent in 1983, and 43 percent in 1984. Of this number, 57 involved securities transactions. These fell into three categories: brokers providing false information to clients to encourage trading, the "churning" of client accounts (engaging in excessive trading as a means of generating commissions), and issuing prospectuses with misrepresentations. For example, a client sued Harris, Upham after a broker with that firm told him of a pending takeover of a furniture warehouse chain; the takeover rumor was false. The client's total losses from acting on it came to $2.6 million. In 1985, activity related to RICO prosecutions picked up, as prosecutors and litigators fixed upon the law as a superb instrument to terrify business-people.

This new activity did not sit well with many disparate organizations. The American Civil Liberties Union, the National Association of Manufacturers, and the American Federation of Labor-Congress of Industrial Organizations (AFL-CIO), among others, objected to the uses to which the law was put. The law and its use also had critics in the legal profession. Chief Justice of the United States William Rehnquist told a Brookings Institution seminar in April, 1989, that civil RICO was being used in ways that Congress never intended, implying that its constitutionality might be tested and found wanting. In two of the most important cases to be heard by the Supreme Court, however, the Court did not strike down civil RICO prosecutions. A majority in both cases instead threw the matter back to the legislature. RICO may have been a poorly drafted statute, it concluded, but rewriting was a job for Congress, not the courts. Four justices pronounced the wording of the law unconstitutionally ambiguous.

Casting about for means to thwart corporate raiders, target companies started turning to civil RICO. There was talk of using RICO against T. Boone Pickens during the contest for control of Unocal, but nothing materialized. In 1986, officials at the Staley corporation spoke of "extortion" and "bribery," and two parts of its complaint dealt with racketeering activity.

The most important use of RICO, however, was made by Rudolph Giuliani, the U.S. attorney for the Southern District of New York who in the late 1980's led the campaign against Wall Street malefactors. In 1988, he invoked RICO against the investment bank of Princeton/Newport. The prosecution destroyed that company, though it later was found innocent of wrongdoing. Government seizure of assets played a large part in destroying Princeton/Newport. Giuliani's biggest attack was against the investment bank of Drexel Burnham Lambert and its star banker, Michael Milken.

Threatened with RICO action, Drexel agreed to pay $650 million in fines and restitution and to place Milken on a leave of absence. To some, this penalty seemed to be overkill, since the slightest doubt of Drexel's ability to remain in business would, in effect, force it out of business. Ultimately, Drexel did file for bankruptcy in 1990. It was the biggest casualty of RICO, though probably one of the last, because the law was used only sparingly thereafter.

Bibliography

Bailey, Fenton. *Fall from Grace: The Untold Story of Michael Milken.* Secaucus, N.J.: Carol Publishing Group, 1992. Contains a harsh criticism of RICO and an analysis of its use. Bailey is a British journalist who had access to Drexel files.

Bruck, Connie. *The Predators' Ball.* New York: Simon & Schuster, 1988. An early exposé of Drexel and Milken, generally supportive of the use of RICO. Bruck gained entry to Drexel, and this book is the result of investigative journalism.

Kornbluth, Jesse. *Highly Confident: The Crime and Punishment of Michael Milken.* New York: Morrow, 1992. Written with Milken's cooperation, this is a highly personal pro-Milken and anti-Giuliani account of the demise of Drexel Burnham Lambert and the incarceration of Milken. Kornbluth concentrates on the human side of the story and demonstrates only a slight knowledge of RICO.

Sobel, Robert. *Dangerous Dreamers: The Financial Innovators from Charles Merrill to Michael Milken.* New York: J. Wiley & Sons, 1993. Contains an account of the passage of the RICO statute and analysis of how it was used. Valuable for insights into the early and later views of how RICO should be employed.

Stewart, James. *Den of Thieves.* New York: Simon & Schuster, 1991. Stewart is generally sympathetic to RICO and believes its use was justified in certain criminal and civil cases. Stewart was an editor of *The Wall Street Journal* with ties to Giuliani.

Robert Sobel

Cross-References

The U.S. Stock Market Crashes on Black Tuesday (1929); Insider Trading Scandals Mar the Emerging Junk Bond Market (1986); The U.S. Stock Market Crashes on 1987's "Black Monday" (1987); Drexel and Michael Milken Are Charged with Insider Trading (1988); Dow Jones Adds Microsoft and Intel (1999).

CONGRESS PASSES THE FAIR CREDIT REPORTING ACT

CATEGORIES OF EVENT: Finance and consumer affairs
TIME: October 26, 1970
LOCALE: Washington, D.C.

The Fair Credit Reporting Act caused policies to be implemented to ensure the proper maintenance and disclosure of credit information

Principal personages:
WILLIAM PROXMIRE (1915-   ), a senator from Wisconsin
RICHARD H. LEHMAN (1948-   ), a congressman from California
ALAN J. DIXON (1927-   ), a senator from Illinois
ALAN CRANSTON (1914-   ), a senator from California
ESTEBAN EDWARD TORRES (1930-   ), a congressman from California

Summary of Event

The Fair Credit Reporting Act (an amendment to the Consumer Credit Protection Act of 1968), was passed by Congress on October 26, 1970, and became law in April of 1971. Senator William Proxmire of Wisconsin was instrumental in the passage of this legislation.

Section 602 of the Fair Credit Reporting Act (FCRA) outlined the need for this law. First, the banking system is dependent upon fair and accurate credit reporting. Inaccurate credit reports directly impair the efficiency of the banking system, and unfair credit reporting methods undermine the public confidence essential to the continued functioning of the banking system. Second, elaborate mechanisms exist to investigate and evaluate creditworthiness, credit standing, credit capacity, character, and general reputation of consumers. Consumer reporting agencies have assumed a vital role in assembling and evaluating consumer credit and other information on consumers. There is a need to ensure that consumer reporting agencies exercise their responsibilities with fairness, impartiality, and a respect for consumers' right to privacy.

The FCRA had four primary objectives. They were to establish acceptable purposes for which a consumer credit report may be obtained; to define the consumer's rights regarding credit reports, with particular emphasis on giving consumers access to their reports and procedures for correcting inaccurate information; to establish requirements for handling an adverse credit decision that resulted in whole or in part from information contained in a credit report; and to define the responsibilities of credit reporting agencies.

In general, it was the realization by Congress that consumer credit has had major impacts on economic activity as a whole that spurred the legislation. Consumers' inability to obtain credit for expensive items such as automobiles and large appliances negatively affected economic factors such as employment, production, and income, ultimately magnifying the business cycle, particularly in downturns. Financial institutions, as the grantors of consumer credit and the users of information supplied by credit reporting agencies, weighted their credit decisions heavily on the information supplied. Timely, accurate, and intelligible information was necessary for proper credit decisions. Consumers also needed to be protected from ramifications resulting from inaccurate, untimely, or improper credit information.

Consumers by far were the most heavily affected by the passage of this legislation. Consumers rely heavily upon consumer credit as a means of purchasing expensive items and raising their standards of living by purchasing goods for current use with future income. Reporting agencies faced higher costs as a result of the legislation but gained a greater reputation for accuracy and usefulness.

The following information is usually contained within a consumer credit file: name; address; previous address; Social Security number; date of birth; employer; length of employment; previous employment; credit history including creditors, balances, and payment patterns; and public filings such as mortgages, chattels, marriages, divorces, collections suits, and bankruptcies. The FCRA made all information within a consumer's credit report accessible to the consumer.

Consumers can get access to their credit files in several ways. If a consumer is denied credit on a credit application, the lending institution is required to mail a detailed letter outlining the reasons for denial and including the name, address, and telephone number of any reporting agency consulted. The consumer may take this letter to the reporting agency within thirty days of the date of the letter to discuss and obtain a free copy of the report. A consumer who has not been denied credit may obtain a copy of his or her file from the local reporting service for a nominal fee. A consumer must provide proper identification in order to obtain a copy of his or her credit file. The FCRA identifies the type of material available to the consumer. The consumer has the right to know all the information in the file, with the exception of medical records. This includes names of people or companies that have obtained the report within the past six months and the names of those who received the report for employment purposes within the past two years.

The FCRA greatly benefits consumers by allowing them to dispute information contained within their files. Erroneous or inaccurate information can be contested and asked to be verified by the reporting agency. The consumer has the right to place within the credit file a consumer statement outlining his or her interpretation of negative information. This statement is then part of the file and is presented to future users. The consumer statement is usually limited to one hundred words. The FCRA limits the amount of time that unfavorable information can be reported on a consumer. Seven years is the maximum, with the exception of bankruptcies, which are reported for ten years.

In some instances, an investigative credit report may be compiled on an individual. It includes all the information mentioned above. In addition, it includes information on the character, reputation, and living style of the consumer. This information is obtained from interviews with friends, associates, and neighbors. The consumer has the same rights of access to this report as to an ordinary credit file.

The final major area that the FCRA addresses is consumers' right to privacy. Credit information is basically for use by the consumer, the reporting agency, authorized credit grantors, employers, and insurance companies. To restrict dissemination to proper users, those who request credit information must prove their identity and their reason for wanting access to a consumer's credit file. For users who obtain information under false pretenses, the law provides for fines of up to $5,000, prison sentences up to one year, or both. The same penalties apply to officers and employees of reporting agencies who misuse information. Consumers are allowed to pursue civil litigation against reporting agencies and are entitled to compensation for any financial injury, extra penalties imposed by the court, court costs, and attorney fees. Consumers can discuss complaints with credit reporting agencies by contacting the Federal Trade Commission.

Impact of Event

Consumers were not the only parties affected by the FCRA. Reporting agencies assumed a more clearly defined fiduciary responsibility to act in good faith and trust. Their goals are to maintain timely and accurate files on consumers, handle disputes in a timely manner, and investigate complaints and inaccurate information on consumers. They must also ensure the confidentiality of their information while still making it available to the proper users. Failure to follow proper procedures and guidelines can result not only in consumer complaints but also in lawsuits, fines, or even imprisonment for employees of reporting agencies.

Consumer credit grantors also were affected by the FCRA. Lenders need to be careful when disclosing credit information. It must be both timely and accurate. Letters denying credit must be sent out on time, and procedures need to be in place to handle direct requests made to the organization. Lenders need to be careful with outside requests so as to not be viewed as credit reporting agencies. The final area lenders must address is the use of information for decision-making purposes. Many lenders place great weight in consumer credit decisions on the information obtained from credit files. It is essential that lenders have reliable information in order to make proper credit decisions. Lenders also use credit reporting agencies to screen borrowers. This works in two ways for lenders. It improves their credit quality by eliminating marginal borrowers and also gives them access to potential new customers. Lenders are bound by privacy laws and are forbidden to give copies of reports to consumers or other lenders.

The FCRA had major ramifications for consumers applying for credit, credit reporting agencies, and lenders who relied upon information for decision-making purposes. The emphasis of this act was that information contained within a credit file must be timely and accurate, accessible to all concerned parties, and inaccessible to unconcerned parties. The FCRA and subsequent amendments dealt with these issues.

On September 13, 1989, the United States House of Representatives Subcommittee on Consumer Affairs and Coinage of the Committee on Banking, Finances, and Urban Affairs met to discuss multiple concerns regarding the FCRA. Chairman Richard H. Lehman summarized the concerns. He stated that the act had existed essentially without amendment for nearly twenty years and that the credit reporting industry apparently had been successful in convincing Congress that it worked well in its present form. He noted, however, that people had concerns about privacy and other aspects of their rights under the act. There had been complaints about the difficulty of getting inaccurate information removed from credit files, the length of time to get disputed information reinvestigated, name mix-ups, and denials of credit being based upon the number of inquiries in a credit report. He also noted that Vice President Dan Quayle had had his credit report made available with what appeared to be insufficient checks by the credit reporter of the purpose intended. Finally, Lehman noted that $104 billion in consumer installment credit was outstanding when the act was passed. By 1989, that figure had reached approximately $700 billion.

On October 22, 1991, the United States Senate Subcommittee on Consumer and Regulatory Affairs conducted hearings on the FCRA. In his opening statement, chairman Alan J. Dixon expressed reasons for the hearing. Consumer credit had increased sixfold since the act was first introduced, and the number of reports had increased fivefold. A revolution in computer technology had changed not only the shape of the credit reporting industry but also methods of record keeping and dissemination of consumer data. Witnesses at the hearing were asked to comment on credit report inaccuracies, complaints about errors and obsolete information, consumer access to reports and knowledge of rights, privacy issues and prescreening, enforcement of the FCRA, and credit repair organizations.

At this hearing, Senator Alan Cranston of California noted that he had introduced to the Senate a companion bill to legislation in the House of Representatives proposed by Richard H. Lehman. Cranston's bill proposed education of consumers about the credit reporting process, greater protection of privacy rights, and response to the massive changes in information technology and business credit needs. The meeting was concluded with the members of the subcommittee assuring Dixon that they were looking forward to passing the necessary amendments to the FCRA.

On October 24, 1991, the United States House of Representatives Subcommittee on Consumer Affairs and Coinage met to discuss the FCRA. Chairman Esteban Edward Torres conducted the hearings. The primary purpose of the meeting was to overview legislation (H.R. 3596) introduced earlier in the week by the chairman to reform the FCRA. His legislation addressed problems primarily pertaining to lack of privacy induced by the use of computer technology, the rampant inaccuracy of information contained within credit reports, and the imbalance of power between business credit grantors and consumers. After much debate and testimony, Torres concluded the meeting by stating that it appeared that reform was essential. He ended by stressing the impacts these injustices had upon many Americans, particularly consumers.

The FCRA was passed, and later amended, to enhance the proper maintenance and use of consumer information for credit, employment, and other related purposes. It outlines the responsibilities for all parties involved in the granting of consumer credit. In its inception in the early 1970's, it dealt with relatively small volumes of information and limited technology. In the late 1980's, the amount of information and technology had increased to the point where the original intentions of the law were compromised. This led Congress to hold many hearings and pass amendments to the original law to bring it back into compliance with its original intentions.

Bibliography

Beares, Paul. "Regulation of Consumer Credit." In *Consumer Lending.* Washington, D.C.: American Bankers Association, 1987. An excellent book dealing with all phases of consumer credit. Written from a banker's perspective, but easy reading for the layperson. Discusses in detail the process of granting consumer credit. This chapter in particular focuses on legislation and regulation.

Cole, Robert H. "Regulation of Consumer Credit." In *Consumer and Commercial Credit Management.* 8th ed. Homewood, Ill.: Irwin, 1988. This chapter discusses consumer credit regulation in detail. Chapter 9 in the same volume details the operations of credit reporting agencies.

U.S. Congress. House. Committee on Banking, Finance, and Urban Affairs. Subcommittee on Consumer Affairs and Coinage. *Fair Credit Reporting Act: Hearing.* 101st Congress, 1st session, 1989. Hearings discussing problems, loopholes, and noncompliance by credit reporting agencies.

U.S. Congress. House. Committee on Banking, Finance, and Urban Affairs. Subcommittee on Consumer Affairs and Coinage. *Fair Credit Reporting Act: Hearing.* 102d Congress, 1st session, 1991. Hearings discussing pending legislation designed to modernize and amend the FCRA. Discussions include abuses and reclarifications of the intended purpose of the original act.

U.S. Congress. House. Committee on Banking, Finance, and Urban Affairs. Subcommittee on Consumer Affairs and Coinage. *Give Yourself Credit (Guide to Consumer Credit Laws).* 102d Congress, 2d session, 1992. A detailed guide covering consumer credit regulations. Uses a question-and-answer approach. Written in everyday language. Actual consumer situations are included. Chapter 5, "Your Credit File," is directly applicable to this article.

U.S. Congress. Senate. Committee on Banking, Housing, and Urban Affairs. Subcommittee on Consumer and Regulatory Affairs. *Fair Credit Reporting Act: Hearing.* 102d Congress, 1st session, 1991. Senate hearings and testimonials relating to proposed amendments prompted primarily by the explosive growth of consumer credit, in conjunction with implementation of computer technology as a means of managing credit information.

William C. Ward III

Cross-References

The Federal Reserve Act Creates a U.S. Central Bank (1913); Congress Passes the Consumer Credit Protection Act (1968); Congress Prohibits Discrimination in the Granting of Credit (1975); Congress Deregulates Banks and Savings and Loans (1980-1982); Bush Responds to the Savings and Loan Crisis (1989).

THE ENVIRONMENTAL PROTECTION AGENCY IS CREATED

CATEGORIES OF EVENT: Government and business; consumer affairs
TIME: December 2, 1970
LOCALE: Washington, D.C.

A large consensus on the need to consolidate the many programs designed to protect the environment led Congress to approve President Nixon's proposal to create the Environmental Protection Agency

Principal personages:
RICHARD M. NIXON (1913-1994), the president of the United States, 1969-1974
JOHN D. DINGELL (1926-   ), a congressman
RUSSELL E. TRAIN (1920-   ), the chair of the Council on Environmental Quality
ROY L. ASH (1918-   ), the chairman of the President's Advisory Council on Executive Organization
PARKE C. BRINKLEY, the president of the National Agricultural Chemicals Association

Summary of Event

The nature and extent of governmental involvement in setting environmental policy was dramatically changed by two nearly concurrent developments. First, the passage of the National Environmental Policy Act of 1969 established the President's Council on Environmental Quality (CEQ). The second development was initiated on July 9, 1970, when President Richard M. Nixon forwarded a plan to Congress to create an independent Environmental Protection Agency (EPA). The plan required consolidation of several programs from the Interior Department (for example, water quality administration and pesticide research programs), the Department of Health, Education, and Welfare (for example, air pollution control and solid waste management), the Department of Agriculture (for example, pesticide registration, licensing, and monitoring functions), the Federal Radiation Council (for example, setting of radiation standards), and the CEQ (for example, ecological research).

Subsequent congressional hearings and floor debates led to the formal endorsement of President Nixon's plan. Hearings were conducted under the auspices of the House Government Operations Subcommittee on Executive and Legislative Reorganization and the Senate Government Operations Subcommittee on Executive Reorganization and Government Research. Individuals providing supportive testimonies included Russell E. Train, the chairman of the CEQ, Roy L. Ash, the chairman of the President's Advisory Council on Executive Organization, and Parke C. Brinkley, the president of the National Agricultural Chemicals Association.

Train stressed that the EPA would contribute to the effectiveness of efforts to reduce pollution. He indicated that its authority would stem from previously enacted legislation such as the Clean Air Act; the Federal Water Pollution Control Act; the Solid Waste Disposal Act of 1965; the Federal Insecticides, Fungicide, and Rodenticide Act, and the Atomic Energy Act. Additional authority would come from selected administrative units such as the Council on Environmental Quality, the National Air Pollution Control Administration, the Federal Water Quality Administration, and the Bureau of Sports Fisheries and Wildlife. Ash testified that the programs for combating pollution were spread across several agencies at that time and that this fragmentation did not serve the public interest. He envisaged that the EPA would have a 1971 budget of $1.4 billion and approximately six thousand people on staff. He also indicated the following EPA objectives with regard to pollution control: to conduct research and to set standards, to formulate coordinated policy, to recognize new environmental problems as they arise and develop new programs to address them, to integrate pollution control and enforcement, to simplify tasks of state and local governments, and to clarify the responsibility of private industry. Other testimony focused on the advantages to industry and to Congress of dealing with only one agency on pollution control matters.

The House Government Operations Committee endorsed Nixon's reorganization plan on September 23, 1970. Although most House members favored the plan, John D. Dingell (D-Michigan) contended that the new EPA could be a source of new delays and wastes rather than enhancing the effectiveness of pollution control efforts. He criticized the plan because it excluded water and sewer programs in the domain of the Department of Agriculture and the Department of Housing and Urban Development as well as the environmental programs of the Defense and Transportation departments. He sought establishment of a cabinet-level Department of Environmental Quality instead of the proposed EPA. The House eventually endorsed the plan by defeating a veto resolution opposing the creation of the EPA. In the Senate, the Government Operations Committee presented a report expressing its endorsement for the establishment of the EPA. The reorganization plan became effective on December 2, 1970.

Impact of Event

The EPA has been forced to cope with enormous performance expectations. The agency was created at a time of popular dissatisfaction with earlier attempts at pollution control. Responding to demands from the electorate for effective efforts to protect the environment, Congress passed several legislative measures that were ambitious in scope and that served to heighten expectations of what the EPA should deliver. In addition, the EPA's considerable authority stemmed from a legislative mandate to establish and administer standards for industry aimed at protecting the environment in the United States. In a report titled *Research and Development in the Environmental Protection Agency*, the Environmental Research Assessment Committee of the National Research Council elegantly summarized the far-reaching scope and importance of effective environmental policy for industry. The report noted that once agents have been released into the environment as by-products of production, natural processes acting on them can cause changes in the quality of the ambient environment. These changes have potentially adverse consequences for human health and welfare, weather and climate, managed and natural ecosystems, and the use of resources for alternative purposes.

Because environmental protection is a multifaceted and complex topic, it is difficult to assess the risks and costs associated with any decision or policy. Such assessments often are confounded by value judgments (for example, the tradeoff between "necessary" economic progress and "acceptable" environmental damage), conflicting viewpoints (for example, the differing agendas of industry and environmental groups), and a genuine lack of knowledge (for example, uncertainty over the thresholds of exposure to substances likely to harm human beings, and a clear understanding of the causal links between the intensity and duration of environmental pollution and societal costs such as birth defects, poor health, and premature deaths). Decisions and actions of the EPA thus were fated to become the subject of debate.

Creation of the Environmental Protection Agency was one of the lasting achievements of Richard R. Nixon's presidency. (White House Historical Society)

An objective appraisal of the EPA's decision-making impact should consider the benefits directly attributable to the agency and the costs at which they were achieved. The EPA claimed that emissions of lead, carbon monoxide, and sulfur oxides respectively fell by 97 percent, 41 percent, and 25 percent between 1970 and 1990. Although these benefits appear impressive, they can be attributed in part to factors largely unrelated to environmental regulation.

Cost implications further undermine the benefits associated with EPA regulations. The EPA grew into a massive bureaucracy several times larger than its size at inception. In 1992, it accounted for an operating budget of $4.5 billion and a staff of eighteen thousand. The EPA itself estimated that compliance with its regulations cost Americans $115 billion in 1990, or an annual pollution control cost of $450 per person per year. That figure was a remarkable 2.1 percent of the country's gross national product. That figure was higher than corresponding percentages for most Western European countries and was more than twice the 0.9 percent of GNP spent by the United States in 1972. Furthermore, the EPA's 1992 budget represented one-third of the entire annual spending on federal regulatory bodies.

The burgeoning cost estimates focus attention on value judgments associated with lives saved as a direct consequence of EPA regulations. Some studies show that the cost of saving one life through EPA regulations ranges from $100 million to as much as $5.7 trillion. More generous estimates of the number of lives saved lower this cost. EPA critics such as John Goodman of the National Center for Policy Analysis have questioned the wisdom of incurring such astounding costs, noting that regulating for health is a policy at war with itself, since the reduction of living standards associated with increased regulatory costs will cause additional deaths. Even if the

EPA's claims regarding lives saved were accurate, the price paid to save one life through environmental regulation could cover the cost of many other lives at risk from other causes, such as malnutrition.

Businesses have often exploited environmental politics and policies to hurt competitors or to discourage new competition. Ethanol manufacturers, for example, formed a strategic alliance with environmentalists to hurt the oil industry. This alliance influenced the 1990 amendments to the Clean Air Act in a manner designed to enhance demand for their alternative fuel. Many businesses share the view that the EPA possesses sweeping and potent authority that can unreasonably restrict their operations. This view has some merit. Federal agencies usually have either broad authority covering virtually all industries or focused power that deeply affects operations of specific industries. In contrast, the powers of the EPA are unparalleled in both breadth and depth. Nevertheless, some aspects of environmental pollution are less amenable to direct EPA control than others.

Although the EPA derives its authority from several congressional statutes focused either on protecting the environment or on protecting the public against health hazards, the agency does not carry unlimited powers to achieve statutory goals. On the contrary, the EPA is constrained by procedures and limitations that may not be consistent across statutes. As one illustration, the Clean Air Act states that the EPA's decisions concerning ambient air quality should not focus on economic or technical considerations but on protection of public health. In contrast, under the Federal Environmental Pesticide Control Act, the EPA cannot cancel the registration of a pesticide because it poses an unreasonable risk to the public unless the impact of cancellation on economic factors such as prices of agricultural commodities and retail food prices have been considered.

The political ramifications of environmental policy decisions are formidable. Political realities may inhibit EPA regulatory actions even if they are essential from a public interest standpoint, and even if they are mandated by law. Often, EPA policy is influenced heavily by extraneous considerations such as the likelihood of legal challenges. Because almost four out of five EPA decisions are litigated, it appears that environmental policy is shaped more by court orders and settlement negotiations than by EPA directives. For example, one area that has witnessed controversy and litigation involves the Comprehensive Environmental Response, Compensation, and Liability Act (CERCLA) of 1980, more widely known as Superfund. Essentially, Superfund is a large trust fund, financed through tax dollars and levies on petroleum and certain chemical products, that the EPA utilizes to clean up toxic spills and hazardous waste sites. The law also empowers the EPA to pursue parties responsible for these environmental hazards and to get them to reimburse the fund for cleanup costs. This has led to much resentment, because in some cases the parties held responsible were only tenuously linked to the object of the cleanups for which they were forced to pay.

Additional constraints on the EPA are imposed by Congress, through the large number of committees that supervise EPA activities, and the White House, through control over key appointments and budgetary oversight through the Office of Management and Budget. Taken together, the preceding political factors may have significantly undermined the effectiveness of U.S. environmental policy. Some policy regulations overtly subordinate environmental protection goals to political feasibility. For example, EPA regulations discourage the replacement of old plants by holding them to lower pollution standards than new plants. This may be irrational both economically and environmentally, but it is politically essential.

Key functions of the EPA include establishing standards to control and safeguard the environment and conducting research that contributes meaningfully to environmental decision-making. These tasks pose special challenges. First, establishing standards is a difficult undertaking given the enormous imbalance between the current level of knowledge and the amount of work that remains to be done. Of the approximately seventy thousand chemicals in the EPA Toxic Substances Control Inventory in the early 1990's, information concerning health implications was available for only ninety-six hundred. Second, although the EPA's research should aim to provide scientific bases for environmental decision-making, such research is not likely to be perceived as objective by the regulated parties. Given the high frequency of litigation in environmental matters, the EPA is likely to draw on findings from EPA-initiated research programs to bolster its arguments in an adversarial legal setting. Unfortunately, the validity of sound EPA-initiated research may appear suspect because the EPA is a participant in a litigated, adversarial regulation process.

Other evidence suggests that the bulk of available environmental research and knowledge may not be effectively used by the EPA for decision-making purposes. The Environmental Research Assessment Committee reported in 1977 that environmental research and development is actively pursued by many agencies other than the EPA, including the departments of Agriculture; Commerce; Health, Education, and Welfare; and Interior. The National Science Foundation and the Energy Research and Development Administration are among the other agencies that contribute. Although most of these research efforts could help decision-making at the EPA, the report found detailed information on the efforts lacking.

In summary, environmental regulation is an extremely vital and complex area. Enforcing environmental policies often constrains industrial operations; therefore, businesses usually resist or oppose EPA directives via judicial means. Environmental regulation is also an enormously costly enterprise. Because of pervasive value judgments in this area, it is not surprising that some people advocate the abolition of the EPA, calling for a replacement with another system based on common law and torts. Others see the effect of the EPA as beneficial.

Bibliography

Brimelow, Peter, and Leslie Spencer. "Should We Abolish the EPA?" *Forbes* (September 14, 1992): 432-443. Evaluates common law and torts as an alternative to the bureaucratic approach for tackling environmental problems.

_____. "You Can't Get There from Here." *Forbes* (July 6, 1992): 59-64. An informative performance assessment of the EPA. Analyzes the complexity of environmental legislation, focuses on cost/benefit factors, and critically appraises the EPA's bureaucratic approach to solving pollution problems.

Committee on Environmental Decision Making. *Decision Making in the Environmental Protection Agency*. Washington, D.C.: National Academy of Sciences, 1977. A useful assessment of the EPA's decision-making framework.

Environmental Research Assessment Committee. *Research and Development in the Environmental Protection Agency*. Washington, D.C.: National Academy of Sciences, 1977. A detailed and insightful account of the EPA's research policies and practices.

Washington Environmental Research Center. *Managing the Environment*. Washington, D.C.: U.S. Government Printing Office, 1973. Although dated, this source contains informative articles on a variety of environmental management topics.

Siva Balasubramanian

Cross-References

Congress Passes the Motor Vehicle Air Pollution Control Act (1965); The Banning of DDT Signals New Environmental Awareness (1969); The Three Mile Island Accident Prompts Reforms in Nuclear Power (1979); Bush Signs the Clean Air Act of 1990 (1990).

NIXON SIGNS THE OCCUPATIONAL SAFETY AND HEALTH ACT

CATEGORY OF EVENT: Labor
TIME: December 29, 1970
LOCALE: Washington, D.C.

The Occupational Safety and Health Act of 1970 gave the federal government the responsibility of establishing and enforcing safety standards in the workplace

Principal personages:
RICHARD M. NIXON (1913-1994), a conservative Republican president who strongly supported the passage of legislation to improve safety in the workplace
HARRISON A. WILLIAMS, JR. (1919-   ), the principal author of the Occupational Safety and Health Act
GEORGE P. SHULTZ (1920-   ), the secretary of labor during the hearings on the bill, a strong supporter of the legislation
JIMMY CARTER (1924-   ), the Democratic president who, in the late 1970's, undertook a substantial revision of OSHA procedures

Summary of Event
On December 29, 1970, President Richard M. Nixon signed the Occupational Safety and Health Act, mandating that the U.S. Department of Labor establish health and safety standards in the workplace with the goal of achieving the "highest degree of health and safety protection for the employee." This was one of a series of statutes, sometimes referred to as "public interest labor laws," that began with the Landrum-Griffin Labor-Management Reporting and Disclosure Act of 1959. The purview of OSHA

is expansive, involving both health and safety standards. In the 1970's, the Occupational Safety and Health Administration (OSHA), created by the act, stressed direct government regulation of safety in the workplace. In the 1980's, OSHA extended its efforts to the communication of information, primarily through the labeling of hazardous chemicals.

OSHA enforcement involves inspections, financial penalties, and recourse to criminal prosecutions. The act grew out of growing concern for issues related to the environment and awareness of dangers in the workplace, particularly asbestosis (a lung disease caused by breathing asbestos particles), respiratory diseases among cotton workers, and various forms of cancer. Between 1964 and 1969, the injury rate in manufacturing increased by almost 25 percent. Efforts to address black lung disease had been addressed in the Federal Coal Mine Health and Safety Act of 1969. Other acts had been passed to protect certain workers, such as longshoremen and construction workers, but the OSHA regulations superseded these laws and extended to many previously uncovered sectors. Causing considerable controversy were situations in which employers knew of dangers but workers did not.

The high cost of safety made it unlikely that standards would be met unless mandated by government statute. It was also hoped that OSHA would alleviate some of the problems associated with state-administered workers' compensation programs. Some injuries were not compensated or were not adequately compensated, yet the costs of workers' compensation programs were very high. Advocates of new regulations proposed injury prevention as a way of reducing compensation payments. In addition, it was argued that workers' compensation programs might cause people to feign injuries, be less cautious, or stay out of work longer than necessary. By increasing time at work and reducing expenditures on workers' compensation, increased safety would be better for the individuals directly involved and for society as a whole. It was also pointed out that since employers paid into the workers' compensation program and since benefits to workers differed among states, the cost of injuries was not uniform among the states. As a result, incentives for employers to provide safe workplaces were not the same. In addition, a given safety standard might have different costs in different states, depending on such factors as wage rates and prevailing technology in use. Secretary of Labor George Shultz pointed to the increasing incidence of workplace injuries and the costs of medical care and workers' compensation claims as evidence of the need for passage of the OSHA law. In congressional hearings it was pointed out that in some European countries national standards had been imposed, but they had met with mixed results. In sectors such as steel and chemicals, the U.S. safety record was far better than that of the United Kingdom, even though the latter country had a national safety program.

The Senate bill (S. 2193) created the National Institute of Occupational Safety and Health (NIOSH) in the Department of Health, Education, and Welfare; and an independent Occupational Safety and Health Review Commission. The first two agencies were to conduct inspections and investigations, and the third was intended to hear appeals by employers relating to the decisions of the first two agencies. A 1978 Supreme Court decision prevented OSHA from conducting inspections without cause, limiting the ability to catch violators in the act. The decision, however, allowed for warrants permitting inspections. States maintained the right to establish their own safety programs provided that they received prior approval from OSHA. State standards therefore had to match those at the federal level or provide greater protection. OSHA provided workers with a form of redress beyond that provided through collective bargaining agreements. Equally important, the Supreme Court ruled in *Alexander v. Gardner- Denver* (1974) that workers could seek statutory redress even after making use of the grievance procedures established in a collective bargaining agreement.

The mandate of the OSHA law represented a shift from issues of cost efficiency in production to equity. The goal was to eliminate injuries in the workplace without explicit consideration of costs and benefits. The legislation represented a movement away from a system for determining reparations after an accident to an approach intended to set standards that would prevent accidents. OSHA brought to the forefront a number of issues central to the future of industrial relations in the United States. Previous legislation such as the Fair Labor Standards Act of 1938 and its amendments set limits on wages, hours, and other conditions of employment, but the way production was conducted was left to be decided by employers and workers. The theory of "compensating wage differentials" argued that unsafe, high-risk jobs would require higher wages to attract workers. Workers who chose those occupations would be compensated for the risk by higher wages. In cases in which the allocation of workers among jobs was unacceptable, unions, through collective bargaining, would negotiate a package of wages and safety standards mutually agreeable to both the employer and the employee.

The justification for direct government intrusion into the way production was conducted rested on two premises. To the extent that the way goods are produced affects people other than the employer and the employee, the interest of those others may justify a role for the government. As an example, exposure of pregnant women to certain chemicals may be a health hazard not only to them but also to their future children. Society may feel compelled to limit such exposure in the interests of the unborn even if the women are willing to risk exposure. OSHA policies sought to control the social costs of unsafe workplaces. A second justification arises in cases in which the risk of disease or injury is not known or is underestimated by the worker. In this context, workers are unable to make informed decisions. From a purely monetary perspective, there may even exist incentives for employers to conceal true risks from employees. In this case, the role of the government may take the form of setting standards or providing information.

Impact of Event

From its very passage, the OSHA law was plagued with problems. The act provided no penalties to employees who were careless or deliberately unsafe, only an encouragement to act safely. The act provided for sanctions against employers including citations and fines. When corrective measures prescribed by OSHA were not adhered to, the agency had recourse to the courts. In 1972, twenty-four hundred citations were issued under the act. The number increased to forty-three thousand in 1973. Companies found it especially difficult to understand what OSHA expected and how the OSHA standards were to be implemented. The Subcommittee on Labor of the Committee on Labor and Public Welfare of the United States Senate held numerous oversight hearings at which employers vociferously addressed the uneven enforcement of the act, the trivial nature of many standards, and the excessive costs of adherence to standards. Enforcement efforts have been criticized for unevenness and for responding to the preferences of the political party in office.

Since the mandate of OSHA can be carried out either by state programs or at the federal level, any assessment must look at the two distinct modes of implementation. Although states were allowed to establish their own mechanisms for enforcement, standards were to at least equal those at the federal level. In part, the federal statute was a response to the failure of state programs to adequately address the problems of workplace injuries, yet the statute allowed for state implementation of the program for two principal reasons. First, some legislators were concerned with states' rights, particularly in the light of problems with implementing federal programs. Second, there were more than two thousand state inspectors, with millions of dollars spent on safety by states. The federal government was not interested in dismantling the state programs or assuming this additional cost.

In September, 1991, a fire at an Imperial Food Products poultry plant in Hamlet, North Carolina, killed twenty-five workers who were trapped in the factory after the employer had locked the exit doors from the outside.

OSHA found serious deficiencies in the enforcement of standards at the state level, precipitating an examination of the state programs. Particular attention was paid to the failure of states to adjust their standards to changes in federal rules. States with separate programs included Alaska, Arizona, California, Hawaii, Indiana, Iowa, Kentucky, Maryland, Michigan, Minnesota, Nevada, New Mexico, Oregon, South Carolina, Tennessee, Utah, Vermont, Virginia, Washington, and Wyoming, in addition to Puerto Rico and the Virgin Islands.

At the federal level, critics of OSHA have come from many camps. Employers have argued that OSHA rules and regulations are trivial and have led to large increases in the cost of doing business. Organized labor has at times argued that the standards are not stringent enough, while in other cases, in which the standards have led to job losses, unions have argued that the standards are too strict. In 1990, maximum fines for each violation were raised from $10,000 to $30,000, and willful violations that led to death were changed from misdemeanors to felonies.

Despite annual expenditures in the early 1990's of approximately $400 million, there is little evidence that OSHA has had the effect of reducing injuries in the workplace. Two explanations are given for the ineffectiveness of OSHA. Some argue that the penalties for violating safety standards are so low that it is more profitable for firms to violate the standards and pay fines if caught rather than make changes to meet standards. In addition, the likelihood of a firm being inspected is very small, so the chances of being caught are very low. The second explanation is that OSHA has concentrated on standards for machinery and equipment while ignoring the human aspect in many accidents. Safe machines do not ensure a safe workplace in the absence of safe operation and supervision. The question is why Congress has continued to support OSHA.

Two factors seem to explain continued support. One is that OSHA has been able to increase compliance. In other words, it is able to impose penalties that reduce the likelihood of firms repeatedly violating standards. It can force compliance even if that does not translate immediately into fewer injuries. A second factor is the significant indirect influence of OSHA on the structure of American industry. Large firms and unionized firms tend to be safer in part because of the ability to bear the costs of increased safety and also because of economies of scale associated with safety. An expenditure to make a machine safer will be more cost effective if the machine is used by ten people rather than by one person. OSHA, by concentrating on sectors with the greatest incidence of injuries, intrudes most on small, nonunion operations. As a consequence, costs are driven up in these firms, giving large firms and unionized firms cost advantages. These are the same firms that are able to influence political decisions the most. It comes as no surprise that these firms support continuation of OSHA. Support may come in the guise of promotion of safety, but large firms also gain a cost advantage as a result of safety and health regulation.

A number of lessons have been learned from experience with OSHA. One is the need to consider cost effectiveness in establishing safety standards. In this context, the move toward performance-based regulatory policies was inevitable. In October, 1978, Eula Bingham, director of OSHA during the Jimmy Carter Administration, modified or eliminated almost a thousand OSHA regulations. President Ronald Reagan's efforts to deregulate led to further reductions in OSHA efforts. The total budget for OSHA went from $97 million in 1975 to $248 million in 1989. By 1989, despite the increase in budget, the staff was still smaller than in 1980, with most of the reduction being enforcement personnel.

During the Reagan Administration, the Office of Management and Budget (OMB) was given oversight power. OSHA had to submit proposed reforms to the OMB, which could then hold up implementation. A 1986 court decision required that OMB not restrict OSHA when it faced a statutory deadline. Unions used this rule on behalf of OSHA to get regulations on formaldehyde and lead, among other job hazards. The Office of Management and Budget has estimated that the regulatory costs of OSHA were $2.7 billion in 1987 and $12.7 billion in 1989. The growth in OSHA is evidenced by the following statistics. In 1972, there were 28,900 inspections, 89,600 discovered violations, and $2.1 million in penalties. In contrast, in 1989, there were 58,400 inspections, 154,900 discovered violations, and $45 million in penalties.

Bibliography

Bartel, Ann P., and Lacy Glenn Thomas. "Direct and Indirect Effects of Regulations: A New Look at OSHA's Impact." *Journal of Law and Economics* 28 (1985): 1-26. Data for the 1974-1978 period show no significant effect of OSHA on injury rates.

Gray, Wayne B., and Carol Adaire Jones. "Longitudinal Patterns of Compliance with OSHA in the Manufacturing Sector." *The Journal of Human Resources* 26 (Fall, 1991): 623-653. This empirical study looks at the pattern of response to the regulatory efforts of OSHA.

U.S. Congress. Senate. Committee on Labor and Public Welfare. Subcommittee on Labor. *Legislative History of the Occupational Safety and Health Act of 1970.* 92d Congress, 1st session. Senate document 2193. Documents the various amendments to the bill and the positions of interested groups.

Viscusi, W. Kip. *Fatal Tradeoffs*. New York: Oxford University Press, 1992. A detailed economic discussion of how risk is evaluated. Empirical evidence is used to examine the effectiveness of OSHA in the 1970's and 1980's. The author is the leading economic authority on risk in the workplace.

Warren, A. C., Jr., ed. "Occupational Safety and Health." *Law and Contemporary Problems* 38 (Summer/Autumn, 1974): 583-757. A collection of eight articles looking at the legal and economic aspects associated with the implementation of OSHA.

John F. O'Connell

Cross-References

The U.S. Government Creates the Department of Commerce and Labor (1903); Congress Passes the Pure Food and Drug Act (1906); Roosevelt Signs the Fair Labor Standards Act (1938); The Landrum-Griffin Act Targets Union Corruption (1959); The Three Mile Island Accident Prompts Reforms in Nuclear Power (1979); Bush Signs the Clean Air Act of 1990 (1990).

THE UNITED STATES SUFFERS ITS FIRST TRADE DEFICIT SINCE 1888

CATEGORY OF EVENT: International business and commerce
TIME: 1971
LOCALE: The United States

In 1971, the United States suffered its first trade deficit since 1888, importing more than it exported, on its way to becoming a net debtor nation by the end of 1987

Principal personages:
RICHARD M. NIXON (1913-1994), the president of the United States, 1969-1974
RONALD REAGAN (1911-   ), the president of the United States, 1981-1989
ARTHUR BURNS (1904-1987), the chairman of the Board of Governors of the Federal Reserve System, 1970-1978

Summary of Event

In 1971, the United States suffered its first balance of trade deficit since 1888, importing $2.26 billion more in goods and services than it exported. The United States recorded a surplus on its trade account in only two of the following fourteen years. In 1973 and 1975, the United States exported $911 million and $8.9 billion more, respectively, than it imported. Between 1980 and 1987, the U.S. trade deficit virtually exploded, growing at a compound annual rate of 29.7 percent, from $25.5 billion in 1980 to $159.5 billion in 1987, the year in which the United States became a net debtor nation, owing more to the rest of the world as a whole than it was owed.

To understand the causes and significance of these developments and events, it is necessary to understand the rudimentary elements of balance of payments accounting and theory. The balance of trade is a part of the overall balance of payments. The balance of payments is a bookkeeping system that records all transactions between nations, including the flows of physical goods and services as well as the financial flows between nations. As a flow concept, the balance of payments must have a time dimension. In general, balance of payments statements are reported on an annual or quarterly basis. They can be reported in terms of the country in question versus the rest of the world or versus a particular region or a particular country. For example, the United States Department of Commerce reports the balance of payments for the United States in its *Survey of Current Business* on a quarterly and annual basis. The U.S. balance of payments is reported relative to the rest of the world and relative to various regions and countries.

A nation cannot simply import more than it exports. It must pay for any excess of imports over exports in one of several ways. It can use up foreign assets that were the result of past investments, spend foreign currency reserve balances or gold reserves it had accumulated in the past, or borrow. A relatively small percentage of imported goods takes the form of gifts or aid from one country to another; these imports do not have to be paid for.

Concern about trade deficits centers on the fact that they cannot continue indefinitely. Eventually, reserves of foreign currency and assets will be used up, and other countries eventually will become resistant to lending to trading partners that, because of persistent trade deficits, show little evidence of being able to earn the foreign currency to pay back loans through selling goods and services on the international market. Persistent trade deficits may indicate the need for a reduction in living standards in the deficit country. In simple terms, a trade deficit indicates that a country is consuming and investing more than it produces. Reducing the trade deficit may require reducing consumption of goods and services, thus lowering the standard of living.

The foregoing information about the balance of payments should aid in understanding the history of the United States' balance of trade. In 1960, the United States had a surplus on its balance of trade of $4.9 billion. The value of the United States' exports in that year was one-third higher than the value of its imports. By 1964, the surplus on the U.S. balance of trade had peaked at $6.8 billion. Exports in that year were 37 percent greater than imports.

In 1960, imports and exports were only 2.9 percent and 4.0 percent of the gross national product of the United States, or total value of all goods and services produced in the country that year. U.S. imports and exports were 11 percent and 16 percent, respectively, of world trade, making the United States an important part of the international marketplace.

This asymmetric position—the United States was important to the world economy, but the converse was not true—allowed the United States, the largest trading nation in the world, to operate as though it were a "closed economy" for purposes of domestic macroeconomic policy. A closed economy is one that is closed off from international markets. Because foreign trade was so small relative to the level of U.S. production, policymakers could ignore the effects of international transactions on the U.S. economy when analyzing proposed policies.

In 1964, there was little evidence to indicate that in just seven years the United States would suffer its first deficit in eighty-three years in its balance of trade. The balance of payments problem of the moment was a capital outflow from the United States. The subsidiaries of U.S. multinational corporations, foreign corporations, international agencies, and foreign governments were using the U.S. capital markets to raise funds to finance foreign projects. Dollars were flowing out of the United States, and the rest of the world was becoming more indebted to the United States.

From 1964 to 1971, the United States' imports grew at a compound annual rate of 13.3 percent, while its exports grew at only a rate of 8.3 percent. In 1971, the United States suffered a $2.6 billion deficit in its balance of trade, the first such deficit since 1888.

The reversal in trading position of the United States can be traced to at least one cause. In the late 1960's, the United States' international competitive position deteriorated as the country's domestic inflation rate, the rate of increase of prices, accelerated. Americans were willing and able to pay higher prices for American goods. Because foreign prices as a whole did not rise as rapidly as did American prices, goods produced in the United States became relatively more expensive. This caused potential foreign buyers to shun American goods, reducing U.S. exports. At the same time, foreign goods appeared increasingly attractive to American buyers because of their relatively lower prices. Imports therefore increased. A combination of falling exports and rising imports led naturally to a balance of trade deficit. The trade deficit thus can be traced to the relatively high inflation rate in the United States.

Impact of Event

The worsening balance of trade position of the United States led to worldwide concern. In May of 1971, a wave of speculation began that the deutsche mark was going to be allowed to increase in value relative to the dollar. Confidence in the dollar waned, and by early summer the fundamental weakness in the U.S. balance of payments became apparent. A widespread belief developed that even though the United States suffered from a high rate of unemployment and sluggish growth, inflation was not being brought under control. Normally, policymakers perceive inflation as a cure for unemployment and vice versa; the problems are not supposed to coexist. Confidence in the dollar ebbed further.

Various suggestions came from monetary policymakers including Arthur Burns, chairman of the Board of Governors of the U.S. Federal Reserve System. As chairman of the Board of Governors, Burns directed policy related to the functioning of the U.S. banking system and markets for U.S. treasury bonds. On August 15, 1971, President Richard M. Nixon announced his selection from among the various policy suggestions offered. The United States would suspend the privilege of converting U.S. dollars into gold as well as imposing a 10 percent tax on imports. Major world currencies at the time were all convertible into gold at fixed prices; suspension of convertibility meant that the United States recognized that the dollar had fallen in value relative to gold and relative to other currencies. Suspension of convertibility lowered the desirability of the dollar. Foreign countries would not be as willing to take dollars in exchange for goods knowing that dollars could no longer be traded for gold on demand. This effect, combined with the tax on imports, was intended in part to lower the trade deficit.

The dollar was the world's principal reserve currency at the time, meaning that it was the primary currency used in international exchanges and in settling debts. The exchange rates, or values, of most of the world's currencies were defined in terms of the U.S. dollar as part of the Bretton Woods System, under which countries had agreed to maintain the values of their currencies within narrow bands. It was clear that the dollar had become overvalued relative to most major currencies, with the agreed-upon fixed rates of exchange making the dollar appear more valuable than it in fact was. The questions were how much the dollar's value had to fall and how the fall could be achieved. Two alternatives were to allow the dollar to find its own value in the world market, thus eliminating fixed exchange rates, or to negotiate a new set of fixed exchange rates.

The latter alternative was chosen. The Smithsonian Conference was convened in Washington, D.C., in December of 1971 in an attempt to save the Bretton Woods System of fixed exchange rates. Representatives of the ten largest industrial nations in the Western world reached an agreement, known as the Smithsonian Agreement, to devalue the U.S. dollar by 8.57 percent, which was accomplished by raising the official price of gold from $35 to $38 per ounce. The Smithsonian Agreement, moreover, allowed currency values to fluctuate 2.25 percent above and below the fixed rates, allowing some flexibility before the rates would need adjustment.

In June of 1972, the new regime of exchange rates established only six months earlier began to collapse. By the second quarter of 1973, the world's major currencies were "floating." Rather than being fixed in terms of relative values, the world's major currencies traded for each other at rates determined by daily market transactions in the international market for foreign exchange. The Bretton Woods System, which had been dying a slow, agonizing death, finally collapsed.

The early 1980's witnessed the United States moving very rapidly from being the world's largest net creditor nation to being the world's largest net debtor nation. At the end of 1980, the United States was a net creditor to the rest of the world in the amount of $393 billion. By 1987, the United States had become a net debtor; by the end of 1991, it had accumulated $362 billion in debt. Essentially, this debt was incurred to pay for excesses of imports over exports.

The twin deficit theory argues that the tax cuts of the early 1980's, promoted by President Ronald Reagan, were not followed by spending cuts of equal magnitude. The U.S. government therefore ran huge fiscal deficits and had to borrow to finance its spending. The increased demand for funds by the U.S. government put upward pressure on interest rates, attracting foreign investors in search of higher interest rates. The inflow of capital into the United States and the increased demand for U.S. dollars resulted in an increased value of the dollar as measured against the major currencies of the world. The high value of the U.S. dollar made U.S. exports expensive to the world and made imports cheaper to Americans. A product with a given dollar price becomes more expensive to a foreign buyer as the value of the dollar increases relative to other currencies. This change in the prices of American goods relative to prices in the rest of the world led to a tendency for the U.S. trade deficit to increase.

The U.S. dollar rose in value throughout the early 1980's, and imports grew at astounding rates. The United States ran ever-larger trade deficits, and the value of the dollar kept rising, contrary to accepted theory, which predicts that a country running a trade deficit will find the value of its currency declining. As other countries accumulate a currency, the theory predicts, they will find it less attractive to accumulate even more and will be less willing to take it in trade for goods. That currency therefore should fall in value, rather than rise in value as the U.S. dollar did. Government borrowing apparently offset the effects on the dollar that resulted from trade deficits.

The trade deficit of 1971 thus signaled the beginning of a variety of problems in the U.S. economy. Policymakers faced increasingly unpleasant choices in overcoming trade deficits, debt to foreign countries, government budget deficits, inflation, unemployment, and slow economic growth. The multitude of goals and problems meant that some would have to be ignored.

Bibliography

Federal Reserve Bank of Atlanta. "Atlanta Fed Research Points to Validity of Twin Deficits Notion." *Economics Update* 4 (July-September, 1991): 6-7, 10. This brief article presents arguments for the twin deficit theory, reviews previous research, and presents a review of the Atlanta Fed's current research on this topic.

Howard, David H. "Implications of the U.S. Current Account Deficit." *Journal of Economic Perspectives* 3 (Fall, 1989): 153-165. Reviews some of the current empirical literature, concluding that the trade deficit is caused by an insufficiency of domestic savings. Concludes that the United States has gone from the position of a large net creditor to one of a large net debtor. The Feldstein Horioka Puzzle, the high correlation of saving and investment across countries, is discussed. Concludes that evidence indicates that capital is not very mobile internationally.

Pigott, Charles. "Economic Consequences of Continued U.S. External Deficits." *Federal Reserve Bank of New York Quarterly Review* 13 (Winter/Spring, 1989): 4-15. Concludes that the U.S. trade deficit is fundamentally a result of the imbalance between savings and investment. Policymakers cannot ignore it simply because some of the dire consequences predicted have not come to pass. Actual consequences include job loss and overcapacity in U.S. manufacturing during the early 1980's and slow U.S. domestic growth in more recent years. The most dire consequences could include a significant increase in the real U.S. long-term interest rate, which in turn could reduce both the future level of investment and productivity growth.

Scholl, Russell B., Raymond J. Mataloni, Jr., and Steve D. Bezirgaian. "The International Investment Position of the United States in 1991." *Survey of Current Business* 72 (June, 1992): 46-59. Discusses the difficulties in determining the net international investment position of the United States, concluding that the country became a net debtor in 1987, rather than in 1985 as reported earlier.

Solomon, Robert. *The International Monetary System 1945-1981.* New York: Harper & Row, 1982. This book is excellent, well written, and easy to understand. Solomon spent many years at the Federal Reserve System. His perspective, as both a participant in and an objective observer of developments in the international monetary system, is unique.

Yeager, Leland B. *International Monetary Relations: Theory, History, and Policy.* 2d ed. New York: Harper & Row, 1976. An excellent source for anyone interested in international finance. Contains a wealth of information.

Daniel C. Falkowski

Cross-References

The United States Establishes a Permanent Tariff Commission (1916); The General Agreement on Tariffs and Trade Is Signed (1947); Mexico Renegotiates Debt to U.S. Banks (1989); The North American Free Trade Agreement Goes into Effect (1994).

THE SUPREME COURT ORDERS THE END OF DISCRIMINATION IN HIRING

CATEGORY OF EVENT: Labor
TIME: March 8, 1971
LOCALE: Washington, D.C.

In Griggs et al. v. Duke Power Company, *the Supreme Court ruled that employers could not require qualifications for jobs that were discriminatory in effect unless those qualifications were proved necessary for the job*

Principal personages:
WILLIE S. GRIGGS, a black worker who led the class action suit
WARREN BURGER (1907-1995), the Supreme Court justice who delivered the *Griggs* decision
HUBERT H. HUMPHREY (1911-1978), a U.S. senator who supported the Civil Rights Act of 1964
JOHN TOWER (1925-1991), a senator who sought amendments allowing job tests
HERMAN TALMADGE (1913-   ), a senator who was concerned about Title VII of the Civil Rights Act
ASA PHILIP RANDOLPH (1889-1979), a black union leader and lifelong enemy of employment discrimination
LYNDON B. JOHNSON (1908-1973), the president of the United States, 1963-1969
MARTIN LUTHER KING, JR. (1929-1968), a black leader and organizer of Operation Breadbasket
JESSE JACKSON (1941-   ), a King aide who led the boycott of biased employers

Summary of Event

Legal challenges to the constitutionality of Title VII of the federal Civil Rights Act of 1964 brought the case of *Griggs et al. v. Duke Power Company* before the U.S. Supreme Court for argument in December, 1970. The Court's decision, read by Chief Justice Warren Burger, was rendered on March 8, 1971.

Beginning in 1866, the American Congress enacted a series of civil rights laws that ostensibly safeguarded citizens' nonpolitical rights, notably those personal liberties guaranteed to U.S. citizens by the Thirteenth and Fourteenth Amendments to the Constitution. The Civil Rights Act of 1964 became law amid the turbulence of the 1960's associated with the "Black Revolution," campaigns for the rights of women, battles for alternative life-styles, environmentalism, and bitter debate over the Vietnam War. The Civil Rights Act of 1964 represented the most sweeping legislation of its kind.

President John F. Kennedy, contrary to his political instincts, launched the civil rights bill in June, 1963, five months before his assassination. Anxious to build the Great Society, President Lyndon B. Johnson, Kennedy's successor, was deeply committed both personally and politically to the principles embodied in the bill. So, too, were liberal members of the Congress, some of whom, including Hubert H. Humphrey, Michael Joseph Mansfield, and Carey Estes Kefauver, were veteran civil libertarians, while others including Samuel James Erwin had become dedicated converts.

The real initiatives for fresh civil rights legislation lay outside the White House and Congress, most notably among black leaders. By 1963, Martin Luther King, Jr., and young aides such as Jesse Jackson had begun their dramatic peaceful assaults on segregation in various Southern cities. Almost simultaneously, they had launched Operation Breadbasket, a grass-roots effort to bring an end to discriminatory practices that kept substantial numbers of African Americans out of the work force and gravely handicapped their economic opportunities. It was this type of discrimination in particular that was dealt with in Title VII of the 1964 Civil Rights Act.

Although hiring discrimination affected many groups, the plight of African Americans, the nation's largest minority, was singularly bad in the early 1960's, and in some regards it was worsening. Long a leader against discrimination in trade unions and a proponent of equal employment opportunities, the president of the Brotherhood of Sleeping Car Porters, Asa Philip Randolph, outlined the effects of hiring and job discrimination to a U.S. Senate subcommittee in 1962. Randolph pointed to the relatively small number of skilled black workers in the nation, to segregation and racial barriers in trade unions and in apprenticeship programs, to a disproportion-

Chief Justice Warren Burger delivered the Court's Griggs decision and spoke out forcefully against discrimination in hiring. (Supreme Court Historical Society)

ate concentration of black workers in unskilled occupations, and to new technologies that were diminishing industry's need for unskilled labor. He noted that the percentage of black carpenters, painters, bricklayers, and plasterers, for example, had declined precipitously since 1950. In addition, the unemployment rate for black workers was nearly three times the rate for whites.

Such was the background against which Willie S. Griggs and thirteen fellow black coworkers at the Duke Power Company's Dan River Steam Station in Draper, North Carolina, brought a class action suit against their employer. All the black workers at the Dan River Plant worked in the Labor Department, in which the highest paying jobs paid less than the lowest paying jobs that whites held in the plant's four other departments. Promotions within departments were normally made on the basis of seniority, and transferees into a department usually began in the lowest positions.

In 1955, the Duke Power Company began requiring a high school diploma for assignment to any department except Labor. When the company eliminated its previous policies of segregation and stopped restricting black workers to the Labor Department, a high school diploma remained a prerequisite for transfer to other departments. In 1965, the company announced that for new employees, placement in any department except Labor was dependent on the achievement of adequate scores on two professionally designed high school equivalency tests. It was in this regard that the *Griggs* case invoked Title VII of the 1964 Civil Rights Act. The workers argued that black workers were less likely than whites to pass the tests but that performance on the tests was unrelated to ability to perform jobs.

The longest debate in American legislative history had preceded passage of the Civil Rights Act. Congress had laboriously made clear its intent in regard to Title VII: It was to achieve equality of employment opportunities and to remove previous barriers that had favored identifiable groups of white workers. No part of the act barred employers from utilizing "neutral" tests, practices, or procedures in selecting or promoting employees.

Delivering the opinion of the Supreme Court in the case, Chief Justice Warren Burger reiterated these congressional objectives. Speaking for a unanimous Court, Burger declared that even when an employer's tests, procedures, or practices were "neutral" in their intent, they could not be maintained if their effect was to freeze the status quo of prior discriminatory employment practices. What the Civil Rights Act and Title VII proscribed were any "artificial, arbitrary, and unnecessary barriers to employment" when such barriers served to discriminate on the basis of race, color, religion, sex, or any other impermissible classification. Burger acknowledged that the test requirements instituted by the Duke Power Company were intended to improve the overall quality of its work force. The Chief Justice noted, however, that employment practices that could not be shown to be related to job performance and that disproportionately excluded black workers from employment opportunities were clearly prohibited. An employer's good intent or absence of discriminatory intent, Burger continued, did not redeem employment procedures or testing mechanisms that operated as "built-in headwinds" for minority groups and were unrelated to measurements of job performance. Burger emphasized that the purpose of Title VII was to protect the employer's right to insist that any job applicant, black or white, must meet the applicable job qualifications. Title VII in fact was designed to facilitate hiring on the basis of job qualifications rather than on the basis of race or color.

Impact of Event

Title VII of the Civil Rights Act of 1964, however strongly President Johnson and liberal members of Congress felt about its objectives, did not miraculously abolish ingrained discriminatory hiring and employment practices. Despite the vast powers that Johnson derived from being the head of the country's largest employer, the federal government itself, and from having some control over billions of dollars in federal contracts, his power was circumscribed. The federal bureaucracy, many observers noted, was lethargic, and the country's great corporations and unions could not lightly be antagonized, particularly because the president required their support to attain other goals of his Great Society. After appointing Vice President Hubert H. Humphrey, one of the country's leading civil libertarians, to lead the President's Committee on Equal Employment Opportunity in February, 1965, Johnson abruptly removed him the following September. Taking this as a signal of presidential will, the agencies charged with implementing fair employment policies tended to drift.

There were gains, most notably in the changed public attitudes about race. Whereas in 1944 only 45 percent of whites polled believed that African Americans should have as good a chance as whites to secure jobs, in 1963, 80 percent espoused that belief. The U.S. Civil Service Commission increased the percentage of black workers in government jobs, principally in the Post Office. The Civil Rights Commission, however, found that the enforcement of nondiscrimination provisos in government contracts was almost nonexistent, and the Equal Employment Opportunity Commission (EEOC) that had been created to oversee applications of Title VII struggled without enforcement powers. Operation Breadbasket, initiated by Martin Luther King, Jr., and conducted largely by his aide, Jesse Jackson, had boycotted businesses until they opened jobs to black workers, but its efforts and success gradually diminished. Black unemployment ran four to five times as high as unemployment among whites. The problem was especially severe in inner cities.

By the early 1970's, there were signs of improvement. Enforced or not, the Civil Rights Act of 1964 encouraged employers to hire more black workers. This cause was aided by labor shortages of the 1960's as well as improvements in the education of black labor force entrants. Moreover, by 1972, Congress had granted the EEOC power to initiate legal action against businesses showing evidence of employment discrimination, and major offenders were soon forced to comply with Title VII's mandates. For these reasons, among others, black men nearly tripled their employment in white collar jobs. Black women also gained in employment generally, with strong gains in white collar jobs. Accordingly, the gap between white and black incomes narrowed significantly. The median income of black employees, for example, had been 59 percent of that of whites in 1959. By 1969, the proportion had risen to 69 percent. Employed black women, during the same period, raised their median income to 93 percent of that of white female employees, although women generally were paid less than were men.

By March, 1971, when Chief Justice Burger delivered the Court's decision in the *Griggs* case, some observers believed that despite the Civil Rights Act of 1964, the gap in opportunities between blacks and other Americans was widening. Increases in the numbers of black high school dropouts, black welfare recipients, and black women giving birth out of wedlock, as well as in venereal disease, drug abuse, and crime among African Americans, seemed to substantiate such assertions. According to some observers, the African American population had taken on the configurations of a distinct underclass.

As indicated above, however, there was heartening evidence that black workers were closing economic gaps between them and mainstream white society. Challenges to hiring and promotional barriers through Title VII and an empowered EEOC were important contributing factors to the hastening of this process. The liberal position taken by the Burger Supreme Court in giving specific weight to Title VII's objectives in the *Griggs* case also undoubtedly strengthened federal and state attacks on employment discrimination. To many black leaders, such decisions proved the worth of the 1964 Civil Rights Act. As Roy Wilkins told the Fifty-fifth Annual Convention of the National Association for the Advancement of Colored People (NAACP), the principal value of the act was the recognition by Congress that African Americans are constitutional citizens, recognition necessary to begin the pursuit of happiness through political, social, and economic progress. Wilkins might have gone further. As legal scholars observed, the *Griggs* decision went beyond the Constitution. The Constitution prohibited only intentional discrimination, and the illegality of such discrimination had for decades been beyond legal question. After the *Griggs* opinion, legislation such as the 1964 Civil Rights Act's Title VII was interpreted to prohibit de facto discriminatory effects of employment practices as well.

Bibliography

Auerbach, Jerold S., ed. *American Labor: The Twentieth Century.* Indianapolis: Bobbs-Merrill, 1969. Commentary and documents presented clearly by a labor historian and other specialists. Part 4 is particularly relevant, dealing with civil and economic rights, race, segregation, employer and union job discrimination, and the impacts of automation. Part 3 also deals with major labor legislation.

Berger, Morroe. *Equality by Statute: The Revolution in Civil Rights.* New York: Octagon Books, 1978. A clearly written, intelligent survey of subject. Chapter 4 examines efforts to reduce employment discrimination in New York State as a mirror of national problems. Chapter 1 details creation of the EEOC and increments to its powers. Chapter 5 is an acute analysis of the effects of law in controlling prejudice and discrimination.

Blasi, Vincent, ed. *The Burger Court: The Counter-Revolution That Wasn't.* New Haven, Conn.: Yale University Press, 1983. The main thesis linking these expert analyses of the Burger Court is that it continued its work much in the same liberal spirit in regard to civil rights as its predecessor, led by Chief Justice Earl Warren. The *Griggs* case is treated in chapters 6 and 7, in context with analogous cases. Contains photos and biographies of Burger Court justices.

Hall, Kermit L., ed. *The Oxford Guide to United States Supreme Court Decisions.* New York: Oxford University Press, 1999. Multiauthored collection of essays on more than four hundred significant Court decisions, with supporting glossary and other aids.

Matusow, Allen J. *The Unraveling of America: A History of Liberalism in the 1960s.* New York: Harper & Row, 1984. An outstanding survey. Richly detailed and critical but well balanced. Places the *Griggs* case in context with a gamut of racial and employment problems. A fine historical survey, clearly written and engaging.

Schwartz, Bernard, comp. *Civil Rights.* 2 vols. New York: Chelsea House, 1970. Consists of federal legislation, extracts from congressional debates, and Supreme Court decisions, with commentary by the compiler. An outstanding work for the background and context of Title VII.

Whalen, Charles, and Barbara Whalen. *The Longest Debate: A Legislative History of the 1964 Civil Rights Act.* Washington, D.C.: Seven Locks Press, 1985. Written by an outstanding congressman and civil libertarian with his columnist wife. This is an informative, engaging commentary and excerpting of testimony on an extraordinarily complex and politically difficult bill. Ample discussion of the EEOC and Title VII.

Clifton K. Yearley

Cross-References

The Wagner Act Promotes Union Organization (1935); Roosevelt Signs the Fair Labor Standards Act (1938); The Taft-Hartley Act Passes over Truman's Veto (1947); The Civil Rights Act Prohibits Discrimination in Employment (1964); The Pregnancy Discrimination Act Extends Employment Rights (1978); The Supreme Court Rules on Affirmative Action Programs (1979); *Firefighters v. Stotts* Upholds Seniority Systems (1984); The Supreme Court Upholds Quotas as a Remedy for Discrimination (1986).

AN INDEPENDENT AGENCY TAKES OVER U.S. POSTAL SERVICE

CATEGORY OF EVENT: Government and business
TIME: July 1, 1971
LOCALE: Washington, D.C.

The Postal Reorganization Act of 1970 replaced the U.S. Post Office Department with the semi-independent U.S. Postal Service, established to modernize mail delivery, make operations more efficient, and be self-supporting

Principal personages:
RICHARD M. NIXON (1913-1994), the president of the United States, 1969-1974
FREDERICK R. KAPPEL (1902-1994), the head of the President's Commission on Postal Organization under President Lyndon B. Johnson
LAWRENCE O'BRIEN (1917-1990), the postmaster general under President Johnson
WINTON M. BLOUNT (1921-   ), the postmaster general under President Nixon

Summary of Event

President Richard M. Nixon signed the Postal Reorganization Act on August 12, 1970. The reorganization was the culmination of an effort begun during the administration of Lyndon B. Johnson, when the President's Commission on Postal Organization, popularly known as the Kappel Commission, recommended that the Post Office Department be made independent and self-supporting.

The U.S. Postal Service, as an independent, government-owned agency, replaced the Post Office Department. An eleven-member commission managed the service. The commission was composed of nine governors who were appointed by the president and confirmed by the Senate. Their terms were staggered, and no more than five governors could come from one political party. Also serving on the commission were the postmaster general and a deputy postmaster general, both of whom were appointed by the governors. The postmaster general was no longer a member of the president's cabinet. The new agency was phased in during 1971.

The Postal Service was freed from the financial control of Congress and was authorized to issue bonds for capital improvement. A limit of $10 billion was placed on outstanding debt, with a $2 billion annual limit on new issues. Proceeds of bond issues were initially used to modernize buildings and automate processes. The service was expected to move toward self-sufficiency but would continue to be subsidized until able to break even. The subsidy took the place of large rate increases.

Significant improvements were made to operations. Political appointments of local postmasters were replaced by a merit system. Specific criteria were established for hiring and promotion. Postal workers were given the right to negotiate for wages and benefits. Binding arbitration would be used to settle labor disputes. As part of the Reorganization Act, postal workers received an 8 percent pay raise.

The cost of stamps was raised to eight cents for first-class mail. A similar increase was instituted for bulk mail. Increases for second-class mail would be phased in gradually. A five-member Postal Rate Commission would have the authority to set future rate increases, with Congress retaining the right of veto.

New services were provided to customers, including the Priority Mail next-day delivery system and Mailgrams, letters sent by telegraphs. To handle customer complaints, an Office of Consumer Advocate was established. The entire operation was decentralized. Regional directors were given greater autonomy, and the number of regions was reduced to five.

In 1970, the Post Office Department handled more than eighty-seven billion pieces of mail, making it the largest postal operation in the world. It was also the largest civilian government agency, employing more than 750,000 workers, a payroll comparable to those of General Motors Corporation and American Telephone and Telegraph (AT&T). The Post Office Department was plagued by problems in all phases of its operation. A deficit of $2.6 billion was expected in 1970. The operation relied heavily on manual work, with clerks able to hand-sort only eighteen letters a minute. The Post Office relied on the airlines and Amtrak to deliver intercity mail. Route cutbacks slowed down the mail. Coast-to-coast delivery took ten days, and intracity delivery often took two days. Second-class mail delivery of newspapers and magazines was frequently delayed by as much as ten days.

The problems of the Post Office Department were widely believed to be caused by political influence. Postmaster jobs were filled by political appointees, and within-the-ranks promotion was considered unlikely for someone without political connections. The inefficiency and the lack of capital improvements were blamed on Congress, which often failed to appropriate funds for automation or building improvements. Within the Nixon Administration, there was a strong desire to implement modern management techniques throughout government operations, including the Post Office.

Working conditions for postal workers were below the standard of industry of the time. The Post Office experienced a turnover rate of 23 percent, lower than the industry average of the time. It took thirteen weeks to hire a new worker. Post Offices in some large cities experienced difficulty filling vacant positions; in 1970, more than nine hundred positions were unfilled in New York City. Post Office jobs started at a salary of $6,176, and the top pay grade was $8,440, reached after twenty-one years of service. Most buildings were not air conditioned. Many had no parking lots or cafeterias, and toilet facilities were often inadequate. Few Post Offices had doctors or first aid available for workers, and accident rates were high.

Prior to the Depression, Post Office Department jobs were desirable. After World War II, there was increased labor competition from industry, and the Post Office had difficulty attracting workers. The department, under the Civil Service System, was not able to pay differential rates in high-cost areas such as New

A weary mail carrier rests inside a storage box in Los Angeles in early 1971—only months before the U.S. Postal Service was created to make delivery operations more efficient. (R. Kent Rasmussen)

York City. In 1970, 10 percent of that city's postal workers qualified for welfare. After three years of service, garbage collectors in New York City were paid more than postal workers with twenty years of service.

The idea of reorganizing the Post Office Department originated with Lawrence O'Brien, who was postmaster general in the Johnson Administration and who believed that the Post Office should be made independent and self-sufficient. President Johnson established the President's Commission on Postal Organization and appointed Frederick R. Kappel, former chairman of AT&T, as chairman of the commission. In June, 1968, the commission recommended that the Post Office Department be reorganized and placed on a self-sufficient basis. President Nixon's postal reform message on May 27, 1969, endorsed the proposal. Opposition reached a peak in March, 1970, when the New York postal workers staged an illegal strike. Congress added a binding arbitration clause to the legislation. In April, 1970, the American Federation of Labor-Congress of Industrial Organizations (AFL-CIO), with George Meany as bargainer, reached an agreement with the government to end the strike. On August 12, 1970, President Nixon signed the Postal Reorganization Act, which authorized the creation of the U.S. Postal Service. On June 26, 1971, an eight cent first-class stamp was issued with the U.S. Postal Service emblem, and on July 1, 1971, the service was born.

Impact of Event

The Postal Reorganization Act shifted control of the postal system from Congress and the president to the managers of the new U.S. Postal Service. This provided immediate political advantage to the White House and Congress, which no longer could be directly blamed for the failings of the system.

Until 1979, the Postal Service ran annual operating deficits. In 1979, the service reported an operating surplus of $470,000. Deficits occurred even though postal rates rose significantly after reorganization. The cost of mailing first-class letters rose 150 percent from 1970 to 1977, with similar increases for second-class and bulk mail.

Firms were able to compete with the Postal Service to deliver bulk mail, but not first-class mail. After 1971, this competition accelerated. The business community showed concern about the increased cost of bulk-mail advertising and other kinds of business mail. The bulk-mail industry was the most affected by the change. After 1971, costs of bulk mail continued to rise, and service did not measurably improve.

Firms that entered the bulk-mail business at the time of reorganization were able to offer lower rates because they delivered advertising mail door to door. No mailing labels or sorting was necessary, thus reducing costs. Leading firms included Independent Postal Systems of America of Oklahoma City, Oklahoma; Consumer Communications Services Corporation of Columbus, Ohio; American Postal Corporation of Los Angeles, California; Pacific Postal System of San Francisco, California; and Continental Postal Service of Charlotte, North Carolina.

Some firms began delivering their own bills to customers. Virginia Electric and Power Company was able to deliver its own monthly bills for as little as five cents apiece in urban areas at a time when the Postal Service charged eight cents. Under the Reorganization Act, it was legal for firms to deliver their own first-class mail.

The greatest concern within the Postal Service was the increased competition from the United Parcel Service, which soon had half of the small-parcel delivery market. The competitive advantage United Parcel Service enjoyed resulted from its reputation for reliable, consistent, and rapid delivery and from its ability to charge lower rates than those of the Postal Service.

Management improvements in the new Postal Service focused on improving airmail service, with a goal of next-day delivery for airmail. Airlines depended on airmail for revenue. After reorganization, the Postal Service was able to negotiate terms with carriers. There was fear within the airline industry of the resulting increase in competition. Airmail standards set by the Postal Service were next-day delivery for destinations within six hundred miles, with all other deliveries to be made within two days. The Mail Express program was inaugurated, with door-to-door delivery by courier.

The Postal Service experienced a 35 percent increase in productivity from 1970 to 1980. According to the Postal Service's own reports, by 1980 the system succeeded in delivering 95 percent of first-class mail within one day. Intercity mail traveling less than six hundred miles was delivered within two days 86 percent of the time, and cross-country mail was delivered within three days 87 percent of the time.

The first U.S. Postal Service bonds were issued in October, 1971, in the amount of $250 million. The bonds were issued for capital improvement, with two areas of initial focus. A bulk mail system was designed to include twenty-one processing centers using modern technology, computers, and conveyor systems. The second project was a letter mail code sort system. A pilot plant was built in Cincinnati, Ohio, and used optical scanning equipment and other technologies to sort mail.

After the reorganization, there were significant cuts in headquarters and regional staffs. The new agency started with $3 billion in assets and

$1 billion in cash, which could be invested in U.S. government securities. In 1972, the service ordered a hiring freeze in an attempt to reduce costs. Labor contracts did not allow a reduction in force, so inducements for early retirement were offered. Experienced postal managers responded to the offer, significantly reducing the Postal Service deficit for 1973. The loss of experienced managers, however, resulted in deterioration of service and public criticism. The backlash resulted in additional hiring and subsequent growth of the deficit.

Postal unions were able to negotiate no-layoff clauses in their contracts; nonunion postal employees did not have such protection and significant reductions in work-force levels occurred. From 1970 to 1980, the number of full-time-equivalent postal employees declined by forty-six thousand. After 1971, wages increased at a higher rate than that of other government workers, primarily because of cost-of-living adjustments included in union contracts. During the inflation-plagued 1970's, postal wages more than doubled.

Federal Express was founded in 1971 as a competitor to the government's mail operation. The reorganization of the Postal Service and the emergence of Federal Express and other overnight delivery services revolutionized the way business mail was sent and received. In 1980, Mail Boxes Etc. of San Diego, California, extended innovations in service to the individual consumer. For hundreds of years, it had been believed that mail delivery must be provided by a protected government monopoly. The 1971 reorganization of the Postal Service challenged that basic belief and made possible advances in mail delivery and processing.

Bibliography

Blount, Winton Malcolm. "Overhauling the Mails: Interview with Postmaster General Blount." *U.S. News and World Report* 68 (May 4, 1970): 46-51. An interview with the postmaster general at the time reorganization was under consideration by Congress. Shows the extent of operational considerations and the optimism of Post Office Department management for reform.

Fleishman, Joel L., ed. *The Future of the Postal Service.* New York: Praeger, 1983. Good critical analysis of the effects of reorganization on government, labor, business, and the communications industry. Includes international comparisons as well as detailed economic information. Recommends further restructuring and management improvements.

Fowler, Dorothy Ganfield. *Unmailable: Congress and the Post Office.* Athens: University of Georgia Press, 1977. A highly readable history of the Postal Service from the appointment of Benjamin Franklin as postmaster general in 1753 to the formation of the U.S. Postal Service in 1971. Covers the important role the Postal Service has played in American history and the relationship between Congress and the postal service. Good focus on the dynamics that led to reorganization.

Fuller, Wayne E. "The Politics and the Post Office" and "Epilogue." In *The American Mail: Enlarger of the Common Life*. Chicago: University of Chicago Press, 1972. A history of political control of the Post Office, from establishment to reorganization in 1971. A balanced report that illuminates both positive and negative aspects of this control. The epilogue recounts the congressional debate leading to passage of the Reorganization Act.

Nixon, Richard M. *Nixon: The Second Year of His Presidency*. Washington, D.C.: Congressional Quarterly, 1971. Contains Nixon's statements on the postal reorganization, the postal strike, and the settlement of the strike.

_____. "Toward a Better Postal Service." In *Setting the Course, the First Year: Major Policy Statement by President Richard Nixon*. New York: Funk & Wagnalls, 1970. Contains Nixon's policy statements on the need for reorganization. The chapter outlines the structural and political problems inherent in the Post Office Department as well as the basic objectives of reform.

Sandford, David. "Post Office Blues, the Mail That Costs More and Comes Sometimes." *The New Republic* 162 (March 21, 1970): 19-22. Focuses on customer frustration with Post Office Department performance prior to reorganization. Particular emphasis is placed on problems experienced by weekly news magazines regarding delays in second-class mail delivery. Inequities in the rate structure are covered.

Tierney, John T. *Postal Reorganization: Managing the Public's Business*. Boston: Auburn House, 1981. An in-depth study of the reorganization of the Postal Service, from a broad perspective essentially favorable toward the system. Focuses on managerial initiatives within the postal system and the changing dynamics of labor relations. Also shows the effects of competition on the operation of the postal service.

_____. "Untangling the Mess in the Post Office." *Business Week*, March 28, 1970, 78-80. A survey of the problems plaguing the reorganization of the Post Office Department. Covers all aspects, including labor, systems performance, management, and political influence. Comparison with other nations is included. Good coverage of the political concerns that led to reorganization.

Alene Staley

Cross-References

The U.S. Government Creates the Tennessee Valley Authority (1933); Amtrak Takes Over Most U.S. Intercity Train Traffic (1970); AT&T Agrees to Be Broken Up as Part of an Antitrust Settlement (1982); *Time* magazine Makes an E-commerce Pioneer Its Person of the Year (1999).

NIXON SIGNS THE CONSUMER PRODUCT SAFETY ACT

CATEGORY OF EVENT: Consumer affairs
TIME: October 28, 1972
LOCALE: Washington, D.C.

The Consumer Product Safety Act established an independent agency of the federal government to investigate the causes of product-related injuries and to develop regulations to control their occurrence

Principal personages:
WARREN GRANT MAGNUSON (1905-1989), a U.S. senator from California and a member of the Senate Committee on Commerce
JOHN E. MOSS (1913-1997), a U.S. senator from California and a member of the Senate Committee on Commerce
RICHARD M. NIXON (1913-1994), the thirty-seventh president of the United States
CHARLES PERCY (1919-   ), a U.S. senator from Illinois, the sponsor of the bill

Summary of Event

The Consumer Product Safety Act of 1972 (CPSA) established the Consumer Product Safety Commission (CPSC) as an independent agency of the federal government. The CPSC was given authority to identify unsafe products, establish standards for labeling and product safety, recall defective products, and ban products that posed unreasonable risks to consumers. In order to ensure compliance with its directives, the CPSC was given authority to impose civil and criminal penalties, including fines and jail sentences.

Prior to the enactment of the CPSA, attempts to reduce hazards associated with consumer products were fragmented and produced uneven results. Federal, state, and local laws addressed safety issues in a limited, piecemeal manner. Industry self-regulation was occasionally attempted by trade associations, testing laboratories, or other standards-making groups. Competitive economic forces often delayed or weakened the establishment of standards, and the inability of the industry legally to enforce standards once they were set often made these attempts little more than window dressing. In 1967, members of Congress decided that there had to be a consistent approach to the problems of injuries resulting from the use of consumer products.

The House of Representatives and the Senate enacted PL 90-146 in June, 1967, creating the National Commission on Public Safety. The commission was given the responsibility of identifying products presenting unreasonable hazards to consumers, examining existing means of protecting consumers from these hazards, and recommending appropriate legislative action.

In June, 1970, the commission reported the magnitude of the problem: 20 million people were injured each year because of incidents related to consumer products; 110,000 people were permanently disabled from such accidents; and 30,000 deaths resulted each year. The cost to the country was estimated to be more than $5.5 billion a year. The commission suggested that consumers were in more dangerous environments in their own homes than when driving on the highway. The commission outlined sixteen categories of products as providing unreasonably hazardous risks to the consumer. Architectural glass used for sliding doors in homes caused approximately 150,000 injuries a year; the commission recommended that safety-glazed materials be required for this use. Hot-water vaporizers that were capable of heating water to 180 degrees repeatedly caused second- and third-degree burns to young children. High-rise bicycles with "banana" seats, high handlebars, and small front wheels encouraged stunt riding and frequently resulted in injuries. Furniture polish with 95 percent petroleum distillates was packaged in screw-cap bottles, colored to resemble soft drinks, and attractively scented; many children who drank it suffered fatal chemical pneumonia. Power rotary lawn mowers sliced through fingers and toes and sent objects hurtling toward bystanders. Other products that the commission identified as posing unreasonable potential hazards to consumers included color television sets, fireworks, floor furnaces, glass bottles, household chemicals, infant furniture, ladders, power tools, protective headgear (especially football helmets), unvented gas heaters, and wringer washing machines.

The commission maintained that it was not entirely the responsibility of consumers to protect themselves, because they could reasonably be expected neither to understand all the existing hazards nor to know how to deal effectively with the hazards. Although consumers were becoming increasingly successful at receiving compensation for injuries through common law, manufacturers in general had not responded by taking preventive measures.

The commission suggested that a national program was needed to prevent further accidents and injuries. At hearings before the U.S. Senate Committee on Commerce on June 24, 1970, the National Commission on Public Safety recommended that an independent agency, the Consumer Product Safety Commission, be formed. Hearings were held between May of 1971 and February of 1972. These hearings allowed individuals representing both businesses and organizations concerned with health and safety issues to testify. Competing legislation included proposals to give the responsibility for oversight to the existing secretary of health, education, and welfare rather than to an independent agency. One proposal would have permitted the adoption of an existing private standard as a federal safety standard; this proposal, however, was criticized on the grounds that it might result in the acceptance of private standards that were inadequate or anticompetitive. Witnesses at the hearings testified on the problems of hazardous household products, the function and effectiveness of state and local laws, and the role of advertising and the need for public education and debated whether the American economy would reward or punish producers of safe consumer products, which were likely to carry higher prices. Manufacturers, legislators, college professors, attorneys, publishers, representatives of trade and professional associations, engineers, and physicians provided information and opinions on the proposed legislation.

The process brought about intense lobbying and heated debates. Companies saw the CPSC as a potential source of harassment, with government decisions affecting their industries. Sponsors of the legislation complained that regular government agencies listened too closely to the very industries that they were directed to regulate and ignored the voice of the consumer. Long filibustering sessions and angry accusations nearly killed the legislation. Observers claimed that key sponsors could have brought the issue to a vote sooner but were not present when votes on stopping the filibustering were taken. The Richard M. Nixon Administration publicly supported the legislation, but key aides supported the filibustering. The Grocery Manufacturers of America, a business lobby, distributed information kits on how to fight the bill in Congress, calling the legislation a threat to free enterprise. Opponents warned of the authority the agency could have, claiming that it had the potential to turn against the consumer, side with big business, and increase the costs of products to consumers.

Impact of Event

As it was passed in 1972, the Consumer Product Safety Act charged the CPSC with four main tasks: to protect the public from unreasonable risks of injury associated with the use of consumer products; to be of assistance to consumers in evaluating and comparing the safety of consumer products; to develop uniform safety standards for consumer products; and to encourage research and investigation into the causes and prevention of product-related deaths, illnesses, and injuries. "Consumer products" were defined both as things sold to customers as well as things distributed for the use of customers (such as component parts). Specifically excluded were tobacco and tobacco products, motor vehicles and equipment, pesticides, firearms and ammunition, aircraft, boats and equipment, drugs, cosmetics, and foods, as these fell under the jurisdiction of other existing agencies. Responsibility for a product was extended to include producers, importers, and, basically, anyone who handled the product in the stream of commerce.

The CPSC established a National Electronic Injury Surveillance System (NEISS) in order to collect and investigate information on injuries and deaths related to consumer products. NEISS is a computer-based system tied into more than one hundred hospital emergency rooms. The information in this system allows the commission to compute a product "hazard index." Products with the highest hazard indices—such as cleaning agents, swings and slides, liquid fuels, snowmobiles, and all-terrain vehicles—are targeted for further studies and possible regulation. The CPSC is authorized to perform in-depth studies on accidents and to investigate the effects and costs of these injuries to individuals and the country as a whole. If the CPSC believes there is significant cause, it can investigate the industry and product in question with the goal of encouraging voluntary industry safety standards or initiate mandatory safety standards of its own. If CPSC investigators believe that safety standards are required, they will research the product, develop test methods if necessary, and propose an appropriate safety standard. Proposals for appropriate standards are also solicited from the affected industry. Interested organizations, individuals, and industry representatives testify during open hearings on the proposed standards. After the hearings, the standards may be modified or enacted as proposed. Products that fail to meet the standards within a set period of time (from one to six months) may be pulled from store shelves, and manufacturers may face fines as well as jail sentences. If adequate safety standards cannot be designed, court action may be taken to have the products banned. So that unreasonable demands are not placed on a small company, fines for violations may be limited, or establishments of particular sizes may be given extensions of time in which to comply with regulations.

The establishment of specific standards is a process that is frequently viewed with concern by the manufacturers involved. When changes in manufacturing, product design, or labeling are suggested, manufacturers' associations respond with proposals, which include estimates of the additional costs necessary to implement the changes. Cost/benefit criteria are considered to determine if the benefits of a proposed action can be justified by the attendant costs. This not an easy issue to revolve. For example, the changes that were contemplated in the design of power lawn mowers included locating pull cords away from chokes and throttles, installing footguards, redesigning exhaust systems, and installing automatic cutoffs. The enacted changes increased the price of the power lawn mower to the consumer by an average of twenty-two dollars.

Manufacturers, legislators, and administrative figures all were aware of the potential power of CPSC. The establishment and enforcement of standards had the potential to raise the costs of manufacturing and, consequently, increase prices to consumers. Regulations had the potential to limit the types and quality of consumer products on the market. Passing the Consumer Product Safety Act did not bring an end to the debate. The CPSC's first action was to establish flammability standards for mattresses. As soon as the new regulations were established, the CPSC was promptly taken to court both by manufacturers' associations and by consumer groups unhappy with the standards. Manufacturers claimed that they were being unfairly asked to absorb the costs of switching materials and conducting new testing procedures; the problem, the manufacturers alleged, was really caused by careless cigarette smokers. Consumer groups claimed that the standards were not strict enough, since small manufacturers were given additional time during which they could sell mattresses that did not meet the flammability standards if such mattresses were prominently so labeled. Consumer groups wanted only safe mattresses on the market, without a time delay. In spite of the potential for unlimited power claimed by opponents, the CPSC—a watchdog agency—soon became the watched.

Critics of regulatory agencies argue that solutions to safety problems cost money and that these costs will be passed along to consumers. Direct costs, such as those involved in retooling, testing, labeling, and changes in personnel and material, are relatively easy to determine. Trade associations and manufacturers argue that government standards actually limit consumers' freedom of choice, increase costs, put people out of work, and lead to excessive governmental control. Many associations advocate self-regulation in order to preempt government involvement. Consumer-protection advocates contend that if self-regulation could solve the problem, there would not be any problem. They also argue that costs are inevitable when safety is concerned. Indirect costs, including hospital and doctors' fees, time lost from work, and pain and suffering from injuries, must be paid, whether by injured consumers, insurance companies, or manufacturers. Regardless of who pays directly, the ultimate cost is passed on, whether to the consumer or to the public as a whole.

Bibliography

Burda, Joan M. *An Overview of Federal Consumer Law.* Chicago: American Bar Association, 1998. Practical guide prepared by the American Bar Association.

Commerce Clearing House. *Consumer Product Safety Act: Law and Explanation.* Chicago: Author, 1972. Contains the text of the law and an overview of its meaning and intent.

Evans, Joel R., ed. *Consumerism in the United States: An Inter-Industry Analysis.* New York: Praeger, 1980. The history of consumerism is examined in ten industries. The roles of consumer groups, industries, individual companies, and the government are explored. Describes the effects of consumerism and legislation and the reactions by the businesses studied.

Katz, Robert N., ed. *Protecting the Consumer Interests.* Cambridge, Mass.: Ballinger, 1976. An edited version of papers presented by the National Affiliation of Concerned Business Students. Chapter 10, "The Consumer Product Safety Commission: Its Clout, Its Candor, and Its Challenge," by R. David Pittle, is an especially valuable essay.

Mayer, Robert N. *The Consumer Movement: Guardians of the Marketplace.* Boston: Twayne, 1989. A history of consumerism as a social movement, with an examination of the factors that affect the success of regulatory action. Attempts to quantify the economic impact of consumer-protection policies.

Office of the General Counsel, ed. *Compilation of Statutes Administered by CPSC.* Washington, D.C.: U.S. Consumer Product Safety Commission, 1998. Unofficial compilation of laws relating to the Child Protection and Toy Safety Act assembled for consumer use. Indexed.

U.S. Consumer Product Safety Commission. *Regulatory Responsibilities of the U.S. Consumer Product Safety Commission: Study Guide.* Washington, D.C.: Government Printing Office, 1976. Developed as a training manual for entry-level inspectors. Easy to read. Excellent definitions, with detailed lists and explanations of products that are specifically not covered by legislation. Has quizzes and answers.

Sharon C. Wagner

Cross-References

Congress Passes the Pure Food and Drug Act (1906); Nader's *Unsafe at Any Speed* Launches a Consumer Movement (1965); The United States Bans Cyclamates from Consumer Markets (1969); The Banning of DDT Signals New Environmental Awareness (1969); The U.S. Government Reforms Child Product Safety Laws (1970's).

THE UNITED STATES PLANS TO CUT DEPENDENCE ON FOREIGN OIL

CATEGORY OF EVENT: International business and commerce
TIME: 1974
LOCALE: Washington, D.C.

In 1974, responding to disruptions in world oil supplies, the Federal Energy Administration formulated plans to reduce U.S. dependence on foreign oil, plans that later became national legislation

Principal personages:
RICHARD M. NIXON (1913-1994), the president of the United States, 1969-1974
GERALD R. FORD (1913-   ), the president of the United States, 1974-1977
JIMMY CARTER (1924-   ), the president of the United States, 1977-1981
RONALD REAGAN (1911-   ), the president of the United States, 1981-1989
JAMES R. SCHLESINGER (1929-   ), the secretary of the Department of Energy, 1977-1979

Summary of Event

In the late 1960's and early 1970's, the economy of the United States became dependent upon oil imports, especially from the Middle East. The growth of American dependence on imported oil was made dramatically clear by the disruption in world oil supply caused by the Arab oil embargo of 1973-1974. The embargo prompted Congress to pass the Emergency Petroleum Allocation Act of 1973, implementing a number of policies designed to reduce U.S. dependence on foreign oil. The act also created the

Federal Energy Administration (FEA) to implement and enforce the legislation and to formulate policies to reduce dependence on oil imports. A number of the FEA's recommendations, developed in 1974, were passed into legislation in the Energy Policy and Conservation Act of 1975. These statutes and regulatory policies laid the foundation for a continuing federal role in the domestic oil and natural gas industries.

American oil companies had been developing oil and gas reserves in the Middle East since the mid-1930's. By the mid-1950's, American domestic demand began to outpace domestic oil production. At the end of 1955, imported oil accounted for less than 15 percent of America's domestic energy consumption, but the figure was growing rapidly. As the American economy began to demand increasing amounts of petroleum, the relationship between the United States and the Middle East continued to grow.

In 1972 and 1973, oil production in the United States (excluding Alaska) declined by about 360,000 barrels each year. This came at a time when American demand for oil was increasing dramatically. The American population had increased 30 percent since 1950, but energy consumption had doubled. Almost all the increases in U.S. energy consumption were filled by oil imports. In 1970, foreign oil accounted for 22 percent of domestic consumption; by 1973, 36 percent. In 1970, the United States imported 3.2 million barrels of oil per day; by 1972, that figure had risen to 4.5 million barrels. In the summer of 1973, months before the Arab oil embargo, the United States was importing 6.2 million barrels of oil each day, largely from the Middle East.

In 1971, federal control of oil and gas prices was instituted as part of the federally mandated general freeze on wages and prices. This action was a response to an inflation rate of nearly 5 percent per year. Although most of the price controls ended by 1974, continuing public disenchantment with oil and gas shortages and price increases meant that price controls on the domestic petroleum industry would continue in various forms until 1981.

The members of the Organization of Petroleum Exporting Countries (OPEC) met in Kuwait City on October 16, 1973. The OPEC ministers decided to raise the price of a barrel of OPEC oil, which had become a measure of world oil prices, from $2.90 to $5.11. In January, 1974, OPEC raised the price again, to $11.65 per barrel. Many of the Arab oil-producing nations also had embargoed shipments of oil to the United States in October of 1973 in retaliation for U.S. support of Israel.

The prospect of the exhaustion of domestic oil stocks, together with the Arab oil embargo, portended disaster for the American economy. On November 7, 1973, President Richard M. Nixon announced that if preventive measures were not taken, the American economy would soon fall 10 percent short of its energy needs. Nixon called for Project Independence, a series of policies designed to eliminate U.S. dependence on imports by 1980. Many oil industry executives and policy experts believed the goal to be unrealistic.

Nixon called for voluntary conservation of energy and lower thermostat settings, lower standards for air quality to aid factories and the auto industry, reduced highway speeds, acceleration of the building and licensing of nuclear power plants, incentives to increase the production of coal and lignite, a halt on changing utilities from coal to oil, increased oil production on the outer continental shelf, and increased production from the federal naval petroleum reserves. Although the coal, lignite, and nuclear power options were slowed by environmental concerns, in the next two years Congress passed legislation calling for a national 55 mile per hour speed limit and tax breaks for home insulation. Congress also passed legislation to speed up the Alaskan pipeline project.

More comprehensive legislation was needed, however, to address the immediate problem of the shortage in petroleum supplies. As domestic oil supplies became scarce in late November, 1973, political action groups representing the independent and smaller refiners, transporters, and marketers called for the federal government to allocate limited crude oil stocks for the immediate future, a plan that would be designed to ensure fairness in crude oil stocks while also preserving competition.

On November 27, 1973, Congress passed the Emergency Petroleum Allocation Act (EPAA). A primary goal of the EPAA was to aid vulnerable end-users of oil. This meant federally mandated allocations of crude and refined oil to small and independent domestic refiners, transporters, and marketers. This policy often meant that integrated companies with large crude oil stocks had to sell oil at controlled prices to their less-well-supplied competitors. The EPAA also continued the complex series of price controls on domestic oil and provided for gasoline rationing. To implement, administer, and enforce these policies, the EPAA authorized the president to create a federal energy agency.

Accordingly, President Nixon created the Federal Energy Administration (FEA) to implement and enforce the provisions of the EPAA. The FEA also endeavored to develop a workable set of policies from the energy initiatives proposed in Project Independence. The FEA devised a number of proposals to reduce U.S. dependence on foreign oil and completed its report in November, 1974. Some of these proposals that would soon become federal legislation included higher fuel efficiency standards for automobiles, higher efficiency standards for electrical appliances, and standards for home and office insulation and heating and cooling equipment.

Impact of Event

Gerald Ford became president of the United States in August, 1974. He proposed federal decontrol of oil and natural gas prices in the hope that rising prices would spur domestic oil production. To maintain some control on oil prices, Ford proposed a Windfall Profits Tax. Ford also proposed large-scale development of coal mines, coal-fired power plants, and synthetic-fuel plants. Ultimately, these plans were canceled or scaled down.

Congress included some of Ford's proposals in the Energy Policy and Conservation Act (EPCA) of 1975. Instead of decontrol of petroleum prices as Ford advocated, however, the EPCA continued the complex and contro-versial price controls on oil and gas. Federal allocation of domestic oil and natural gas continued as well. The FEA was given authority to implement and enforce the new regulations. The attempt to control prices and allocate oil and gas proved to be just as complex, controversial, and difficult as under the EPAA.

The EPCA gave increased powers to the president to intervene in the domestic petroleum industry. The president could require power plants to use coal, if available, rather than oil; order the development of new coal mines; and further allocate and appropriate domestic stocks of oil and gas. The president could also order mandatory conservation measures and rationing of oil and natural gas.

The EPCA required higher fuel efficiency standards for a host of prod-ucts, including automobiles and electrical appliances. The EPCA required manufacturers of electrical appliances to label their products with informa-tion on their energy efficiency. The EPCA also mandated fuel-efficiency standards for automobiles that later became the Corporate Average Fuel Economy (CAFE) standards. The new standards established by the EPCA mandated that the average fuel efficiency of a new car would have to double over a ten-year period, from 13 miles per gallon to 27.5 miles per gallon.

Another significant aspect of the EPCA was the establishment of the Strategic Petroleum Reserve (SPR), in which the federal government, together with the American oil companies, would establish reserve oil stocks for emergencies in the case of a future disruption in world oil supplies. The EPCA also called for U.S. participation in the International Energy Program, whereby Great Britain, Japan, West Germany, and the United States would all develop reserve systems that they could coordinate and share in the event of another oil supply disruption. The EPCA ratified American participation.

President Jimmy Carter came into office in 1977 also committed to reducing American dependence on foreign oil. In April, Carter announced several goals, including a reduction of oil imports to one-eighth of total energy consumption by 1985. In an effort to reduce demand for energy, Carter proposed the Crude Oil Equalization Tax, which would have taxed oil at the wellhead, and instituted a new pricing system. The Carter Administration hoped that this new pricing system would let oil prices rise gradually to discourage consumption and reduce dependence on foreign crude oil. Carter also submitted to Congress the Department of Energy Organization Act; Congress approved the bill in August, 1977. The bill created the Department of Energy (DOE) and placed most of the previous energy agencies under the DOE umbrella, including the Federal Energy Administration, the Energy Resources and Development Administration, and the Federal Power Commission. Carter appointed James R. Schlesinger, the secretary of defense in the Nixon Administration, to be the first secretary of energy.

The Iranian revolution of January, 1979, removed large amounts of petroleum from world markets, pushing prices up to $30 per barrel and bringing on a second oil price shock and supply disruption. OPEC used the opportunity to raise its prices. By December, 1979, the price was above $30 per barrel; in some spot markets, it was $45 per barrel.

The whirlwind of congressional activity and executive actions taken during the Nixon and Ford administrations had done little to reduce American dependence on foreign oil. The complex set of energy regulations was of little help to President Carter in the crisis of 1978-1979. The American economy was still dependent on imported oil for nearly half of its energy consumption in the last years of the 1970's.

In the midst of the severe worldwide inflation of oil prices, pressure increased for the Carter Administration to decontrol U.S. prices. The ensuing price increases would, the government hoped, make domestic exploration economical. In April, 1979, Carter announced a phased process of decontrol of oil prices over thirty months. To satisfy consumers, Carter proposed a new tax on American oil companies that became the Windfall Profits Tax Act of 1980.

Ronald Reagan assumed the presidency in 1981 strongly committed to reducing federal regulations. In his first month in office, Reagan formally ended the federal pricing system, lifting all the controls on oil and gas. The Reagan Administration also pledged to reevaluate the Department of Energy, which had become a political symbol of overregulation. President Reagan considered abolishing the DOE but finally decided to reduce its budget.

It was not long after federal decontrol of prices occurred, however, that world oil prices began to fall. Beginning in 1981, world oil prices began a five-year deflationary trend. By 1983, oil prices had fallen to below $30 per barrel. Price deflation also reduced the political and economic threat of high prices and gasoline lines. As the American economy recovered from the oil shocks of 1973 and 1979, controversy over imported oil also abated. The Reagan Administration, previously concerned with removing federal hindrances to economic growth, took the opportunity to push through Congress a measure that increased the federal tax on gasoline by five cents. It was hoped that this act would check potential increases in consumption caused by falling prices while also raising revenue to meet mounting federal expenditures.

Ironically, falling oil prices on the world markets in the early 1980's resulted in large part from OPEC's success in raising prices in the 1970's. Higher prices made oil production in non-OPEC areas, such as the North Sea, Alaska, Mexico, and the southwestern United States, more economically feasible. The U.S. national economy still depended on foreign oil for approximately 25 percent of its petroleum requirements. Greater non-OPEC production, however, was creating a glut of oil on the world market, leading to price deflation.

With the price of oil falling and supply on the rise, public and private alternative fuel programs became uneconomical. In 1981, the Reagan Administration slashed federal funding for solar energy programs as well as the Synthetic Fuels Corporation, established by Carter. American oil companies cut back their shale oil and coal gasification projects.

In 1990 and 1991, the United States, under United Nations auspices, militarily intervened in a conflict involving Iraq, Kuwait, and Saudi Arabia. The action was motivated in part by a desire to keep Middle Eastern oil flowing to the United States, which still had not eliminated its dependence on foreign oil.

Bibliography

Bradley, Robert L. *Oil, Gas, and Government: The U.S. Experience.* Lanham, Md.: Rowman & Littlefield, 1996.

Feldman, David Lewis. *The Energy Crisis: Unresolved Issues and Enduring Legacies.* Baltimore, Md.: Johns Hopkins University Press, 1996.

Krueger, Robert B. *The United States and International Oil: A Report for the Federal Energy Administration on U.S. Firms and Government Policy.* New York: Praeger, 1975. Presents policy options considered in the 1970's. Also contains brief but informative histories of federal and state regulation of the petroleum industry and of U.S. diplomacy with the oil-producing nations of the world.

Melosi, Martin V. "Energy Intensive Society, 1945-1970" and "Scarcity Decade—1970's." In *Coping with Abundance: Energy and Environment in Industrial America.* Philadelphia: Temple University Press, 1985. These chapters give an excellent overview of the formation of energy policy, detailing the forces behind the growing federal regulation of the energy industries in the United States after World War II.

Nash, Gerald D. *United States Oil Policy, 1890-1964* Pittsburgh, Pa.: University of Pittsburgh Press, 1968. Although Nash's work does not cover the 1970's, it is a good source for readers seeking an introduction to the subject of public policy regarding the oil, coal, and natural gas industries.

Sherrill, Robert. *The Oil Follies of 1970-1980: How the Petroleum Industries Stole the Show (and Much More Besides).* Garden City, N.Y.: Anchor Press/Doubleday, 1983. The best source for a detailed treatment of the politics of petroleum regulation in the 1970's. Shows the ways in which the divergent segments of the American political economy shape energy policy.

Vietor, Richard H. K. *Energy Policy in America Since 1945: A Study of Business-Government Relations.* New York: Cambridge University Press, 1984. This work covers the oil, coal, and natural gas industries and their regulatory relationships with federal and state governments. Contains useful and detailed analysis of the issues of imports, price control, and allocation.

Yergin, Daniel. *The Prize: The Epic Quest for Oil, Money, and Power.* New York: Simon & Schuster, 1991. Covers many aspects of petroleum issues, including actions and policies of oil producing and consuming nations, international relations, and the business strategies of oil firms. Best in its treatment of the international aspects of the petroleum industry, this work also has concise coverage of domestic regulatory policy.

Bruce Andre Beaubouef

Cross-References

The Supreme Court Decides to Break Up Standard Oil (1911); The Teapot Dome Scandal Prompts Reforms in the Oil Industry (1924); Atlantic Richfield Discovers Oil at Prudhoe Bay, Alaska (1967); Arab Oil Producers Curtail Oil Shipments to Industrial States (1973); The Alaskan Oil Pipeline Opens (1977).